SKIPPER STORIES

True Tales from
Disneyland's Jungle Cruise

DAVID JOHN MARLEY

Belle's Library
Publishing

Cover Art by Trevor Kelly

ISBN
Printed in the United States of America

This book is dedicated to my wonderful daughters,
who never seem to get tired of hearing daddy's Jungle Cruise stories.
Olivia and Cordelia Marley, this one is for you.

CONTENTS

Introduction:
A Bad Reputation

Years ago when I was a skipper, I was at a meeting backstage at Disneyland with about thirty random cast members and six managers. While everyone else was serious, I sat in the back of the room with the only other skipper there and we cracked each other up. After one particular burst of laughter, I saw one of the managers lean over to our manager, point toward us, and ask a question. We couldn't hear her entire reply, but we did hear her say "Jungle Cruise." He then nodded his head as if that explained everything.

That one moment tells you everything you need to know about how Jungle Cruise skippers are viewed by the rest of the people at Disneyland.

Skippers are generally seen as loud, overly energetic, and self-amusing trouble makers. If this book does nothing else, it should prove that reputation correct.

Why does the Jungle Cruise produce the wildest cast members at Disneyland? The Jungle Cruise is much more than the sum of its audio-animatoric parts. Every attraction at Disneyland is designed to give guests the same consistent experience, but the Jungle Cruise changes from boat to boat and skipper to skipper. In fact, it is the wise-cracking skipper that is the heart of the Jungle Cruise. They are the crucial element, the show editor, entertainer, narrator, and guide. Not only is the skipper the heart of the attraction, the 10 minutes they're with guests is usually the most time a guest will spend with a cast member during their entire stay at the park.

What I like the best about skippers is all of them have a story to tell. I haven't met a single one yet who hasn't. I have interviewed skippers from just about every era of the history at Disneyland. This book features the skippers in their own words. Historians call this oral history, people speaking about their experiences without any filters. The words in this book are their own; I have only edited them to remove repetition, grammar, and the occasional swear word (this is a book about Disneyland, after all). As far as I know, this is the first time a Disneyland attraction has been covered in this way. The book only scratches the surface of the many amazing stories about both the Jungle Cruise and Disneyland itself.

Normally, in this kind of work the historian doesn't interject very often. I have tried to make sure that the events described actually happened. A few of the cast members that I interviewed, including some that left the park more than 15 years ago, wanted their stories kept anonymous. A few of the current skippers in this book had their interviews approved by Disney Media Relations, and I appreciate the company's cooperation with the project.

I've taken the liberty of sharing stories from my years working at the Jungle Cruise because my girls always want to hear them. I have mixed my own stories among those of my fellow skippers. I'm pretty sure that this book is the closest thing I'll ever have to an autobiography.

SKIPPER STORIES GLOSSARY

100: Attraction unable to open with the rest of the park.

101: Attraction closed for any reason (medical emergency, fire, mechanical breakdown, etc.).

3 Shot: Used for mechanical failure onboard the boat.

4 Shot: Used for a medical emergency. All boats forward of the sound of four shots are supposed to move full speed to the dock to make way for the boat with the medical emergency on board.

6 Shot: Used when one or both of the Jungle Cruise boat's guide rails came off the underwater track.

Adventure 1: The radio call sign for the most senior manager at Adventureland currently available.

Attraction: All of the rides, shows, and displays at Disneyland are called attractions.

Boat Storage: As the name implies, an area where boats are stored off stage, now behind a huge wall that opens and closes. It is essentially a channel that runs half the length of Main Street. In the 1990s it became a break area for skippers.

Cast Deployment System (CDS): A computerized system implemented in the late 1990s as a way to save expenses by eliminating the need for a lead at each attraction. The CDS system was designed to increase efficiency by having a computer determine the most optimal way for each cast member to use their time. While still used park wide, the CDS system was a total failure at Jungle Cruise.

Cast Member (CM): Any Disneyland employee is called a cast member.

- *Lead*: An hourly CM who runs an attraction as a manager and is always in costume. The lead is almost always a ride operator and not a salaried member of management. A lead can also work at their attraction as a ride operator. Every attraction usually has four main leads, ranked A to D, with a number of other leads not regularly in rotation.

- *Manager*: A salaried CM who oversees all the attractions of a land and usually dresses in business casual attire. At Disneyland, Adventureland/Frontierland is run as one business unit. Most managers will have worked as hourly CMs at some point and each attractions manager gets trained on all the attractions in their area.
- *Ride Operator (RO)*: Self explanatory.

Cat Walk: The narrow dock that lies between the main dock and the jungle. The cat walk can only be reached via boat.

City Hall: This Main Street building is the headquarters of Guest Relations, where guests can get a birthday sticker, a note to use the handicapped entrances to rides, and most importantly for skippers, to make an official compliment or complaint.

Deadhead: Taking a boat around the jungle without guests. This is done when something in the jungle needs to be inspected by a lead or later in the day when the dock becomes overcrowded and it is faster to send an empty boat out than to have guests sitting on a boat waiting to reach the exit dock.

De-Rail: The technical term for when one or both of a boat's guide rails comes off the track.

ER (Early Release): This is a request that a CM will make to leave work early. At Jungle Cruise there was an ER List which was first come, first served. So, if you were ER1, there was a good chance you could leave work early. ER 5? Slim chance.

Front Load: The front door of the Jungle Cruise boat. The front-load skipper stands with his back to the skipper driving the boat and faces the skipper at rear load. The front position loads guest into the right side and center section of the boat. It is also their responsibility to make sure that boats are not getting backed up at the dock.

GC Shift: Guest Control Shift usually means working crowd control for parades, Fantasmic, or a special event.

Inn Between: The cast member-only restaurant located backstage behind the Plaza Inn restaurant.

Jungle Central: The radio call sign of the lead cast member at Jungle Cruise, or whoever happens to be in the shipping office.

KA (Knowledge Assessment): A test, usually multiple choice, that cast members are given at the end of various parts of their training process.

K Lot: The CM parking lot on Katella Avenue. Since 1998 most CMs park there and take a tram to the employee entrance to the park.

Land Locking: A policy begun in 2003 that restricts CMs to one particular land. Prior to this, a CM could work at any attraction anywhere in the park.

LOG: See OG.

Max/Maxing: To "max" is to take a longer break than allowed.

OG (aka LOG or SOP): OG stands for Operation Guidelines and is the rulebook concerning a particular attraction. For a Jungle Cruise skipper, to be non-OG means you're not doing jokes from the script.

PA (Performance Assessment): A final test given by a lead or manager to make sure the newly trained CM knows how to do every aspect of their job, including all safety and emergency procedures. At the Jungle Cruise, the PA usually lasts more than an hour.

Plaid: A plaid is a person from City Hall/Guest Relations. They are called plaids due to the plaid shirts or vests that they wear. They usually accompany celebrities around the park.

Points: The attendance system of the Disneyland Resort is based on points. If you receive too many points in a year you may be suspended or fired. It is normally 3 points to call in sick and 1.5 points if you're late to work.

Presenteeism: A policy of strict enforcement of the points system. Begun in 2004, this policy led to hundreds of Disneyland cast members being fired, resulting in manpower shortages. But it lowered the park's operating costs since the replacement cast members made less than the people they were replacing.

Princess Rotation: A rotation without a boat or dock position. This is rare and only used on very busy days. The "princess" is in charge of strollers, working at greeter, and occasionally getting into a boat to relieve a tired skipper.

Rear Load: The back door of the Jungle Cruise boat. The loading skipper faces both the front load and driving skipper. They load the left side of the boat. At the beginning and ending of each day, rear load is the only load position open, since the entire boat can be loaded from that rear door.

Rotation: Every attraction has its own rotation system, and the Jungle Cruise has perhaps the most unique. While many attractions have one single rotation (greeter, load, unload, etc.), the Jungle Cruise has as many as five rotations running at a time, each with up to four people. Each rotation is focused on a particular boat.

- *2-man*: One person on a dock position, one on the boat. This is usually only done the first and last hour of the day, since neither can take a break. Technically, this isn't even a real rotation, it's just a 3-man waiting for the third skipper to arrive.
- *3-man*: One person on dock, one in the boat, one on break. This is a skipper's favorite rotation because they get a 20-minute break every hour instead of a 15 minute break.
- *4-man*: The most common rotation when the park is busy during the day. It has one dock position, two boats, and one person on break. A skipper shares their boat with one other skipper and they take turns on break or at the dock position in cooperation with the other boat.

Set Up: As in "grab a set up." A set up includes an ammo box with a microphone, gun, ammo, and occasionally an air horn.

Shipping Office: The office for the Jungle Cruise, located on the dock. This is where the lead can normally be found.

Shuttle, The: The name of the vehicle that transports CMs from the K Lot, or other parking area, to the CM entrance to Disneyland.

Skiff: A small boat used by the lead or maintenance to quickly access the jungle. Until the early 2000s, the Skiff was located near the dock and had a small outboard engine. Later it was moved to a hidden spot in the Indian elephant bathing pool and its engine was removed.

The Skip Phrases: These are simple phrases used mostly at the dock and are mostly self-explanatory.

- *"Move it up, Skip."* Used when a skipper is wasting time at unload or is in the way.
- *"Hit it, Skip."* Used at the loading dock when the boat is clear to leave.
- *"Hold it up, Skip."* Used when asking a skipper to stop their boat to load a special guest.
- *"Kill it, Skip."* Used in an emergencies when a guest or CM falls into the water near a boat.
- *"Back it up, Skip."* Used when a boat is coming off the catwalk or moving from the dock back to storage.

SOP: See OG.

TDA: The Team Disney Anaheim building is the center of park operations, casting, and Disneyland University. The beautiful building was designed by Frank Gehry and opened in 1995.

Theme Park 1: The radio call sign for the manager who in charge of operations at the park.

Track Switch: There are three track switches at the Jungle Cruise, all of them between Trader Sam and the exit dock. The forth track switch, the "Dominguez Switch," was removed with the Indiana Jones renovation in the mid 1990s. Before 1995, these switches were manual and each in their own location. After 1995, a central console was put in to control all the switches.

Trader Sam: The infamous "head salesman" of the jungle is also the attraction's mascot. Leads and managers will leave notes for the CMs signed "TS". He is also the place with a lighted warning to skippers about track switches. Often boats will stop at Trader Sam while track switches are being moved.

WDI: Walt Disney Imagineering, the company started by Walt Disney that creates all of the attractions and shows for the Disney parks.

Westside/Eastside: Disneyland is split into two halves which has created a decades long rivalry. The Eastside includes Fantasyland, Toontown, and Tomorrowland while the Westside is considered to be Main Street, U.S.A., Adventureland, Frontierland, New Orleans Square, and Critter Country.

Westside Diner/The Deck: A CM-only restaurant located underneath New Orleans Square, and the site of a large underground kitchen serving all the restaurants above it. This restaurant was primarily used by Westside CMs. The diner was shut down in the early 2000s and repoed years later in a new location.

CHAPTER ONE

JUNGLE DREAMS

Many people dream of working at the Jungle Cruise, but not everyone gets the chance. In 1996 I went through Disneyland University with a funny, outgoing guy who wanted to work on Jungle Cruise, too. At the end of day two, when we were told our assigned lands, I was given Adventureland and he got Tomorrowland. He argued and begged but nothing changed and I never saw him again.

While I think just about everyone in southern California, or the world for that matter, dreams of working at Disneyland, there are those who want to work a specific attraction, and nowhere else. For a select few, that dream is working at the Jungle Cruise.

Of course I wanted to be a skipper on the Jungle Cruise! It's the best job at Disneyland. To be honest I think I passed it by my father [Disney Legend Claude Coats] casually, "Gee, Dad, I'd really like to be a skipper at the Jungle Cruise," and I left it at that. And I must admit that Dad must have mentioned it. He wouldn't have been pushy about it at all because he was such a laid-back guy, but he may have mentioned it to somebody and bingo.

Alan Coats, 1960s

I was living in Portland, Oregon, and McDonalds was handing out free Disneyland tickets as part of a promotion for Splash Mountain, even though the ride wasn't open in time for the promo. I was 17 and my friend was 15 and his parents let us take a Greyhound bus to California to go to Disneyland for the week by ourselves. This was during spring break of my senior year. It was a great trip and we thought we would record our whole journey on tape, so we had our pockets full of cassette tapes; this was before digital recorders. We didn't have a camera or a video camera or anything, just this tape recorder to record our trip. And we came back and we were listening to the Jungle Cruise. We both made copies and we would listen to the Jungle Cruise trip over and over again. A couple weeks later I thought, "I know what I'm going to do after high school. I'm going to get a job at Disneyland and work the Jungle Cruise since I already know the script."

Fred Martin, 1980s

Only 1 in 10,000 people are doing a job that they were born to do. I know that I was born to work at the Jungle Cruise. My high school yearbook was filled with comments that said, "Good luck on the Jungle Cruise...you'll be great!" People just knew that's where I was going.

David Schoenwetter, 1990s–2000s

Like most kids in southern California, Disneyland was a big part of my life. Still, it was my sister who turned my affection for the park into a life-long obsession. When I was 7 years old my sister, who was then 16, took me to Disneyland for the day. I remember virtually nothing about that trip, except for one moment that is still as clear as a bell. We were in line for the Jungle Cruise and a skipper started talking to me.

"Where are you from?" he asked.

"Orange." I answered. My answer seemed to surprise him, perhaps since Orange is only about 6 miles from the park.

"What brings you here today?"

"I don't know, my sister just brought me here."

At this point the skipper looked at my sister, then bent down and whispered in my ear, "Be careful, one day she's going to ask you for something."

I nodded my head, convinced that the skipper had done me a favor. It was at that exact moment, with him kneeling next to me on the dock, that I decided that one day I was going to be a Jungle Cruise skipper.

David John Marley, 2000s

Jungle Cruise was the reason that I wanted to work at Disneyland. I left my old job, where I was a manager, and they gave me an exit interview and asked why I was leaving. I told my boss that I was going to follow my dream and work at the Jungle Cruise. His reply was, "That is a great dream!"

Ben Case, 2000s

I have a picture of my first trip to Disneyland when I was 3 and it is of me at the Jungle Cruise. The Jungle Cruise was the entire reason that I came to work at the park.

Chris Ramirez, 2000s

It's one of my greatest accomplishments. I feel it was the peak of my life. I think the first time that I wanted to become a skipper was when I was 19 years old. I went on the ride with my brother and that's when I realized that this was a dream job. It wasn't something that I felt I had to do, it seemed more like a fantasy job. When I was in college someone said to me, "You like Disneyland so much, why don't you just go work there?"

So I got trained over a weekend and I went back to class on Monday morning. The professor asked us, "What did you all do this weekend?" I raised my hand and told her that I got my dream job. She looked at me and said, "No, you didn't, that's impossible." And I said, "No, I really did. I'm a Jungle Cruise skipper now." Everyone in the class laughed.

That moment showed me how some people think it's just impossible to do something that you really want to do. How often does it happen you get a job that you're really proud of? It's rewarding, it's fun, you feel special, you can walk around with your head held high.

I didn't take it for granted. I realized that this was probably the best job I was ever going to have and I was only 21 years old. I realized I wasn't going to be there forever, so I had to take advantage of the opportunity.

Joey Hurley, 2000s

I wanted to be a skipper since I was a toddler. I grew up in Long Beach on a kind of Disney street. We had one of the candy shop guys down the street with his wife. He remembers being at the park the last time Walt Disney visited. Our neighbors across the street had a son named John; he was in college when I was little, and he was a Jungle Cruise skipper. As a kid I called him Jungle John and I remember that he had a cool car. This was the mid 1980s. He always seemed to be dating pretty girls. I was only five, but even then I knew that was cool. Then I went on the Jungle Cruise and I loved it and realized that this was what I wanted to do. I never saw his spiel, but I was hooked. I thought that if I had a job at Disneyland, this is the one to have.

Joshua Sudock, 2000s

I always wanted to work Jungle Cruise. I remember riding it once at night and the skipper was hilarious and I thought that if I ever worked at Disneyland it would be at Jungle Cruise. Plus, I loved the whole pseudo-1930s jungle *African Queen* look. I love the time period.

Trevor Kelly, 2000s

The Jungle Cruise was my first attraction and I remember working my interview to get it. I wore clothes that looked like the Jungle Cruise and

I tried to be funny. I wanted to work at Disneyland so bad, but I really wanted Jungle Cruise. I was so happy when at Disneyland University I got my paperwork and it said Jungle Cruise and the script was attached to the back. They used to give it to you right away, before training. They stopped doing that because technically it was illegal to ask people to read the script off the clock.

Kaz Liput, 2000s

I had read David Koenig's *Mouse Tales* book and wanted to get trained on Jungle Cruise. I asked a manager and he was surprised that anyone wanted to go there. It was just not fun; people didn't enjoy it, from what I was hearing. I think most of the skippers had been there for a while and had gotten burned out. I got there at the end of the Narrations Department era and so they were still saying "make a whacky costume and a whacky character" and some people had no interest in doing that. Some people would bring props from home and do crazy things. So I got trained right after the guns got taken away.

Chris Ramirez, 2000s

As a kid I remember riding the Jungle Cruise and not being that into it. But my parents would drag me on it anyway. I think as a kid Adventureland kind of scared me. Pele in the Tiki room was terrifying. I remember fire shooting out of her head and I would run screaming and crying. So I was on the Jungle Cruise with my parents, and like I said not into it, and the skipper did the "have to go to the bathroom" joke at the dancing natives and it made me really laugh. I was around 5 years old at the time. To a little kid, a joke about the bathroom is just about the funniest thing in the world.

So I got interested in Disneyland more in junior high, and then in high school I got an annual pass and I would often come to the park with my friends. By then I liked the Jungle Cruise because it was different every time we rode it. When I graduated high school I went and got a job at Disneyland, but I was only 17 and I couldn't work attractions, so I got a job in foods at the French Market as a busboy. I think that when I worked at the French Market it wasn't a secret that I really wanted to be working at the Jungle Cruise, because when I quit and got rehired a year later, in the fall of 2002, I ran into two people that I used to work with at the French Market, and without saying a word they said to me, "You finally got your dream job at the Jungle Cruise."

Mike Pucher, 2000s

I always loved the Jungle Cruise. There was a boy that was older than me in high school who ended up working there around 1996. We were friends in the theatre department in high school together and I went to see him do the Jungle Cruise and he was amazing. He was so into it and he absolutely sold it. I thought that this looks like the most fun you can have in a job, like, people get paid to do this, that's crazy. So it was something that was always in the back of my mind

Jen Chavez, 2010s

Growing up as a kid, I worshipped Jungle Cruise skippers. It was like what a normal, well-adjusted kid thinks of an astronaut. For many of us, they were the rock stars of our generation. When they were on, they were so on! Prior to working at the park, I was an annual passholder. I repeatedly went on Jungle Cruise and learned the spiels. I collected jokes of my own and took notes. I tried to learn from the best. And in my opinion, from the perspective of an AP, the best skipper at that time was Benny LeMaster. From the outside looking in, he was just the most extroverted. As a person he's rather guarded, but he had this very outgoing skipper persona, and I was just in awe of him. He was so funny and he'd really push the envelope. I was like 16 years old, I was often there by myself, I just got my drivers license. So I'm driving really far away from home just to see these guys clowning around on the boats. I would think to myself, "How are you getting away with this? This is the coolest thing I've ever seen."

Michael Libby, 2000s

One day I going to the park and I stopped by the Jungle Cruise. Scott was the lead that day, and I told him, "I want to be a skipper here, I want to transfer over from The World of Disney store, but I'm not sure I'll fit in a boat." So he's really nice and he got me into a boat and let me stand there in front, and I thought, "Okay, it's a tight fit, but I can make it work." Scott was very nice and accommodating to me that day.

Kipp Hart, 2000s–2010s

The Jungle Cruise was always the go-to attraction for me as a kid. I'd ride it once during the day and then once at night. You'd get two different experiences that way. Jungle Cruise was always the best. I told people that I wanted to work at Disneyland, work Jungle Cruise, and then work my way to WDI.

Kevin Lively, 2010s

When I interviewed I told her honestly the only attraction I was interested in was Jungle Cruise. I had a job at the time so I wasn't nervous about not working and it was something I really wanted to go for. She said, "Well, I have openings in Adventureland, so I can hire you in there." And I said OK. It worked out beautifully for me.

Jen Chavez, 2010s

Not everyone had as easy a time getting to work at the Jungle Cruise as Jen Chavez. Getting the job you actually want at Disneyland can be difficult. At times the selection process seems maddeningly random. People who would later become legendary skippers were originally sent far away from the Jungle Cruise and some spent a year or more trying to get to the ride of their dreams.

So I went to Disneyland without the intention of working at Jungle Cruise. I just wanted to get in. They put me in the parking lot, and so I worked for a year in the parking lot. I usually worked a position called RT which stands for rear tram. Before there was an automated spiel it was my job to spiel to the guests. We had to spiel about Disney California Adventure and explain what would be in the park, and of course we would make fun of it, too. I had a great time spieling on the tram. I would do jokes and impressions and voices and the guests would love it; often they would applaud at the end. I only liked the job when I was spieling; every other aspect of working the parking lot was awful. Setting up cones and standing there directing traffic with a flashlight was just horrendous. I had to get into the park, so I asked to be transferred.

Joey Hurley, 2000s

When I finished my master's degree in 1995 I wanted to buy an old Corvette to reward myself and my wife said, "Hey, why don't you go work at Jungle Cruise like you've always wanted, and you can make money rather than spend money." I wasn't sure how to get hired, but I sure felt qualified. By chance I had a friend in Walt Disney Imagineering who worked on creating the Indiana Jones Adventure. He took us to Club 33 and a soft opening ride on Indy one night. Unbeknownst to anyone, I had a plan. When we walked by Jungle I ducked into the shipping office hoping to talk to a lead. Instead, I met Bruce Kimbrell, the senior manager in the area. I handed him a tailored, tongue-in-cheek resume on why I'd be a perfect Jungle Cruise Skipper. He let us ride the attraction and invited me to come to an open casting call that he was going to be at the next day. I was hired that day.

David Schoenwetter, 1990s–2000s

I started in 1998. Jungle Cruise was my first choice, but I didn't get it; I got sent to Subs. That turned out to be a fantastic thing because it was their last summer. I drove the last sub for the last guest on the last day of operation.

Every single time cross–training came up I told them that I wanted Jungle Cruise, and they would say, "Yeah, but your availability makes you a perfect fit for the Eastside, or this attraction or that attraction." And I kept telling them, "Yeah, but I want the Jungle Cruise." It took a couple of years before they finally said I could have it.

Joshua Sudock, 2000s

I got Jungle Cruise, but I was still in high school and couldn't do the training, so they moved me to Pirates. I drove to Disneyland and met the person who did the scheduling and told them that I wasn't going to work at Disneyland unless it was at the Jungle Cruise. So with a couple of clicks with a mouse I was back on Jungle Cruise.

Trevor Kelly, 2000s

When I got hired in at Disneyland for the first time in 1996, I begged and begged to get trained at the Jungle Cruise. However, after my Disneyland University class I was given a form that said "Indy GC," Guest Control for Indiana Jones. So I wasn't working the attraction, but making sure its queue ran smoothly. Indy was still a very new ride in 1996 and the line regularly stretched out to Main Street. I did this and Fantasmic for what seemed like forever. It hurt me to stand at the Indy exit and watch the Jungle Cruise boats go by. I resolved to get on the Jungle Cruise no matter what. I made myself a pest to the lead at Indy GC and the people in scheduling, who never seemed to care.

One day I worked with a guy whose name I sadly don't remember. He had been at the park for years and seemed to know everyone. I worked with him all day at Indy GC. Near the end of our shift, he decided that he'd heard enough about my love of Jungle Cruise. He walked me over to cast member scheduling and demanded that they train me at the attraction immediately. The scheduler checked and people were booked there for the next couple of months. My friend just pointed to the next weekend and said, "Bump one of them and get David on there." The scheduler looked at him, looked at me, then deleted this one guy's name and typed mine in his place. A week later I was a skipper! Ever since that day I've been afraid I ruined some poor guy's life because I took his spot at Jungle Cruise.

David John Marley, 2000s

I knew I wanted to work at Disneyland. It took me three attempts to get hired by Disney. When I applied the third time and got a call back, the only jobs available that I had applied for were hotel bell hop and stores. I wanted to take any job just to get my foot into the door.

I wanted to work Haunted Mansion, mainly. I also wanted Indy and Jungle Cruise. I originally thought that skippers were actors hired by auditions. I didn't know how hiring was done. I thought working the dock was one job and being in the boat was another. So I got on a wait list and eventually got a call that I was being hired into attractions in Adventureland. On the last day of Disneyland University I found out that I was getting Jungle Cruise. That is when I learned that I was going to be in the boat!

Anonymous, 2010s

The first time I hired in and they didn't have the online survey, that personality test that they make you take. I know what they were for; I was a manager once and I've given stuff like that to employees. I came in to apply again when we were moving, so I had a lot of stuff on my mind and this online survey was like a chore to me because it takes forever. And so I got lazy and started answering all the middle-of-the-road questions, and that is suicide. I wasn't thinking about it, I was just thinking of getting it done. I was still the same person who had left the company a few months before.

So I was waiting for the guy to call me in for my interview. He calls me in and he closes the door. Then he tells me, "Based on your online survey we don't have a place for you at Disneyland right now." I told him that I only left a few months ago and I have referrals from all of my old managers that they want me back. He was like a robot; he just stared at me and repeated the exact same sentence. And this is the best part, he was only 25 years old and I was in my mid-40s and he said to me, "Maybe when you get a little more life experience you can come back and reapply in six months."

Kipp Hart, 2000s–2010s

When I rehired in 2002 I told a person at casting that I really wanted to work attractions and I really wanted to work the Jungle Cruise. And they said that they'd see what they could do. So I was at Disneyland University for two days without knowing where I was going and it was torture because I wanted Jungle Cruise so badly. So at the end of the second day when they handed me the little piece of paper that had "Jungle Cruise" on it, it was the best feeling ever. I saved that piece of paper.

Mike Pucher, 2000s

Two years after I left I came back to Disneyland and got rehired to work Indiana Jones. They said I couldn't have Jungle Cruise and I begged and begged, but they wouldn't let me. They told me just to show up and work at Indiana Jones and they would train me at Jungle Cruise as soon as they could. The guy that I was supposed to be trained with at Indy called in sick, and when he came back they gave him Jungle Cruise. I've never been so angry in my entire life.

I was just furious and I went and complained about it. But I should've called in sick for my training at Indiana Jones and it sucked because you had to walk by the Jungle Cruise every day. I would just stare at the boats and just wish I was over there. I didn't want to do button pushing and all the other stuff you have to do it Indy. Working Indy became so easy because you just had to stand there and push a button. I eventually got to like it. There is a better position where you just stand there and say hello to guests; you don't have to do anything or entertain them, it was a nice break. So I guess I cried enough times to the upper management and they put me back at jungle Cruise.

Joey Hurley, 2000s

I had originally hired in to attractions at Critter Country and I was worried because I really didn't want to work Davy Crockett's Explorer Canoes. I told them, "My body is not built for this." I told them that I really wanted a spieling attraction since my major was communications, I study public speaking—can I please have a speaking role? And they said, "Sure, no problem," and they sent me to Splash Mountain.

I trained there for two and a half days before my trainer told the managers, "Yeah, he's not a good person for this." It wasn't a good fit for me, so I asked if I could have a speiling attraction. These managers said, "Sure, just work Fantasmic for a couple of weeks and we'll get you in there." I check my schedule after two weeks and they gave me Winnie The Pooh. So I went to another manager and he got me moved to Opera House.

I loved Opera House. It was while they still had the "Disneyland's First Fifty Magical Years" celebration and I loved it because I was a geek for all of that stuff anyway. So I worked at Opera House for six months and then it went down to get new carpets installed. I remember a scheduler called me and told me that Opera House was going down for at least a month so I had to learn something else. Then she asked, "Is there anything you'd like to work?" I told her, "I'd give my right arm to work Jungle Cruise." And she said, "Alright, you've got it," and it showed up on my schedule the next week.

Kevin Lively, 2010s

Some people got to the Jungle Cruise on accident and ended up loving it.

I had a friend who was a balloon seller at the park and he told me all the ins and outs about the interview process. He said first they will offer you a job in foods, and if you don't take that they'll offer you a job in stores, but don't take that either. Tell them the only thing you want to do is rides because that's the only job at Disneyland that is unique. So I went in for my interview and that is exactly what happened. They offered me foods and then stores. Then the lady says, "I have an opening in attractions on the westside of the park but I don't know what it is, take it or leave it." So I took it. I just knew it was going to be the Haunted Mansion. That was my favorite ride at the park and I always wanted to work there. I thought it would be cool.

I show up for my orientation for two days of training at Disneyland University. I met this lady from the westside and she gave us a tour of that side of the park. Then she took us upstairs to the Adventureland management office and introduced us to the Adventureland manager who told all of us what our jobs are going to be. He starts calling out names and says, "So-and-so, you're going to Pirates; so-and-so, you're going to Haunted Mansion; and the rest of you are going to the Jungle Cruise." I get handed the spiel to Jungle Cruise and I'm told to "come back in two days and have this memorized." And I was so disappointed. I remember looking at the script and thinking there is no way I'm going to remember all of this. I hated having anything to do with talking in front of people. I never ever looked for the spotlight. So I walked out of the park and I was thinking to myself, "This is stupid, I'm just going to quit."

The next day I'm making my regular delivery trip up to LA, and I have the script there in the cab of the truck with me. And I'm trying to remember the jokes. And it was during that drive I realized that I had to face my fears and stop avoiding this kind of thing. So I worked hard, I memorized the spiel, and when I got there had it down pat.

Jeff Rhoads, 1970s

I wanted Indiana Jones, I told them I wanted Indy. I wanted to be a button pusher. I knew what the job entailed, I wanted to wear the fedora. But they told me "since you had such a great interview, we're going to put you on the Jungle Cruise." I have a fear of speaking in front of people. I wasn't a good public speaker at that time. I was only 18. If I had to read something in class, I would break out in sweat and hives. It was horrible.

My first couple of shifts were guest control, and I never went through orientation. I was supposed to go, but I got a call asking me to come in for a guest control shift. So I called my dad, who worked in park security, and said I don't have an ID or a name tag and my dad was my Disneyland orientation. I got to meet all the guys in security and they found a name tag for me and made my ID card and I went out for my first shift and was instantly reprimanded for having my pager out. They asked me what attraction I knew, and when I told them that I was learning Jungle Cruise that next weekend everyone was impressed, so I figured it was a pretty cool place to work.

Jessica Harris–Lopez, 2000s

I wanted Davy Crockett Explorer Canoes, and they asked if I could work days and I said no because I was still in high school. They said I couldn't have Canoes because it was days only. So I got my card that says where you're going to work and it said "Small World" and I said, "Hell, no," so I talked to a guy and he said, "How about the Jungle Cruise?" and I was like, "Okay, as long as I get trained in Canoes.

Andy McGuire, 2000s

CHAPTER TWO

WHAT MAKES THE JUNGLE CRUISE SPECIAL

People dream about working at the Jungle Cruise, but what is it about the attraction that makes it so special? The Jungle Cruise is totally unique. Cast members have to be able to safely drive a boat while they're entertaining people from all over the world. Perhaps more than anything else it is the desire to make people laugh, to give guests a truly magical and unique experience that powers the skipper work ethic.

We had a feeling that we were pretty special because we knew that the Jungle Cruise was making money while some of the other attractions weren't. They liked us because we made money. This made us feel better than other ride operators because we were part of the entertainment.

Warren Asa, 1955

That's what made it exiting—you entertained the guests and you had different guests every day, every boat trip. It never got boring driving the boats around. We worked hard and played hard.

William Sullivan, 1950s

The Jungle Cruise was the best ride to work on at Disneyland. It was comfortable and fun, you had a captive audience, and you were your own boss. Where else at Disneyland could you do that? You had a responsibility to do it right, but you had a captive audience.

Alan Coats, 1960s

It was fun working there, it had its own enchantment. After so many trips around you get tired, but you learn how to get over that. It was easy for me to work at Jungle Cruise than it was at Haunted Mansion. At the mansion you were inside all day, and you had to wear a suit and tie, and that wasn't my cup of tea. That was the place I liked to work the least. Jungle Cruise was fun; I enjoyed it. The crew was the most important part about that attraction. If you had good guests on your boat, that made the day fantastic.

Terry Eaton, 1970s–1980s

I could not believe I was getting paid. There were times I would've paid them to let me do that job. When I was a kid I would go to Disneyland maybe once a month, which at the time seemed excessive to a lot of people. but to me it was never enough—I wanted to go at least once a week. It was so great; you got to ride the ride. You never got to ride the ride while you're working at Haunted Mansion, but you got to be out in the jungle. I loved that, I loved being backstage and wandering around there. Interacting with the guests was always fun. I met great people and I made friends who today are still some of the best friends I ever had. Facebook is responsible for some of that, but many of these guys I've always stayed close to. It was a different time when I worked at Disney; things were a lot more laid-back. We were allowed to do a lot of stuff that you just couldn't do today.

Jeff Rhoads, 1970s–1980s

That was the great thing about the Jungle Cruise: you were allowed to goof around with people, It's not the same as doing guest control on the parades. At Jungle Cruise you're supposed to be clowning around with people.

Fred Martin, 1980s

You'd see couples having a great day and saying "thank you" and you knew you'd made a genuine impact on them. I had great memories from when I went to Disneyland as a kid, so I knew that you could really help them make a great memory. It doesn't get any better than that.

Ron Robledo, 1980s

It felt like I had some special power that I've been given. It was a very special place to work because it felt like a one-in-a-million type of job. There's those special kind of jobs that everybody thinks is a dream job, like being an astronaut or putting oil on a Playboy model. I felt like being a skipper was one of those jobs. I felt cool, I felt like I was really a member of Disneyland. I thought it was so cool that I got to drive the boat and control that audience all alone for eight minutes.

Joey Hurley, 2000s

It was the closest thing you can get to working in an 1980s sitcom where everyone has banded together against this evil corporation. There was Jungle Cruise and then there was the rest of the park, to me at least.

Trevor Kelly, 2000s

Jungle Cruise changed my life. I'd never be doing standup. The friends I've made a Jungle Cruise are invaluable. These are lifelong friends, it's a fraternity. What we have is so unique, you couldn't duplicate it anywhere.

Kipp Hart, 2000s–2010s

Jungle Cruise is the great equalizer for everybody. It didn't matter what your background is, it only mattered if you were funny or not.

Michael Libby, 2000s

Jungle Cruise was the only place I worked at Disneyland where everyone was excellent. There were skippers that took too long or did stuff you didn't like, but they got corrected quickly. Everyone was excellent. There is a bond when you meet a skipper that I never noticed at other attractions or at Guest Relations. I think it was because you had to band together to fight outside forces. We were the redheaded step-children of the park. Nobody else really gets it, so there was a feeling that you had to protect it.

Karen Vogelvang, 2000s

There are no other attractions at Disneyland that combine the personality of the host with the changing experience and humor that Jungle Cruise does. Because of that, we are a singular institution within the resort. The Jungle Cruise is one of the few places where the cast member interaction and banter is part of the show. There are very few other areas outside of characters and entertainment where the cast members have a themed level of personal interaction with the guests. That creates something personal, and on a much deeper level than the guests would experience on a roller coaster, or dark ride. Jungle Cruise skippers are literally talking to you for 10 minutes, as well as our on-dock interactions.

Kyle Crocker, 2000s

That's the thing about Jungle Cruise. It's a desired location. People don't go into casting and beg to work Big Thunder Mountain or Small World. But people cry when they find out that they are going to work Jungle Cruise. Once you're a skipper you're in a fraternity.

Andy McGuire, 2000s

One day I was the lead and I was standing in front of the shipping office. I see friends and families moving through the queues filled with happy anticipation, I see boats filled with laughter coming and going around the river, I see the comedic camaraderie of the skippers moving in and out of rotation. Suddenly I am overwhelmed by the sheer circular movement of it all. It feels like not only the world but perhaps the entire universe was circling around me in that spot at that moment. And it hits me: I'm at the "core of happiness!" Guests are happy, skippers are happy. I was so happy. I was there in the middle of it all and getting paid to do it. It was a surreal, almost spiritual experience, and I knew I was doing what I was born to do.

David Schoenwetter, 1990s–2000s

My favorite part of Jungle Cruise is that each day was completely different from every other day. At Jungle Cruise every boat, every seven-and-a-half minutes, it's completely different. We're learning to play off of the crowd, which is one of my least favorite parts if the boat is pretty bad.

Anonymous, 2010s

Every single audience in a Jungle Cruise boat is different, and that is the secret to keeping your sanity while working as a skipper. If you go in there and you're pre-programmed, you'll lose your mind, and it's not fun and you'll get worn down. I told my trainees that the secret to success at the Jungle Cruise was to use that live audience; it fits the show. We told our trainees that everything they did had to fit the show, and a skipper would talk to their crew. If you had a young teenager on your boat, that was just gold, you could spend the next eight minutes just messing with them to no end. And in doing that you'll make every trip different and your day will go by a million times faster. It just makes life a lot easier and happier. The audience will appreciate it because you took the time to make a memory.

Jungle Cruise is one those things, it's part of the Disney parks DNA, and it's so special and so unique and you'll never be able to replicate it. It's going to change over the years, inevitably, it already is the most changed attraction we've ever done. No attraction has been as updated as the Jungle Cruise. So the scenes might change and the jokes might change, but the fact that you have a live host there interacting with your crew, that is the most bang for your buck you can get. If you're going to have someone just press a button, you might as well have them entertain people. It's the most aspirational job, too; everyone wants to be a skipper.

Kevin Lively, 2010s

At Disneyland all of the operators are paid the same amount; there is no incentive, financially, to do your job well. Zero. And that is apparent very quickly at other attractions, but at Jungle Cruise there is a non-financial incentive to do your job well. Because you want to be good. That is a pretty awesome thing.

Michael Libby, 2000s

Sue Barnaby worked Storybook Land, another popular spieling attraction.

I think the difference between Jungle Cruise and Storybook was that at Jungle Cruise you were performing, you have to entertain this whole boat, You're in the front of the boat so people are looking around, but they are also looking at you. Where at Storybook it's this nice, slow, gentle thing and you're sitting at the back of the boat, and you could do minimal or maximum spieling. People were cool with whatever. If you were in the mood you could make it interesting. People would zone out because they were not focused on you. At Jungle Cruise you are at the front of the boat and constantly interacting with the guests.

Sue Barnaby, 1980s–1990s

Jungle Cruise was exactly whatever you wanted to make of it. You are not stuck in one cubic foot pressing a button all day. Some people are built for that. There are people who work Indy and they own it. They know that attraction like the back of their hand. They live for that attraction, and if you put them in the Jungle Cruise, they freeze up and they hate it. I was the exact opposite of that.

Kevin Lively, 2010s

While the job is famous for being fun, it is also a difficult job. Some attractions require nothing more than sitting at a console and pressing buttons. The Jungle Cruise is both physically and mentally taxing. After an eight-hour shift a skipper is usually exhausted, their throat might be sore, and they have mostly been standing for their entire shift. That is why some cast members hated working at the Jungle Cruise; they could make the same money working at an attraction that was much less demanding.

When I was there it was the place to try to get out of, because spieling is hard; to do it right, it is draining. So doing that all day, every day is just draining. At that time doing a spieling attraction was considered to be a pain in the ass. It was a lot of work and that's where a lot of the new cast members ended up. Everybody wanted to work on what we call the "skate" rides. Working on the *Mark Twain* was a skate because it was so easy. Haunted Mansion and Pirates were still both new and that's where everybody wanted to go. The spiel rides were not where it was at. The idea was that when you got on Jungle Cruise you tried to get out as soon as you could.

Jeff Rhoads, 1970s–1980s

We used to have this old saying at the park, "What are they going to do, put us in the Jungle Cruise?" Some people saw it as a punishment. I think it's because some people thought it was monotonous doing the same trip over and over and over.

Terry Eaton, 1970s–1980s

The repetitive spieling, and they just didn't like it, unless they picked it for summer. Maybe during the winter, but for five days a week every week, they were over it. And then certain people came in later and they loved it. Some of them loved it because they didn't work there too long; it was like their college years. They had great memories and it was lots of fun and then they were gone, back to school or they quit and they had these great memories. But for other people, if you're stuck there five days a week, it just gets repetitive.

Sue Barnaby, 1980s–1990s

I was so tired after every shift. I'd go in, work the night shift, which was always super fun. Then we'd all go to Denny's until 2am, then I'd get up at dawn to go surfing with my boyfriend, then go home and sleep from 10am to 2pm, then get ready for work. I did that my entire summer.

Jessica Harris–Lopez, 1990s–2000s

When you're having a bad day you just start counting the trips and all you can think about is getting through the day. You think, "Okay, three more then I get my break or four more and I get a lunch." You're in a bad mood and just want to go home. That's when it was like a job. I remember many, many days in the middle of the summer working 40 hours a week. It's the middle of the day and it's really hot, and it was so monotonous and you're standing on the dock. It would make me mad because it could be such a fun place to be, but when it is that crowded and that hot, it's just not fun. That's why it hurts so much when it became monotonous because you knew how much fun it could be. It can be better than this and now it's not.

Joey Hurley, 2000s

Once I opened the park with Gerry, and they needed someone to extend to 8pm, so I volunteered, then the lead for Grad Nite needed more people, so I extended again. By the time I left I had been working Jungle Cruise for 21 hours. At the end of the shift, I wrote a note for Gerry saying that I was ER 1 and I would be back at 9:30. Gerry made me ER 1 and I worked until 11:30. I then called out sick for two days. I was exhausted. The funny thing is that they really didn't need me at Grad Nite. I hung out with the lead all night.

Amanda Case, 2000s

Especially in the summer, it is physically exhausting. You're talking all day, you're in the sun. Even though the jungle is the primary role in the whole attraction, you are an entertainer. You are in that role. You need to be energetic and you need to carry that energy for your entire eight-hour shift. Jungle Cruise is an exhausting attraction. So for that I understand why people don't want to work there during the heat or the rainy season.

Another prime reason is stage fright. I know that there are a lot of people who struggle with that. If you are primarily at a dispatch attraction and you get called in for a Jungle shift, people have to mentally prepare for those shifts. The skippers who primarily work Jungle Cruise are the ones that love it. The ones who don't are the ones who only work it every couple of months.

Anonymous, 2000s

Since the Jungle Cruise is focused on the abilities of the skippers, it is only natural that the work culture has changed over the decades. Some traditions came and went, the popularity of working the attractions rose and fell, and even how much freedom skippers were allowed on their boats varied as time passed.

We all had nicknames. Alligator Al seemed obvious to me, so I just used it from the get go. Guys usually had some funny names, they'd take their own name and give it some animal or jungle sounding thing. And they would introduce themselves to their boats that way, "Hello, I'm Alligator Al, and I'll be your skipper and guide." So you would introduce yourself with your name. They all did nicknames.

Alan Coats, 1960s

I worked with guys who had been hired by Walt Disney. Van France, Dick Nunis were still out there. All these guys whose names are now on the windows in Main Street. You'd see them in the cafeteria. The camaraderie at Jungle Cruise was great.

George Trullinger, 1970s–1980s

The Narrations Department was a short-lived experiment in the mid 1990s to have selected cast members work attractions that required them to speak to guests.

Narrations was great. We got to dress up in wild costumes and do characters, we got to learn all about the history of the attraction when they re-did it. We had tons of guest compliments. Our problem was that capacity sucked, but people didn't seem to care. We interacted with the queue like they used to back when Jungle Cruise had a ticket-taker position. It was great because you didn't have to worry about how many people you could get on a boat.

If it wasn't for Narrations and the Jungle Cruise I probably would have quit before that because working there made it fun again. I loved to spiel, I loved guest interaction. There were days where you didn't feel like it, so you'd ask to be sent over to Tiki.

I think the year that I was there was kind of a golden, fun time. People didn't do things to break down the attraction on purpose because everyone wanted to be there. People were having a good time.

Sue Barnaby, 1980s–1990s

At that time [2000] there were so few things that were as cool as they seem. When I got there it was kind of lawless, but we still did our jobs. Our trainer Kaz said that as long as we didn't offend anyone we would be fine. We got guest compliments all the time. We had this book and anytime a guest said anything positive we would write it down as a guest compliment. Paul, one of our managers, would talk to guests and get them to praise the ride and we would write it down.

Chris Ramirez, 2000s

I liked getting there first thing in the morning and going into the shipping office and looking at the clip board to see who else you're going to be working with that day. I don't think I ever had the exact same crew twice. It was cool to meet new people, or see people that haven't worked there in a couple of months, and it was always great to work with your friends. It was kind of like the movie *Animal House*. There was a great chemistry of a great ensemble cast. There isn't any one person that makes it good, it's all these people and the fun they're having together.

Mike Pucher, 2000s

Disney California Adventure opened in 2001 and it seemed that the calibre of people that they were hiring kept diminishing. When I got hired, it was hard to get a job, but in 2001 they took anybody they could get and the quality of service dropped. You saw more people getting termed, getting there late. The Jungle Cruise had a family atmosphere that tried to teach people or get them to move on if they couldn't cut it.

Matt Nerrie, 2000s

By early 2002 that particular crew of skippers just did whatever they wanted to, and whatever they thought was funny. We made jokes about music and culture that had nothing to do with the 1940s. Our jokes related to the fact that the guests were having this very stuffy experience at Disneyland and it was time to let loose a little bit.

Joey Hurley, 2000s

That was my favorite thing about that ride looking back on it: it was populated by people who had no business piloting these boats and being put in charge. There was a whole group of us there for at least a year who had no business running an attraction involving large boats.

Trevor Kelly, 2000s

It was living the life of one big drunken party, hanging out with funny people, and we made fun of everything. Having that constant comedy around you made the sometimes bad aspects of the job palatable.

Matt Nerrie, 2000s

The work culture of the Jungle Cruise changed over time. In 2004/2005 it began to lose its sense of wildness.

When I came back to Jungle Cruise in early 2005 it was a totally different ride, I don't know what happened. There was less trying to entertain your friends and have a good time, And it was more of a job. The attitude was like, "We're going to do 7½ minute trips around the jungle and tell the written jokes." Also, it was a new generation of skippers; everyone I knew from my era had moved on. I got along with these new skippers, but it just seems like their sense of humor was different. We used to be silly, and it seemed like nobody wanted to be silly anymore. Everything just felt more rigid.

Part of the problem was people had seen how great Jungle Cruise was and now everybody wanted to work there because they've heard of this great experience and they wanted to be a part of that, and it didn't pan out, it wasn't the same. It's like they were expecting something to happen, but didn't realize that it was the skippers that make the jungle magic.

Joey Hurley, 2000s

It all started with presenteeism, when they fired tons of people. The summer of 2003 was the end of the good times. Everyone was frightened for their jobs.

Chris Ramirez, 2000s

I think the culture of the Jungle Cruise changed because the turnover was so high, you lose that culture. It didn't happen overnight, it just slowly eroded. In 2005 we had a new script update, and that kind of started it. They told us that we had to pay attention to the script, even though they gave us lots of options, and allowed us to submit our own material. And then when Gerry, the A Lead, transitioned out of Jungle Cruise, that was a big change. That led to opportunities for other people to inject what they thought was their idea of it.

The guy who was the A Lead after Gerry was very instrumental in getting a lot of stuff quelled that we used to get away with. He was a very structured person. He sees a box and that is where everything stays, he can't even step outside the box. If that goes on for a long enough time, you lose the personality of the Jungle Cruise.

Anonymous, 2000s

The internet has ruined the Jungle Cruise. Since everything is being filmed and people post everything, skippers are afraid to do anything that could cost them their jobs, so it has taken away the spontaneity, the sense of a unique experience

Kaz Liput, 2000s

I got there at the tail end of the rogue era [2004], when things were still kind of crazy. I wouldn't even take breaks because I didn't want to miss anything. There was always stuff happening. Always antics! I wanted to take it all in and absorb it. So I would take my lunch, but if I had a break coming up I would just stay on the dock and observe and add to it if I could. It was a good time.

This is my third time at Jungle Cruise, and it has evolved since then. There were a lot more safaris going on. They never happen now, not that I know of. Back then there was a lot more individuality. People had their own characters and now it's more cookie-cutter.

Kipp Hart, 2000s–2010s

This is what one skipper has to say about working there now.

We have fun there. Jungle Cruise is at a high right now, especially with the Jingle Cruise. People didn't used to come to the ride that often. Now we are getting people riding us that used to avoid us. We have fun, but there are a lot more rules and regulations now to cut down on the horseplay. Today, other than playing off of each other, there aren't many shenanigans happening. I just wish that I could have been a part of that wild side of Jungle Cruise.

Anonymous, 2010s

The work culture of the attraction could also fluctuate during a single year.

I noticed a huge fluctuation in the number of people that loved working it to having people just dread being pulled there. I think that is the beauty of the summer time. The summer-time people could pick their shifts and so they really wanted to be there. That made it fun. Whereas in the winter time or the off season people would get pulled there and complain about having five weeks of Jungle. That was my attitude toward Star Tours: "Oh, man, they gave me five weeks of Star Tours, I'm going to kill myself."

Sue Barnaby, 1980s–1990s

Disneyland is famous for strictly enforcing "The Disney Look," which covers everything from hair length to jewelry and nail polish colors. As far as I've been able to discover, the Jungle Cruise was the only place at the park where cast members were able to regularly ignore these otherwise sacred grooming rules.

I let my hair grow long for four months and it was down around my shoulders and I had a Van Dyke goatee beard. I looked like I belonged in the jungle. There weren't the Disney Look grooming standards. I think they started that because of how we looked.

William Sullivan, 1950s

You could show up at the dock a little unshaven or scruffy and you wouldn't catch hell and it was OK. They'd send you home at Fantasyland. At Jungle Cruise they'd just tell you to do it better next time.

Chris Ramirez, 2000s

Karen Vogelvang came to Jungle Cruise after working for years at stores and then Guest Relations, the most "Disney" place in all of Disneyland. She was in for a shock when she stepped onto the dock for the first time.

When I hired into the park in 1999 the Disney Look was strictly enforced. We spent hours on the Disney Look, and that was just for stores. How your body looked, how you can stand or cross your arms, being presentable and open. And Jungle Cruise was totally the opposite—lean on stage, drink on stage, do what you want. Back in Guest Relations, managers would come by with a dime to check the size of your earrings. And I knew girls who were sent home for having highlights in their hair that didn't match, or that were too drastically different. It was so strict. One ring per hand, clear nail polish only.

Jungle Cruise still had the Disney standards. I remember wearing beads and it was fine and I took off my tie and tied it on my belt. I wore my own hat for two years and nobody cared. You didn't have to button your shirt all the way up. In the rest of the park you couldn't roll your sleeves up unless it was Code 90 (meaning the temperature was over 90 degrees) and at Jungle Cruise you could do it if you wanted to. That was huge.

The biggest shock to me was the leaning. That was really weird for me. Drinking water on stage was weird. You could go into the shipping office and drink, but I would hide down low, it felt so wrong to drink in front of guests.

Karen Vogelvang, 2000s

Working at the Jungle Cruise is more complex than most people realize. It is a series of different jobs that require different skills. The way these jobs were divided up has also changed over the years.

Many people don't realize that being a skipper means that you do everything. There are people who ask if you just drive the boat or work on the dock. I had to tell them it was all one thing. People think they are separate skills.

Kristin McGuire, 2000s

However, there was a time when there were separate jobs at the Jungle Cruise.

The summer of 1962 was my first season. We didn't drive the boats everyday. You would get your assignment every morning. You were either a boat driver, a ticket taker, or you did loading or unloading. Those were the four jobs that you did. So one day it would be unload for a day. That's what we did. We also worked other jobs. My first summer the Tiki Room wasn't open, but in 1962 if the park was really busy they'd send us over to Tom Sawyer Island. Our outfits looked enough alike we could do that.

Alan Coats, 1960s

The Jungle Cruise is an old ride system. It dates back to the 1950s. It's very analog and very hands on. The operator does a lot and it makes such a difference. The operator makes or breaks the experience because they are the lens through which guests experience the jungle. This is especially relevant now with virtual reality. In that case the camera directs your view and tells you what to look at and when, while you are in a fixed place in your seat. So the cuts of the camera and the framing of the screen do that for you. However, when there is no frame and you can look anywhere, and you need direction as to what's important to tell a story. So the Jungle Cruise is like virtual reality in that way, but it's VR done well.

Michael Libby, 2000s

For the first twenty-five years of Disneyland history the park rides operated with a ticket system. This meant that each attraction had to have a position of ticket taker. This person was usually the first skipper that guests would come into contact with.

I was the guy who yelled out that bit about "This is an E Ticket. 'E' as in 'Elephant.' 'E' as in 'Euripides.' You-rip-a-dese out of your ticket book." You had to be an extrovert to work on the Jungle Cruise.

William Sullivan, 1950s

The ticket booth could get really hectic, mostly because even though you warn people to have their E ticket ready and out, they didn't when they got to the front. Sometimes people would just hand you the entire book and you had to flip through it and find the right ticket and tear it out. One of the things I liked to do was I would take the tickets and fold them into little boats. And then on my break I would go float them out in the lagoon, For something to do. Until one day I found out that they clogged up a screen that was filtering out the water and the whole river backed up. They couldn't figure out how the tickets got there and I didn't volunteer any information.

Terry Eaton, 1970s–1980s

They kept telling us, "Don't take the tickets, if you're caught with one ticket you will be fired." But every once in a while someone would hand you a ticket from 1956. I had people hand me an A ticket, and explain that it said Jungle Cruise on it and asked if it was still good. So we would still except those, and it was very cool to see them. Eventually, they reduced the size of the tickets. They were about 40% smaller, to save money.

Jeff Rhodes, 1970s–1980s

One popular job was to stand at the entrance and encourage guests to get on the ride. This position replaced the job of ticket taker.

You had to be a showman to get people to come over and ride the ride. Nobody knew what the ride was about, and it was the most expensive ride. I would shout out a spiel so people would get exited about trying it.

William Sullivan, 1950s

Before they took out the center planter in Adventureland they used to have to go stand on the planter and spiel to the guests to get them to come into the Jungle Cruise. That was so fun.

Chris Ramirez, 2000s

I worked there in the summer of 1996 when the line for Indy ran past Jungle Cruise and often out to Main Street. I would get tired of seeing this long line while ours was virtually non-existent. So one time I took down the ropes for the Indy queue and re-attached them to the Jungle Cruise boathouse door and tried to convince the people waiting in line to join us. Nobody moved. They laughed, but they didn't move.

David John Marley, 2000s

I used to stand out there and call it the short cut to Indiana Jones. When I had some unsuspecting guests, I would tell them, "This is a short cut for Indiana Jones. What you do is you go through this boathouse and take a boat ride for 10 minutes. Then, when the boat ride is over, you just go around to your left and into Indiana Jones." People would laugh. Some guests went for it.

Kipp Hart, 2000s–2010s

Working either of the two load positions were perhaps the most important jobs at Jungle Cruise besides driving a boat. The people who worked at load had to keep an eye on the length of the queue, prevent boats from getting backed up on the river, and had to do this while safely loading guests at the same time.

I had a love-hate relationship with front load. I was very good at front load, I had no trouble cramming guests into the boat. It was just a lot of work and it was exhausting. If I had to be at load during a shift in summer when it was hot and humid right there on the water, I'd much rather be at rear load. Dayshift at rear load was a good mixture of activity and intensity for me. Front load I would do a great job, but then I would just go home exhausted.

Mike Pucher, 2000s

Driving the boat is the most iconic part of being a skipper.

The boats were great, it was hard to mess them up. They were such nice boats. The first summer that I worked there they added the Hondo Hattie and the Uci Una and that brought the fleet up to 12 boats. The extension of the elephant bathing pool and veldt made more space so you could add some boats. There were a couple of boats that were always a problem, but most of them were great.

Alan Coats, 1960s

I didn't like dealing with the wheel on the boat. I'm kind of short, and it was designed for someone taller, so that made it a pain in the ass to drive sometimes. I always had a bruise on my arm from trying to reach over the wheel to the throttle. Sometimes I'd get to work and think, "I don't feel like spieling," but then I'd get on the boat and do a full spiel.

Sue Barnaby, 1980s–1990s

I think my favorite part of the ride was when you were at the dock and the boat was loaded and they'd yell, "Hit It, Skip!" and you push the throttle down and off you'd go. That was always exciting. It was my time to do my thing, no one is going to bother me, and I'm going to make these people laugh no matter what. It's the only place at Disneyland where you control the guest experience more than anyone else. It's not pushing a button; the guests look to you to be entertained. So starting that trip was the best.

Joey Hurley, 2000s

The Jungle Cruise also had some weird quirks or traditions on how things were run. They may not have made a lot of sense, but they were tradition.

Many of the more important decisions at Jungle Cruise when I worked there were made by a game of Rock, Paper, Scissors. Usually it involved who got to ER (early release), or moving rotations, and stuff like that. For some reason I got to be really good at the game. So good, that people would demand that I play for their side. One night, the lead pulled me out of the boat so I could represent my four man in a rock, paper, scissors contest to see who got to go down to the three man. I was never defeated and soon I was in a three-man rotation with a twenty-minute break each hour.

David John Marley, 2000s

In the 2001 Disneyland introduced the CDS (Cast Deployment System), a computerized rotation management system. Instead of having a lead create rotations and make sure people are at the correct spots, now cast members would enter their ID and a computer would tell them where to go. The theory behind it was two fold: one, it would decrease costs by possibly eliminating the need for leads (something the park had tried to do before), and two, it would maximize time management because the computer would know exactly when and where to send people. The CDS worked at most attractions where it was placed, but it was a total disaster at the Jungle Cruise. The computer couldn't figure out how to manage a series of 4-man rotations, so it created one huge rotation, which is what is done at all the other rides in the park. The CDS is still the standard today, except at the Jungle Cruise.

We tried CDS at Jungle Cruise and six people went on medical in two days. The way it worked was the whole ride was one big rotation. There were two boats then load position, two more boats then unload, then two boats and front load. So what would happen was you'd start at front load and take three trips, which was typical. But then you'd get bumped into another boat, take three trips, then back on the dock before doing another stint on the boat. So instead of taking three trips and getting a break you were taking twelve. And that was if everything worked perfectly.

What happens when you take a lunch? Because it was early in the CDS era, they had random rotational bumps. And you'd bump in to give someone a break, but if they were in the boat, there was nothing for you to do. Or you'd do 5 trips to get ready for your lunch, then a bump would happen and you'd be kept in the boat, you'd end up doing 20 or 30 trips.

The deal with CDS was getting rid of optimized tasks, so instead of getting a 15-minute break every hour, you'd get one every 2.5 hours. About two-thirds of your time was in the boat. CDS lasted a week, then they tried mini-rotations, going back to how the rotation system worked, but it still didn't work. The other problem with CDS was it would say, "Go bump out Joe at greeter," but at Jungle Cruise it would say, "Go bump out Joe in the Yangtze," and that boat might be in the hippo pool so you'd just hang out.

That was the problem with CDS in general: if there is any gaps in duties, gaps in what it's telling you to do, you're losing efficiency. You're constantly just standing on the dock waiting for your boat to come around. So we were back to four-mans really quick, and there was much rejoicing.

The CDS implementation at Jungle was less than a month. They tried. The full deployment failed. Now for breaks and lunches you have to swipe in and out. I know at other attractions having a 15-minute break every hour is kind of silly, but at Jungle you need it.

Andy McGuire, 2000s

They tried to bring things in from Florida that didn't always work here. CDS, for example, when that became a thing, and every lead and every manager had a hand in it and the ones that were a manual attraction like Jungle Cruise or the rafts, it just didn't work. So they had to go thru several incarnations to prove that it didn't work. This also led to a break between leads and managers where they were less of a team. Having a manager that had worked in attractions before they became a manager was always better. They knew how the parks ran. Some managers that tried to keep the team idea alive often got it beaten out of them.

Kaz Liput, 2000s

When they brought CDS to Jungle Cruise they had to create tasks for you to do so the computer could tell you to do them. Rita was the lead and one of the tasks was that you had to stand in the queue and act like a mannequin. When I did it I took two coconuts and held them strategically in front of my chest and stood there for a good 15 minutes before the lead saw me and I never had to do that task again.

Amanda Case, 2000s

CDS was horrible and everybody was hoarse. Any attraction where you are not available all the time caused problems, and when you are on a boat, you aren't available. You would get a task to relieve someone in the boat, but they just left the dock. Everything freezes for 10 minutes while you wait. They tried two or three evolutions of it, to try to make it work, but it wasn't fun at all.

Matt Nerrie, 2000s

Once CDS came in you didn't know where you were going or when your break was or when your friends were going on lunch. We didn't get paid much so the appeal of work was having fun people and friends to work with and CDS took that away. At Jungle Cruise CDS failed, so we were still able to have freedom and friendships and team spirit.

Chris Ramirez, 2000s

In general Disneyland is kind of a circular mess. They keep trying new things, which fail, and then they go back to the classics. Four-man rotations had been in existence forever, yet they thought they'd find a better way.

Andy McGuire, 2000s

While skipper uniforms have been famously bland since the early 1980s, they used to have the most wild and flamboyant costumes at Disneyland.

We were the only group that got to pick our own outfits. That was fun. I think a third of the drivers were "Hollywood types" who had done some TV and thought that this was a way to keep them in the limelight and help their careers. They were fun to be around. Some had had bit parts in films.

Warren Asa, 1955

The Jungle Cruise had the most comfortable costume at Disneyland. You had this lightweight cotton shirt and cargo pants and a straw hat and these sandals. At nights and in the winter we had more of a uniform with khaki pants and shoes. So I recall there being summer and winter costumes.

Every night we'd turn our costumes in so they could be cleaned. They were always clean, never grungy. The shirts were all different colors; whatever the guy pulled off the rack. At Jungle Cruise we'd wear our name tags on our hats because the Hawaiian shirts were loose and the name tags didn't hang there well. The clothes were so comfortable. The pants had a nice drawstring, so size wasn't a problem.

You kept your hair cut and trimmed, no facial hair. People would complain because they'd see Walt with his mustache and wonder why they couldn't have one. There was a grooming code; you had to look spit polished.

Alan Coats, 1960s

We would go to costuming on really hot days and get short-shorts. We'd get the shortest possible shorts that we could get, another skipper and I, and we would get on the boat and put a leg up on the bench and beckon guests toward us. No guests seemed to be bothered by it. I actually got a compliment from a female guest.

Joey Hurley, 2000s

CHAPTER THREE

WHAT MAKES A SKIPPER

As will become obvious when you read the next chapter on getting trained, not everyone who wants to become a skipper actually gets to be one. Being a skipper takes a certain personality and an ability to adapt to the culture of the dock. For those that make it, there is a bond, a sense of camaraderie that can last long after you've left the river.

What kind of personality does it take to be a skipper? It might be a good idea to ask a psychiatrist about this, but perhaps it's better to let the skippers speak for themselves.

Skippers had no consideration for the larger machine, they lived very much in the moment. I think that's because we worked hard and played really hard. In my entire working career I've never seen people that would all just call in sick for shifts without any concern whatsoever. They'd push the limits on how many calls in they had, justifying things, but at the same time skippers were always willing to put in extra hours at the attraction, they would do double shifts because they enjoyed the work even though it was as exhausting as hell. They'd have a sore throat and be tired, but they'd always stay longer if the attraction needed them. I really appreciate that.

Benny LeMaster, 1990s–2000s

Skippers are more at the extremes. You have the mellow people, and the more intense personalities make for fun. It was a very diverse group. You'd think that Jungle Cruise was a very easy place to work, but because of the very different personalities, if people don't mesh well, it can be a very difficult place to work, Especially if you have preconceived notions of what you're entitled to.

Plus, at Jungle Cruise there are unwritten rules. At Indy if I push the green button the ride goes, but at Jungle Cruise you learn all of the stuff you need to learn, and then you get Jungle boot camp and learn how things work.

Andy McGuire, 2000s

You had to be half goofy to work at the Jungle Cruise. We all had to be extroverts to put on this good of a show.

William Sullivan, 1950s

We made jokes on other rides, but that was the result of having fun. The Jungle Cruise was different because I was going to work to be funny. At other attractions I'd wonder if it was going to be a good day or a bad day and who am I going to work with, but each day at the Jungle Cruise was fun because that was the job. Nobody took themselves too seriously. Those that did, didn't last long.

Cast members at other attractions took themselves far too seriously. Some of the old-timers at Splash Mountain and Pirates had worked with my parents. It wasn't fun for them anymore; they took everything so seriously, they didn't take time to find the fun. I found that the skippers who had been there for a long time still managed to find the fun every day. Being a skipper took the seriousness out of me, too.

Heather Nelson-Wilkins, 2000s

The Jungle Cruise was like a frat house with a sister sorority. We had a frat house and late-night parties and round-robin call in sicks. We had parties and got drunk. I know what it's like to be in a fraternity now. The cool kids versus everyone else. The way we phrased it was the new guys versus the veterans, even though there were people who had been there for years and were never made part of the inside crew.

Chris Ramirez, 2000s

Because you are performing, you must be creative. Working at the Jungle Cruise takes a great deal of creativity. You are not just pushing buttons, you are actively creating magic for the guests.

Ron Robledo, 1980s

People thought that Jungle Cruise skippers should be like Humphrey Bogart, but I thought we should be like Groucho Marx.

David John Marley, 2000s

Some men are born feeling like they are a woman on the inside. They connect to that and they embrace it and they feel comfortable, and that's where they should be even if on the outside they look different. That's how I feel about Jungle Cruise. I connect to it on a spiritual level. When I walk on the dock everything else goes away. I want other people to share that same feeling. I want people to enjoy as much as I do. If they don't, I totally understand it because not everybody connects with Jungle Cruise the same way. When I am there I want everybody to have the same kind of fun and contentment and the peace that I have. It gives me everything. It gives me more than I give back to it. So that's what I like about it. It's kind of the Zen place, and I'm not Buddhist. I just feel like I was meant to be there.

Kipp Hart, 2000s–2010s

Work ethic is hit or miss with any attraction. For a lot of people, especially skippers, this is their first job so they are a little flaky or immature. The one thing I see with skippers is, we have a plethora of attractions, but skippers are proud. When they come in for their shift they have pride in being a skipper; everyone knows what a skipper is. When Jungle Cruise skippers are at work, there is ownership of the attraction. There is a lot of love. There are so many people on social media who brag about working at the Jungle Cruise. They post pictures everywhere. There are people who don't like working the attraction, but they are sure as hell proud about being a skipper. Anyone who knows the attraction brags about it. I haven't seen that with any other attraction. I've seen a few cases here and there, but it is the norm with skippers. Jungle Cruise skippers are their own elite club.

Anonymous, 2010s

While the Jungle Cruise had a clique that could rival the worst moments of high school, once you were in the club, there was a bond between skippers that is even shared between people who never worked the dock together.

Being a skipper there is an instant bond. I would never hang out with some of these people in the real world, but since they were a skipper we have a bond. It's like family. Even meeting skippers from Florida, I feel the connection. Other cast members would talk about their bond and then we'd all tell stories and the other cast members would say, "We had nothing like that." I think it's because we had to be a team and fed off each other and you were performing for people and trying to give a great show. There is something more magical about Jungle Cruise than Disneyland itself.

Kaz Liput, 2000s

The camaraderie is completely different. I made great friends at monorail, and you feel a connection to the monorail trains and the track and you know every bump and part and you get to know the vehicle so well. You can tell if a train is about to go down so you know when to pull it off and replace it. At Jungle Cruise it is so much more about the people. It's a shared experience. You develop bonds and a sense of camaraderie that doesn't exist. I made great friends at every attraction that I worked, Subs, Small World, steam trains, but in terms of bonding over shared experiences there is nothing like the Jungle Cruise.

It's because it's a completely unique experience. What is a trip, nine minutes? That's half a *Simpsons* episode. You fill a boat with 45 people from all around the world, all ages and experiences for half a *Simpsons* episode and you have to keep them engaged. This is the time before cell phones and Google; all eyes are on you, all the attention is on you. If they don't have a good time, if they complain, then it's all on you. It's a lot of fun, but it is also a lot of pressure. So skippers commiserate about their shared experiences out in the jungle. You sit in boat storage and swap stories about your boats. I can't think of any other ride where you have to pour so much of yourself into the job and have it fed back to you. And everyone else is having the same experience. You talk to people on the monorail about your day at the Jungle Cruise and there are aspects they can relate to; loading and unloading guests, handling the vehicle. But in the jungle you are building a relationship with your audience. You figure out where everyone is, meeting them at that level, and taking them on a ride and telling stories. It's no different from what I do now; it's just storytelling.

Joshua Sudock, 2000s

It's like a fraternity and even when you're working with people that you can't stand, you can still have a good time with them because it's a fun environment. It was cool how somebody you would never hang out with outside of work is someone that you can become really close to at work.

Leo Romo, 2000s

I had boats that would make me cry sometimes because I'd be frustrated and the skips would be like, "Go get 'em, go do another one, it'll be fine," and then it would be fine. You never knew what you were going to get; with every boat it was a different experience.

Jen Chavez, 2010s

One day I got called by Frank to come in and fill an absence for a four-hour shift. I said, "Frank, I live two hours away and the car is covered in snow. I'll get there as fast as I can!" I jump in the car, get through parking, shuttle, costuming, and then negotiate my way across the park. I cross the rocks, get to the dock, walk on stage, and immediately Gerry says, "Pull on a boat, we need you." Back in boat storage, I do a safety check, radio check, and finally I'm ready to go and create memories for guests that last a lifetime. Benny LeMaster opens the gates and as I pull out on stage he bursts into song, "Why do birds suddenly appear, every time you are near?" in full show-tune voice. The nearby cast members are laughing and applauding, truly happy I was there. They were like, "The world is fine, Dave is here to help. This will be a great day." Looking back, that was a crazy amount of travel and commitment for a four-hour shift. But, there were no words for how happy I felt.

David Schoenwetter, 1990s–2000s

A bunch of us would sit in boat storage and smoke. My favorite time of day at Jungle Cruise was the late afternoon. There'd be a bunch of us under the canvas awning and maybe five of us smoking. We did lots of stuff together, like the third stop [at K lot parking for cast members]. All skippers got off at the third stop and Indy never had that. A guy named Matt told me that all skippers parked at the third stop. Tomorrowland never did stuff together. They were all old timers and they didn't want to hang out. Meanwhile, at the Jungle Cruise we were all the same age and got along. There was a sense of pride. We would wait at the shuttle for everyone and we'd move in this big group. We'd take over the back of the shuttle and other cast members noticed us.

Chris Ramirez, 2000s

This bond can even last years after someone has left Disneyland.

I was at a Skipper [stand-up comedy] Show a few months ago and you see many of the same people and you just pick up where you left off. Sometimes in my current work I'll run into a former skipper. No matter what, it is clear that there is this skipper bond. I recently ran into a skipper that I haven't seen in seven years, and I'd never seen him in civilian clothes, and I said, "Hey, skip," and we caught up. It was great. It's such a strong community.

Michael Libby, 2000s

And it can exist between people who never worked the attraction at the same time.

One semester at Cal State Fullerton I had a skipper in my class. On final exam day she showed up in her costume, which she'd never done before. She said that she had a jungle shift that started 30 minutes after our final was supposed to be over. As the class took the exam I posted this status on Facebook: "A skipper showed up to take her final in her full Jungle Cruise costume. If she thinks she's going to get extra credit, she is absolutely correct." A few minutes later the man in charge of Adventureland scheduling commented, "She'd better not be late!" I showed her the post when she turned in the exam and she said, "You know that guy!? He terrifies me! I went to call in sick once and he answered so I just hung up and came in to work." I told her, "That was the right decision."

David John Marley, 2000s

Kipp Hart began working at the Jungle Cruise while in his 40s.

When I walked on that dock I felt like a 20-year-old, I didn't feel displaced. I didn't feel out of place. In fact as soon as I got there, there was a natural connection. I have a passion for it and when I got there I knew that I was in the right spot. I connected with the humor immediately and I knew what people were trying to do. A skipper named Matt said that when he first saw me standing in the shipping office he thought, "Who is this old guy?" but then he got it and realized that I was one of them. I assimilated pretty quickly. And you've probably heard this a lot, but your first summer at Jungle Cruise is magical. It's all new.

Kipp Hart, 2000s–2010s

For Disneyland's 45th anniversary I told my manager that I wanted to organize a celebration for skippers both past and present. She approved and I gave a speech to skippers about the importance of what we did at the Jungle Cruise and the balance between having fun as cast, taking care of the guests, and keeping the magic alive. We had cake, it was a great time. I felt I was part of a legacy, a legacy of making people happy. It was something that I'll never forget. We made jackets which were great fake leather.

David Schoenwetter, 1990s–2000s

Out of all the places I have ever worked, I've never seen a place that had a clique as strong as at Jungle Cruise. There is a powerful sense of belonging, which means those that don't belong or don't belong yet can have a difficult time fitting in.

All the rides had cliques. The old timers were on vehicles, they have been there forever and my role was to give them breaks. At Pirates it was fun, but at Jungle Cruise you would hang out and hear wild stories about their boats and people would all share or tell their take on the stories. And I think that being able to talk about which jokes work allowed us to hone our craft. There were Pirate parties, but it never was the same as at Jungle Cruise.

Ben Case, 2000s

The first time I knew that I was "in" at the Jungle Cruise, I had been there a few months and there was this unfunny skipper rolling around on the dock like a fish. I looked at the lead and said, "How often do you think he executes a funny joke?" The lead looked at me and said, "I think about a 100-to-1 ratio is being generous." There was a definite clique and you knew who the cool kids were and who the uncool kids were. It was made very clear. There was lots of hazing out the suck.

Chris Ramirez, 2000s

For the most part, it seemed like I didn't fit in right away. It seemed like after I had been there four or five months that I began to fit in with everyone. That is the magic of the Jungle Cruise; once you are accepted into the crew, you can get along with everyone and you didn't need to be best friends with them to have a good time with them.

I remember when I was really new, it was like my fourth or fifth shift and everyone was going to Denny's and I didn't get invited. There was always this skepticism and caution toward new people. So everyone was standing around as the park closed and everyone was asking each other, "Are you going to Denny's?" and no one was asking me. I remember being bummed that I didn't get asked, But I understood that I wasn't yet in that circle. I wasn't worried that I'd never be allowed in, I just knew that it would take some time for the rest of the skippers to get to know me.

I remember one night I had a closing shift and I took my last boat and there was no line when I left. When I get back to the dock there are no boats waiting and a huge line. I hadn't been at the Jungle Cruise that long, but I knew that this was weird. I had gotten back to the dock about five minutes after the park closed so this line of guests made no sense. So I pulled up to load up the boat and the guests seemed so excited to be getting one last ride before the park closed.

It was a good trip and then I get to the attacking natives and they don't attack and the jungle goes quiet. No backside of water, no lights on Trader Sam. And I was beginning to panic because I was the new guy. I know at the end of the night everybody wants to get out of there. And the Jungle Cruise can shut down really quickly, so I thought they had forgotten about me, shut everything down, and went home. Skippers did not mess around when it was time to leave for the night. I crept around the corner from Trader Sam and I can see that all the lights are out on the dock and in the boathouse. Two boats are tied up at the dock and shut off. And I remember thinking, "I know that I'm new and nobody knows who I am, but I can't believe they would forget that I was out there in the jungle. How could the other skippers not have noticed there were only two boats at the dock? Could they have been in that big of a hurry?"

I stopped spieling. I was just staring at the dock when I caught some movement out of the corner of my eye. I saw someone hunched over in the shadows, then I realized I'm getting pranked. So I decide to play along with it and I slowly approach the dock. And as I do that all the lights come back on and everybody jumps out. That was the first night that I got invited to Denny's. Everybody had a good laugh over pranking the new guy. Apparently, they had already closed the ride when they decided to pull the prank on me. So they reopened the attraction and a few skippers went out into Adventureland and told people they were going to pull a prank on the rookie skipper and they needed some help. All the guests on my boat knew that I was going to get pranked. That was the moment when I felt like I was part of the crew. That was the turning point in my Jungle Cruise experience.

Mike Pucher, 2000s

Getting into the cool club was very arbitrary. A friend of mine got in quickly because he knew people already. It was like high school, it was very random. I think they like people that were naturally at ease with themselves and others. Like when we pranked a new skipper named Jeff, he laughed and said, "Okay, you got me," and that was all it took for him to be in the club.

If you came in and learned your jokes and didn't max on your breaks and got along well with everyone. If you did the basics and didn't steal anyone's jokes. If you liked being there but were not too enthusiastic about being there, you know, it was like high school. Do stuff, but don't get too excited about it. Do lots of good jokes at the dock and when you were new keep your mouth shut and listen. Although there were people who did all of those things and never jelled with anyone. If you did that then you would get invited to stuff off campus. It was very arbitrary. When I came in an old timer told me that I was trying too hard and that I should just be myself and I'll be fine. You ease your way into it. Joking on the dock is a big test. The longer you are there the more you can get away with. There was a lot of watching out for each other. I'm sure every era thinks that they are special, but that was true of our time. There were people who tried so hard to be a part of the cool kids and they tried so hard and it rubbed people the wrong way.

Chris Ramirez, 2000s

There have been a few traditions that have come and gone over the years that keep the spirit of the Jungle Cruise alive. During the 2000s it was common for skippers to take a "Last Boat." It was done on a skipper's last day after the park closed and only friends and co-workers were invited. Some of these could be fun, while others became too wild.

My best trip, my favorite part of working at Jungle Cruise, was when I had to do three last trips because there were so many people there. It was great because I wasn't very popular in school and yet at Jungle Cruise I was very popular. It was a great night. I wish we could have reunions. You know what is weird? Seeing people that I signed off at the Jungle Cruise become managers. When I went back to Disneyland and worked in Critter Country two of my managers were people that I signed off.

Andy McGuire, 2000s

When I was there it was a big deal. It had become a great thing. The Jungle Cruise is like summer camp, it has that vibe, especially among the summer, seasonal people. You take a boat out after the park closes and you can go off script. It was supposed to be more about telling stories and sharing your love of the jungle and it was for skippers only. If there was a well-regarded skipper they might have to take two separate trips. That was a big deal.

Michael Libby, 2000s

Managers always had a love-hate relationship with these last trips. They regularly kept skippers they thought were trouble makers from having a last trip. Finally, their paranoia was proven right.

The person who ended last trips was a skipper named Sherry. I always liked working with her. She was warm and funny and always came back with her boats laughing. It was like playing with Kobe. But she took her last trip and began insulting management and refused to drive the boat back to the dock and security was waiting for her and that was the end of last trips. I was so disappointed. The last trip was about showing love for Jungle Cruise and its skippers, not being all angry and bitter.

Michael Libby, 2000s

Many skippers in my era would do a last trip on their final day at the park. It was a tradition for the departing skipper to take one of both of their shoes and throw them into the gorilla camp. So when you would cruise by the gorillas, you'd always see an ever-changing collection of black shoes there.

David John Marley, 2000s

Another long-lasting tradition was a necklace called the "Spirit of the Jungle."

The jungle necklace was a great tradition. It was a necklace that was passed down from skipper to skipper. It started with a guy named Josh. When he left he passed it down to the skipper that you felt best embodied the spirit of the jungle. So it went to lots of people and then a skipper named Dave got it and kept it. He wants to hang it in Trader Sam's bar, but he kept it. It was a skipper-only thing. There is so much that is generational. So many things that apply only to one generation of skippers. They have something that was only theirs. Like the rope swing in the 90s or the penny bucket or running through the jungle. Wild things like that.

Kaz Liput, 2000s

When I got that necklace, it was instant bragging rights, I wore that thing all of the time. All of the time! Whenever new hires would ask me what it was I'd say, "Oh, no big deal, just the Spirit of the Jungle necklace."

Kipp and I pre-planned what we were going to do. I was going to make this speech about the importance of the necklace and how it's been passed down for generations, then I was going to toss it to Kipp and it would land in the river. We made a copy of the necklace so we could pull the prank. So we did it, and everyone on the boat gasped and freaked out. People were like "Mike, how could you do that?" That was a fun moment.

Michael Libby, 2000s

Not only did skippers have their own traditions, they had their own break rooms. The location changed from time to time. The constant theme of skippers and their break room is of them trying to find a place to relax away from management.

We always went to the balcony above the bazaar, that was our hangout. We would take our breaks there. There was a row of chairs and we would take our 30=minute lunch and if the show was going we could enjoy the music. Or if there wasn't a show we would hang out and talk. I don't think I ever went back to boat storage.

Alan Coats, 1960s

Have you ever heard of JUBA? It stands for Jungle Upstairs Break Area. Above the bazaar there is this little stairway that goes up. It was a place where only Jungle Cruise skippers were allowed. It was our special little place. So my friend and I, this is back when I was trying to make the Jungle Cruise cool again, my friend Lee made this sign that was a beer can pouring into the jungle and it said "Jungle Brews" on the can. And we had this radio and we made tapes to play up there featuring Fast Eddie, the voice of the jungle. We would do this radio show where he'd play songs and after a couple of them he would talk about stuff and so if you didn't know what was going on you'd think it was just a radio, then you hear a commercial for Baboon Bon-Bons or Jungle Brew Beer or After Hours at Ho-Jo's, stuff like that. He would work all of this goofy stuff in. He'd record a two-hour show every couple of weeks. It was an hour on one side and an hour on the other and we'd play it up there, and it was a place to hang out and listen to this fake radio. We all pitched in and bought sodas to keep up there, it was like a little pot-luck thing.

I thought that we needed a place to keep all this stuff safe. It was just sitting out there on the balcony. So I started smuggling in tools and nails and my friend John, who worked in merchandising, we found some drywall and we stole it and brought it to JUBA. You know that whole office up there? John and I built that. On our breaks we'd run up there and hang drywall, we found some insulation and brought that in, too. We made a chest to lock up all of our food and the radio. It was really cool.

One day the Adventureland merchandising lead went up there and saw what we had done (we even had a vent from the air conditioning). She saw what we had done, and she got permission to make it her office. So we only had the inside JUBA for about a year before we lost it.

Jeff Rhoads, 1970s–1980s

At the time I think there was a prohibition against being out at boat storage. I would go out there to linger. In boat storage you are between worlds, between lands. My imagination would go crazy and I would walk back there and it was other-worldly because you'd see the back of Main Street and their stuff and trash cans and then on the other side you'd see this huge jungle. I remember the mechanics were not happy with us being back there. Unless you were coming to get a boat they didn't want you there. When I was new I think someone made a big deal about going back there, so it was special to be able to go back there and get a boat.

Fred Martin, 1980s

We sometimes went to boat storage, but we had three break rooms upstairs in the Adventureland offices. Some skippers would hang out in that upstairs place right across from Jungle Cruise, but that was the Indy guest control office. We'd hang out in the boat storage and sometimes they tried to keep us out of there. We'd sit in the boats back there and take breaks, lay down. It was like that in the Storybook boat storage area, too. Every once in a while at Jungle Cruise some manager would walk by and tell you that boat storage wasn't a break area.

Sue Barnaby, 1980s–1990s

CHAPER FOUR

✕✕✕

TRAINING DAYS

A manager once told me that, as far as she was concerned, once a person is trained at the Jungle Cruise, they are ruined for the rest of the park. She claimed that Jungle Cruise takes a good cast member and gives them bad habits that they then spread to the rest of Disneyland.

For many skippers, training at the Jungle Cruise was their introduction to working at Disneyland. Cast members who came from other attractions could usually get into the swing of things fairly easily, but for brand-new people, it could be rough.

Training new skippers at the Jungle Cruise is a lot more than learning to push the correct buttons at the correct time. Being a skipper means learning how to operate machinery safely, all-important performance skills, as well as learning how to get along with the wildest group of cast members at the park.

Although today Disneyland is synonymous with great training, this wasn't always the case. Today at the Jungle Cruise training takes four full days. In the 1970s it was only two days and according to some skippers in the 1950s and 1960s, formal training was non-existent. The first skippers were simply handed a script a few days before they were to begin work and told to memorize it.

There wasn't any training! There was one session where we met with some supervisors who stood on the dock and gave us a lesson about using the pistol safely. They were really concerned that we pointed the gun straight ahead. They didn't want us to get the gun near the boat where it would get too close to a kid. They didn't want any accidents. He reached up to his eye and took his eye out to make a point about safety. So we got the point about being careful about the pistol.

When I showed up in June 1962 they gave me the outfit. The floral shirt, the cargo pants, the straw hat and the sandals, and I was an instant skipper. I didn't have to audition or do any of that, they just said, "There you go." So I guess they thought I could do it.

The boats were so easy to drive. Just push the lever forward and it goes forward, push it back, it goes back. There were a couple of boats that were funky and you didn't want to have them. As far as training goes, they handed me the script and said "memorize the script" and I memorized it. I reported the first day and they said, "Here's your boat." They never had me audition or take anybody around, they just assumed that I could handle it. I guess I was fortunate. In those days it was much more casual. Disneyland was a family, it was much more fun.

Alan Coats, 1960s

Pete [his trainer] says, "Here's your script and this is how you run the boat. I want you to learn the script and we're gonna put you on the boats." No other training. I just watched what the other skippers were doing and they said, "Off you go."

William Sullivan, 1950s

Training was much more formalized by the 1970s.

The first thing you did was have a class at Jungle Cruise at nighttime. I got there at 5pm and the park was closing at 6pm. I spent half an hour at Disneyland University and then we all walked ourselves to our attractions. We watched the operation, as there still were guests there. We rode the boats a couple of times as passengers. Then the park closed and the guests left and they told us, "Okay, you're doing it," and we started driving the boat. Because the park was closed we went really in-depth on how the attraction worked. We practiced loading people on and off the boat. It was a great way to do things, but by the time I became a trainer jungle they had gotten rid of it. So we did that for a few hours and then they told us to come in tomorrow morning and they were going to show us the daytime operations.

I got to the Jungle Cruise hating to talk in front of people. I did my training and I was scared about having people on my boat and my trainer kept driving us around and around and when he finally put people on my boat I was terrified and I messed up my spiel. I thought I had it memorized, but I kept forgetting stuff. I hacked my way through that spiel and at the end the entire boat applauded. I remember thinking, "How could they possibly think that was a good spiel?" It was horrible. But I thought, maybe they didn't notice, so my very next trip I acted like I was a pro. It just filled me with confidence. At that time you were not allowed to drive the boat before you got signed off, so I would spiel and the trainer would control the throttle. Then after a couple of trips the trainer would move to the back of the boat and you were on your own. It was kind of like walking and chewing gum at the same time.

Jeff Rho, 1970s–1980s

One of the guys that was being trained with me had a South African accent. He told us that he was from South Africa, but none of us believed him. It seemed so fake. I think he just created this character that he was determined to play until the bitter end. He probably had a horrible high school life and he was trying to put all that behind him. It was weird because everybody could see through it, and it eventually alienated him from everyone and he just disappeared. He was around for little bit and everybody would talk about him.

I did my first trip word-for-word from the cassette tape that we had made of a skipper a year earlier when I visited the park. It was fun because the other trainees hadn't even really looked at the script yet. I was ready to take my first boat when I got there. I did a couple of boats with my trainer on board, Then he got off the boat and I took a bunch by myself. It was such a cool feeling to have your first boat. It very quickly became second nature to me; I felt comfortable right away.

Fred Martin, 1980s

I'd never done any public speaking before and I figured that if I wanted to be a stand-up comic I needed to get used to having an audience. When I got hired I thought that if they didn't give me the Jungle Cruise I wasn't going to work there. I was working full time during the day as a graphic artist so I worked Jungle Cruise at night. I thought, what better place to practice doing stand up than at the Jungle Cruise? You get a script, you just have to learn how to entertain people. I thought it would help my comedic timing, which it really did.

Ron Robledo, 1980s

Sue Barnaby, the first female skipper at Disneyland, was forced to spiel to guests before she'd even had a chance to read the script.

We didn't know the spiel and they handed us the script on the second day, but then they threw us in a boat and told us guests are getting on. We didn't even know the spiel, so I went off memory. I had friends that I knew had spiels that had made me laugh. I also ad libbed a lot of stuff, I made it up along the way. On my first trip a couple of times I would say, "Over there is something, I don't know what it is, but it's fabulous." And that was my take on everything that I didn't remember.

When Joy [her friend who she got trained with] got thrown into her first boat with guests she didn't know the spiel either. So she would say things like, "Over there is some kind of elephant. I'm not sure what it is. Work with me people, work with me!" That was her catchphrase for her trip. It was really funny because we were not ready to have guests.

Sue Barnaby, 1980s–1990s

I picked up the script and worked on it. I did 14 trips before they put guests on my boat. I didn't want people on yet, but my lead made me. I was as nervous as heck, but I did a good job and got a kind of standing ovation. And it was all SOP, it was all on the script and it was really successful.

Jessica Harris–Lopez, 2000s

I stopped by Jungle Cruise before I started my training, I went by the dock one day to say hello and to meet people and to tell them I was going to be there soon. And a skipper named Jeremy took me to the training center and he got me a copy of the script. This was so I could start learning stuff early. I took it home with me so I could practice my jokes.

Joey Hurley, 2000s

I got trained with this guy and it was like being trained with a space alien. It was like an alien took human form and was trying to learn how to work at a theme park. He just kind of floated through things. I rode the boat on his PA and we were counting the accents that he was flowing through, and it wasn't even on purpose. I asked him about it and he denied doing accents, but it was like Russian, German, and he did maybe ten others.

Trevor Kelly, 2000s.

On my first day of training I got into my car to head to the park and "Welcome to the Jungle" was on the radio. I just blasted it.

Heather Nelson-Wilkins, 2000s.

I was trained by Kaz and by David Marley. I didn't realize David was training to be a trainer, I thought he was new, too, so I was so intimidated when I saw him give a tour and it was perfect and I didn't want to do it at all.

Karen McGuire-Vogelvang, 2000s.

The final test a cast member takes before they become a skipper is called the PA, or Performance Assessment. During the PA the would-be skipper does every aspect of the job while a lead watches to make sure they do it correctly: loading and unloading guests, emergency procedures, and driving the boat. For some skippers, this process is more difficult than it is for others.

They thought it would be funny to pick on me. They kept pulling me out of the boat. I started my PA at 7:30pm and didn't finish until 11pm. I had to redo my trip because they pulled "Jungle Police" on me four times. I was so mad. They thought it would be funny to mess with me. They pulled out the throttle pin a couple of times. I was so done by the end of it that I ran the squirter and got my trainer wet, then I backed up too far, tripped the sensor, and ran the squirter again. They tortured me.

Kristin Labock-McGuire, 2000s.

I got signed off on Jungle Cruise the night that the Angels won the World Series. I remember being on my lunch break and the Inn Between was packed since it was the top of the 9th inning. And the second that the Angles won, the Inn Between emptied out, it must have been full of people maxing on their breaks. The Angels won, they all cheered, and then they all disappeared. I remember my first trip through the jungle after I got signed off as a skipper; the boat was full of Angels fans. I think the guy I trained with didn't get signed off that day, he needed a fourth day, so I remember it being a little awkward. I remember that the guests were in a great mood that night.

And Kaz, as a trainer, would always take your picture with an instant camera as you came back to the dock on your first solo trip with guests. So I have an instamatic photo of my first trip, and I look so young! When I became a trainer I'd try to bring an instamatic camera with me so I could photograph my trainees on their first trip.

Mike Pucher, 2000s

I had worked at Jungle Cruise in 1996 with the old boats that didn't have governors on them. When I came back in the 2000s I was in my first day of driving the boat and I came roaring into the dock, then I threw the throttle back full and expected to come to a dead stop like we used to do. Now these bigger boats with a governor on them just kept going and going into no man's land. Thankfully, there wasn't a boat there or I would have slammed into it pretty hard. I turned and looked at my trainer, Kaz, and she had a big grin on her face. She said, "I let you do that because I wanted you to know how different the boats are now." I never forgot that lesson.

David John Marley, 2000s

During trainings we were doing deadhead practicing our spiel. It was me and a guy named Aaron (he didn't last very long). So we were doing a deadhead, and when we get to Schweitzer Falls, he says, "There it is, folks, Auschwitz Falls!" And Randy and I look at each other and I said to him, "Did he just say what I think he said?" And Randy said, "I think so." So he does another deadhead and sure enough once again he says, "There's Auschwitz Falls." And we start laughing. Randy stops him and says, "You can't ever say that." The guy's excuse was that he didn't know how to pronounce the word Schweitzer, and so Auschwitz was the next German word that he knew how to say.

Kipp Hart, 2000s–2010s

At Indy the attitude was, "We have to get this many people thru because they've been waiting for so long." Make sure you do step A, then step B. At Jungle Cruise the trainers taught you how to be funny. They treated Jungle Cruise like it was something special and staffed by genuinely funny people.

Chris Ramirez, 2000s

Originally I thought that skippers were hired actors. I didn't know how hiring was done. I thought working the dock was one job and being in the boat was another. So I got on a wait list and eventually got a call that I was being hired into attractions in Adventureland. On the last day of Disneyland University I found out that I was getting Jungle Cruise. That is when I learned that I was going to be in the boat. I'm not shy, I'm an outgoing person, but I don't like being the center of attention. I get horrible stage fright. Training was nerve racking, but by the end of it I was comfortable and by my second day it was like second nature to me.

Anonymous, 2010s

The training that you get at Jungle Cruise, and I'm not talking about the formal training you get when you are new, is a master class in learning how to read people, and connect, and take people on a journey with you. It's pretty cool. I think about Jungle Cruise everyday, not because I'm crazy about skipper culture, but because those tools help me in my job as a reporter. Meeting people where they are.

Joshua Sudock, 2000s

Being the trainee was only part of the fun. Being a trainer at the Jungle Cruise was an honor and a chance to pass on the history and love of the attraction to the next generation. Sometimes this went well, sometimes it didn't.

Having a great trainee is like having a legacy. You teach them how to be a skipper like you. It was like having a child there.

David Schoenwetter, 1990s.

Sometimes you had people show up who had no idea what they were getting into. If they didn't like talking in front of people, it could be intimidating. Once you get the hang of it, it's a great attraction to work at. You learn a lot.

Sue Barnaby, 1980s–1990s

I think it was day one, and it was lunch and this male trainee said that he had left his money in his locker, and I offered to buy lunch for him, but he said he'd go get it. So we were at the Inn Between eating lunch and times passes, over 30 minutes, and he never ever came back. I never found out what happened to him or why he left.

Kaz Liput, 2000s.

It was great that Kaz was my trainer. She was much nicer about me being a Disney nerd than other trainers may have been. I don't think they would've appreciated my geekiness as much, but Kaz was totally okay with it. She didn't mind my excitement about being at the Jungle Cruise. She was a pretty strict trainer; she wanted you to be quality. I remember how that first night she sent us home with the script and told us to come back the next day with our jokes ready to go. As I was practicing my jokes she stopped me because I had contradicted myself. Early in my trip I'd say, When you've been in the jungle as long as I have you start to smell... danger." And then later in the trip I did a joke about it being my first trip. Kaz pointed out the problem with the spiel. She brought a lot of theatrical integrity to the Jungle Cruise, and that was a great way to get started.

Mike Pucher, 2000s

Sometimes a trainer could even get pranked by their own trainees.

I trained a guy named Danny who was a sweet guy and all the girls were in love with him. On his first day he tells me that he's narcoleptic, but he should be okay. I told him that it's okay. It was on the third and final day of training, we're at the Inn Between, and one of the Adventureland managers comes over to talk to me about the trainees and I tell him that they are both perfect to sign off when Danny falls on the floor asleep. It turns out he was faking the whole thing. He was a really good skipper.

Benny LeMaster, 2000s.

Training at Jungle Cruise used to take three days. The first day was all about the Tiki Room and learning how to drive the boat safely and getting the script. On the second day my trainees would ask me if they were going to have guests on their boat that day. I gave them the same answer, "You'll have guests on your boat tomorrow, don't worry about it today." They took that to mean they wouldn't have guests on their boat that day, which was not what I said. All I was telling them was they would have guests tomorrow, but I didn't want them to worry about it today. I didn't want them to worry about today, because they were going to have guests, they just didn't know it.

The second day of training my two trainees would do countless trips practicing their spiel. Later in the day, when I thought they were ready, I would load guests on their boat without warning them. Normally, my trainee would pull the boat up to the load position and I would drag my finger across my throat to tell the loaders that this was a deadhead trip: no guests allowed. Then the trainee would briefly practice docking the boat. When I felt they were ready I would subtly point down to the loaders, telling them to put on guests. Almost every single time, the trainee would park the boat, then turn around to practice docking, only to see guests quickly filling the boat. More often than not the now terrified trainee would look at me in a panic and say, "What do I do now?" My response was always the same, "I'd be funny. I wouldn't put people on the boat if you weren't ready."

David John Marley, 2000s.

I felt a good deal of responsibility. I cared about the Jungle Cruise, and I wanted it to be a great experience for guests. When it came to training, I tried to get people really excited about working there. I remember that Kaz did a great job of teaching the survivor skills, because I think fitting in with the crew was just as important as learning your spiel. I always tried to make sure the people were happy to be working at Jungle Cruise.

Mike Pucher, 2000s

The best skippers were those who would help the rookies and show them the ropes, even if they weren't a trainer.

My friend Jerad was a really good mentor. He used to show up to a lunch when I was training new skippers, usually so that my trainees wouldn't feel terrified of how well everyone seemed to fit together. He'd ask them what jokes they liked, remind them that the really funny skippers didn't start off that way. He told the few female skippers I trained that some of the funniest skippers out on the river were women, and said they should ignore what the guys (both skippers and guests) would say about the girls not being as funny. He liked to help people find their place because other skippers had done the same for him, and that made the prospect a lot less daunting.

Whitney Drake, 2000s

I made fun of pretty much everything, but I always warned my trainees to never mock the statue of Ganesh, the elephant-headed Hindu god that is placed in the Cambodian shrine scene. On the very day that I warned him not to do it, one of my trainees told a mean joke about Ganesh right in front of a group of women dressed in traditional Indian dress. One of the women stood up and screamed, "Do not make fun of my god!" He looked over at me, and I just dropped my head in shame. I think he ended up working at Toontown.

David John Marley, 2000s

Before I worked at Disneyland I was a school bus driver and I worked with this one guy who would always flip the middle finger when you waved at him, but only if you didn't have any kids on your bus. One day I was at the backside of water with a boat filled with guests when I saw a boat coming up to the falls that had two trainers and their four trainees on board. Since I'm tall I often held on to the top rail as I spieled. As the training boat passed I decided to flip them off, being sure to keep my hand above the canopy so the guests couldn't see. I even kept telling jokes so that everything looked normal. I would have gotten away with it except for the horrified faces of my friends and their trainees on the other boat. All of my guests looked at their boat, and then swung back in unison to look at me, trying to figure out what was going on. Those poor trainees had been working at Disneyland for less than an hour.

David John Marley, 2000s

That is part of the joy of becoming a trainer, seeing how bad most people's first boats are.

Anonymous, 2010s

My purpose was to help foster the old school Jungle Cruise, that was my purpose. It was already losing its steam as far as that was concerned. I thought it would be a good opportunity to influence some new skippers, and to get them to go that extra mile and have some fun with it. It's such a fun place to work. It's supposed to be fun, it's not supposed to be all tasks and numbers, it's supposed to be fun.

I did two groups of two and only one from each group made it. The first group was two girls. We get on the boat and one girl couldn't even spiel. I mean even during a deadhead she was too nervous to speak into the microphone. She froze up. We would just drive around for eight minutes. And I told her "You have to be able to talk, that is what we do." She couldn't do it, so we had to recast her at Indy, and she flourished there.

My second trainee group was two guys; one of them is now a lead and a trainer at the Jungle Cruise at Walt Disney World. He was a great kid. The other trainee was late three out of the four training shifts. The third day that he showed up late I told him, "We're done." I told this kid, "Look, first of all it's disrespectful to your training partner, to be late every time. It's disrespectful to me." So I walked them upstairs and talked to a manager. A manager pulls up his personnel file and we find out that he was a restricted rehire and you'll never guess what for: attendance! And they hired him again! So I told a manager to put him somewhere else, and I never saw him again. I don't know where he went.

Kipp Hart, 2000s–2010s

A challenge as a skipper is to make the trip special for every person on every boat. So, during the safety spiel, while guests are loading, you are trying to figure them out. Like, there is a young couple in love, a family who doesn't speak English.... You're trying to build the best possible trip for that unique group of people. You mix and match the jokes for each boat and the guests come away with an experience customized for them. As a trainer I tried to teach new skippers how to do that. You can't just give them all the same show. You want the guests to say, "Holy moly, that was an experience that no one else has ever had and he did that just for me."

David Schoenwetter, 1990s–2000s

This was my favorite prank to pull on my trainees.

Until the mid 1990s there were 12 boats at the Jungle Cruise. When they brought in the new ones, the river only had room for 10 since they were a bit bigger. However, back in boat storage there was still a sign that had all 12 boat names. As I showed my trainees around the attraction I always showed them the sign and told them to memorize the boat names. I would then casually mention a few, and always pointed to the Mekong Maiden, but never mentioned that boat had been gone for 10 years.

On their third and final day of Jungle Cruise training, which was always a late-night closing shift, I would approach one of my trainees and tell them that a lead wanted them to pull on the Mekong Maiden. The rookie would grab a set up and head off to boat storage in search of the boat. My friends and I would hang out in the shipping office and enjoy their increasing panic. First the trainee would try to walk back to me to say the couldn't find it, but I'd wave them back and tell them to stop messing around. Then after a minute or two I would call the boat storage phone and say, "Why are you taking so long? I'm opening the door in one minute, you'd better have the Mekong Maiden ready to go." Then after about 30 seconds I would flick the switch that opened the big boat storage doors and usually the rookie was standing there, waving their arms yelling, "No, no!" After that we would usually let them in on the joke, but not until they were near panicked. Sometimes a guy from maintenance was back there and would tell the rookie that the Mekong Maiden had been gone since the late 1990s.

David John Marley, 2000s

Training managers was always fun. The new ones needed to be trained on the attractions so that they knew what their cast members were doing. It was interesting because you were always in an awkward position where you're telling your boss what to do. So that was uncomfortable.

What is interesting is that since Jungle Cruise is a new-hire attraction, you never know who you are going to get. Sometimes new people would get to the dock and my reaction was, "Do they know where they put you?" I had this one lady, she reminded me of Stephanie Edwards, the red-haired lady who used to host the Rose Parade. We ended up having her play it like a grandmother, and she was great. You know how you train people at Jungle Cruise, you don't have them change their personality, you have them create a spiel that works for them. You can't force it.

I once had this trainee named Mark, and he was a physically big guy but was very soft spoken. I told him that I had found the perfect spiel for him. I told him, you need to do the entire spiel as yourself, very soft spoken. He was kind of like Winnie the Pooh personified. And then when he gets into the hippo pool you just loose it. Then regain your composure at the dancing natives. He never did it, but that would have been awesome.

It's nice to go back to your park and see your trainees, then you see their posts on Facebook, "I'm so happy to be back at Thunder." And I feel so hurt when I see that.

One of my trainees came over from Knott's Berry Farm, and she was excited about two things. The first thing was that she had pockets. She was all, "We have pockets!" I guess they'd had a lot of problems with theft and didn't want their employees having cell phones, so all their pockets were sown shut. The other thing she was excited about was the water cooler. She was all, "We get water!" She was super stoked about those things.

Kevin Lively, 2010s

My weirdest training experience had the most dramatic ending. I trained this couple, which was weird because Disney didn't usually put new people who were dating or married on the same attraction. They had moved here to get a job in animation and figured Disneyland was the best place to start.

They were both shaky at best and all three days were a struggle with them. Driving the boat, being on time, memorizing the script, they had a hard time with all of it. By the end of the third day, the final day of training, they were at least passable, but they were the only trainees I ever had that I wasn't fully convinced would make it. So we went to lunch, and I told them that before I got a lead to do their PA test, they were each going to do a run through for me and when I was happy, then I would get a lead.

We get back to the dock and I tell them to grab a set up and a boat. The guy asked me if I could do it, so they could have a quick smoke. I was a bit irked at the request, but I said okay. So I pull a boat on, get it ready, and they hop in. The guy went first and he forgot jokes, he almost ran the squirter, and was just generally a mess. His mistakes, however, were nothing compared to his girlfriend's. She ran the squirter, forgot jokes, and was just generally terrible. At the gorilla camp she stopped the boat and asked me over the mic, "What am I supposed to say here?" I was literally sitting next to her! Why did she say that over the mic?

By the time we got back to the dock, the guy wouldn't look up at me and she looked ready to die. I was tired and angry, and I let it get the best of me. I took a deep breath, tried to calm down, and then I said, "Hey, remember when I pulled on the boat and you two went to have a smoke? Well, did you smoke crack because those were the worst two boats I have ever seen." With that the girl bursts into tears, runs out of the boat, down the dock, and backstage to boat storage, loudly crying. Then suddenly we hear her throw up. Not just once, either, she repeatedly threw up, right into the river backstage. Her boyfriend runs after her, and all the skippers on the dock, who didn't hear what I had said, just stared at me. I called a manager over and after she spent 45 minutes crying and throwing up, the manager tells her about an "exciting chance to work attractions at Toontown." We tried to get rid of her boyfriend, but he wanted to work Jungle Cruise. I told the manager he'd need at least a fourth day. He was the only trainee I ever had who needed a fourth day, which is usually done by a different trainer.

She never came back to the park. The boy came back, passed his test on the fourth day, and then never came back to work a shift.

A week later, I had a new group of trainees. I met them, as usual at 5am by the cast member gate. As they walked over to me one said, "I heard that you're the trainer who makes his trainees throw up." I suppressed a smile and said, "Yep, so when I say be funny, you'd better be funny."

David John Marley, 2000s

CHAPTER FIVE

TALES OF THE SCRIPT

Jungle Cruise Skippers have a love-hate relationship with the script. What skippers think is funny, and what they think they can get away with saying, is the main source of tension between skippers and Disneyland management. No other attraction gets as many guest compliments as the Jungle Cruise, and no other ride gets more cast member-focused guest complaints. When an attraction like the Haunted Mansion or Space Mountain get complaints, it is almost always about the ride breaking down. A guest complaint about the Jungle Cruise is almost always about something a skipper said or did. A complaint about a mechanical breakdown can be ignored, but a complaint about the actions of a cast member requires immediate attention.

That is the tension that Jungle Cruise has lived with since 1955. On the one hand, you have a ride run by young people who have a craving to entertain, and on the other you have managers trying to make sure that nothing goes wrong. How do skippers deal with a script that they didn't write?

The original script was written by some behind-the-scenes bean counter. I read it, tried to use parts of it. It wasn't a bad tour, it just wasn't me, and it also wasn't most of the other guys.

Warren Asa, 1955

As I recall, our spiel wasn't what you'd think of as a script, it was just a block of words. Here are the animals you're going to see, here is what you can say, maybe. It was pretty boring stuff, so we started tossing in our own jokes.

I made up some jokes, but I can't remember even one of them today. We all added in our own jokes. Some of the guys would go around and sound like pirates. We weren't given any direction, other than make sure the guests were entertained.

Then we had a guy who was a speech writer and would come down and ride the boats. His name was Dave something and he had the driest sense of humor. He would write things for us to say, and we never used any of it. We never liked to see him come around.

William Sullivan, 1950s

The script did have jokes in it, but they were kind of corny. And they did tell us to stick to the script. They'd say, "This is the law and the rule, we don't want anybody coming up with any funny stuff, you stick to the script." Well, nobody did. Some of the guys came up with things that I never would have said. I wasn't a comic, I was an actor, so I went with the show as it was written. The script was revised occasionally and they would show us a few new lines, but it was basically the same thing.

I was a pretty straightforward skipper. I stuck to the script, I didn't do a lot of funny weird jokes, I improvised when I had to when the ride broke down. I did the backside of water and the alligator looking for a hand out. The mother-in-law joke at the dock. There was the men's room laugh. When you got to the dancing natives you'd say, "Those men are not dancing, they are waiting to use the bathroom. They've only got one in their village." All those kind of things would come and go in and out of the script.

Alan Coats, 1960s

I wish I had followed the script more. There is something really special about doing every trip the way it's been done for 60 years. I think I got more laughs because I went off script, but some of those lines just killed. If I had a bunch of annual passholders on my boat, I knew that I had jokes that would just kill. And they'd love it, and I'd get a guest compliment, but I wasn't necessarily doing the Jungle Cruise. But in the moment you love getting the laugh. I don't think that is something that an 18 year old could wrap their head around. I've always felt like the Jungle Cruise should be a more senior attraction. I feel like they should have more reverence for the script and the attraction. I think an older skipper would appreciate how special the ride is and how rare an opportunity it is. When you're 21, your'e going to live forever and you're having fun and you want to keep the guys on the dock happy. Many younger skippers think it's all about them and it's not, it's all about the guests. that's why the Jungle Cruise has staying power, because it resonates with the guests. Skipper culture is fun for us, but I've been on some bad boats.

Joshua Sudock, 2000s

I got to the point after about a year or so where I didn't use a single joke from the script. When I had to train new skippers, I would be on the boat as they spieled, reading it along with them. Sometimes they would ask me, "Was that joke on the script?" and I'd have to check because I paid so little attention to it.

David John Marley, 2000s

The Jungle Cruise is the hero of the story to me. Or maybe the guests are the hero of the story, the ride is the antagonist, and I'm just the side kick. I did a lot of research on the old OG (Operation Guidelines). I read all the old scripts that I could find and a lot of it is still in the old OG but nobody uses it. So I would use the stuff that was approved but nobody used and people thought it was all new jokes and I was like, "No, it's just old stuff people don't use and don't have the energy to put into it, I guess."

Jen Chavez, 2010s

Skippers did occasionally get to add their own jokes to the script. The ability to do so came and went over the years before finally becoming a formalized process in 2004.

I have a book, it's like a log book that the leads used, and they made this one 1978 or 79. This is the approved list of ad lib jokes for the Jungle Cruise. If you had an idea for a joke you write it in this book, and every week or so a supervisor would come by and review the book. If they liked it they would write "OK" by the joke and if not they would cross it out. So the book was organized by sections; you can see here several pages of stuff on Schweitzer Falls. It's pretty cool. There are a few pages that were completely torn out because they didn't want anybody to see what was written there.

Jeff Rhodes, 1970s–1980s

I knew a skipper who was dating a deaf guy who told me that many of the jokes at Jungle Cruise don't translate well into sign language. The puns, which I hate, get translated literally. So at the gorilla camp the joke "Those gorillas were trying to get that Jeep to start, it looks like they finally got it to turn over" in sign language comes out as "Those gorillas were trying to get that Jeep to start, and now it is upside down." When I heard that I tried to come up with jokes for the deaf.

Most of the jokes were me making fun of the translator, who was always a plaid, and then I'd point out that she was forced to translate my jokes about her. I then would say big words and force her to finger spell them. The deaf guests and I thought it was funny; the translator, not so much.

During the summer of 2004 I was honored to be asked to help write jokes and update the script at Jungle Cruise. I spent the summer working with a small group of skippers and an Imagineer; it was the best.

The process was that we'd pitch jokes for a certain scene and the skipper, Imagineer, leads, and manager would decide if they liked the joke. I pitched a joke that many skippers were doing, but nobody was sure who wrote it, or how long it had been there. I know that the joke was there years before I showed up. It's a joke at the scene where the rhino was chasing those guys up a pole. It was the only part of the shoreline that was covered in large rocks. Those rocks went from the water all the way to the rhino. So the joke is, you pull up to the scene, ignore the rhino and the chaos, and say, "Man, look at those rocks! Wow, that's a lot of rocks!" I was instantly voted down, instantly. We were about to break for lunch, so I told them that after lunch I was going to put on a Jungle Cruise costume, take out a boat and do the joke, just to prove it was funny.

So after lunch we were in the boat full of guests, and the eight or nine people working on the new script. I do the "lots of rocks" joke, and the guests laughed really hard. It's funny because you are ignoring all the action and sound to point out rocks. As the guests roared, I looked at the Imagineer. She gave me the thumbs-up sign and I knew the joke was in. After we got off the boat she said, "You know, with that joke, you're encouraging people to ignore a $300,000 piece of animatronics." I replied, "Who cares, that's a good joke."

The lawyers had to approve comedy. So we wrote jokes and the lawyers had to make sure that no one, in any way, was the least bit offended. Luckily for us, the lawyers would sometimes accidentally make them funnier. We had this joke we said as the boat pulled away from the dock. It went like this. "Wave goodbye to all of the beautiful people on the dock. Now wave goodbye to the ugly people on the dock." No one had ever complained, but the lawyers said, "You can't be calling people ugly. It's not Disney." So they changed it to this: "Wave goodbye to all of the beautiful people on the dock. Now wave goodbye to everybody else." We quickly realized that the new version was so much worse. Now the ugly people are not only ugly, but they are too stupid to know that we are calling them ugly.

David John Marley, 2000s

Skipper Jen Chavez worked at Jungle while pregnant and came up with jokes to make the most out of her condition.

We were all trying to think of funny things I could do as a pregnant skipper. When we would do the backside of water joke, I'd say, "It's the eighth wonder of the world, it's the back side of...oh my gosh, my water just broke!" I would get laughs because people were expecting back side of water. It was fun.

There is the joke where I'd say, "I went with my boyfriend to Trader Sam's last night and his wife made stew. Just kidding, I don't have a boyfriend." Then I'd look at the guy closest to me and I'd say, "Do you want to be my boyfriend?" and I would get laughs and then I'd say, "Do you have really good insurance?" and stuff like that and that's the time when you're stretching it out before you hit the dock. "How do you feel about changing diapers and what's your philosophy on circumcision?" It was just fun. But that was kind of it because it was hard to come up with baby-related jokes in the jungle. I just played up the exhausted mom feel.

Jen Chavez, 2010s

Getting material officially added to the script is the goal of any skipper who is truly trying to be funny.

This is what I think was my biggest achievement at Jungle Cruise. When we did the spiel update in 2004, management was adamant that we had to force skippers to stay on the script no matter what. It was just another page in the 50-year struggle to rein skippers in. I was able to convince the managers that if they wanted people to follow the script then they had to give skippers the ability to add jokes. So another skipper named Kaz and I created a system where jokes could be submitted and handed over monthly to Imagineering in Glendale. An Imagineer would then approve or deny the joke, and it would get added to the script. They always changed at least one word, because they said legally the skippers are not writing the jokes, they are. After I left I learned that they give out little awards for people who get their jokes in the official script. I thought that was going to be the thing that made me infamous.

David John Marley, 2000s

While the ability for skippers to submit jokes to the script has now been extended to Walt Disney World in Florida, the process has changed and skippers don't get rewarded for getting a joke on the script.

They have certain times of the year when they open up submissions, and you take a piece of paper and you write your joke down. It's anonymous now, but you used to put your name on it, and they made you sign a legal thing saying that you didn't own this joke anymore. Now it's just anonymous so they don't have to do the legal part. I think they do the first phase upstairs. The leads and managers look through all of the jokes, and they kind of filter it out, and then send the ones they think might be usable off to WDI, then legal takes a peek at it.

Today I have maybe a dozen jokes that are on the official spiel. I use them all to keep my boat unique. I wrote a joke that got on the script for the Indy queue and it goes like this: "Do you know why they call that the Temple of the Forbidden Eye? Because Temple of the Forbidden Me is horrible grammar." What's funny about that is I don't know a lot of the rules of English grammar, so I wasn't even sure that was grammatically correct.

I used to do jokes on the script that were more obscure, and then I'd put my own twist on it. I wrote the Shakespeare joke that you use at the attacking natives. I wrote that when I wasn't even working at Disneyland. I texted it to a friend of mine who was a skipper at the time and she loved it and submitted it.

Kipp Hart, 2000s–2010s

Despite the training and the warnings, the temptation to go off script was often too great to resist. Even the most law-abiding skipper would ad lib when something unexpected happened. Sometimes the jokes eventually made it onto the script, at other times they just got skippers in big trouble.

They had a real issue because skippers started going off script. Skippers would mention products all of the time, and you weren't allowed to do that. For example, in the rain forest they'd say things like, "A day without sunshine is like a day without orange juice," which was copying that Anita Bryant commercial. There were a lot of homosexuality jokes. So it got to the point that supervisors would hide in the jungle and listen to us as we drove by and if they heard something they didn't like they would run back to the dock and get us pulled out of the boat.

There were some jokes that I thought were hysterically funny. For example, as you came back to the dock you say, "Well that's the end of the ride, I hope you had as much fun as my friends did out in the parking lot stripping your cars. Speaking of that, be sure to come back tonight at midnight for our parking lot sale,. 'If you brought it we got it.'" One day a guy's car actually got broken into in the Disneyland parking lot. He complained to the police and said, "Our Jungle Cruise skipper told us this was going to happen."

Other jokes that got skippers in trouble was when they'd drive past the a pile of skulls and say, "You can tell the male skulls from the female skulls because the females skulls are the ones with their mouths still open." Or they would say, "You can tell the male from the female skulls by how they are stacked."

Jeff Rhoads, 1970s–1980s

I got a ton of guest compliments, even a few with the dreaded comment, "I've never heard those jokes before." Then you'd get called up to the manager's office because they wanted to know what you had said. I would reference an obscure joke from the script and tell them that sometimes those bad jokes land well.

Joshua Sudock, 2000s

On the script or off, the most important part of saying a joke was the ability to pull it off correctly. The art of comedy was the key to a successful trip. Some skippers were better at this than others.

My opinion was that some people could tell a joke and make it funny, and other people couldn't. It would be the exact same words, but it was just their delivery that made all the difference between getting a laugh and having people get offended. And it's a finesse thing; it's not anything that you can write out. Even if the job works and everybody laughs somebody's going to come along and not know how to tell it and people will complain.

Jeff Rhoads, 1970s–1980s

There was a skipper, Jeff, who did a trip he called "Spielus Minimus." He was an old-timer and he hated the Jungle Cruise. He always picked Tiki Treehouse because it had minimal guest interaction. So at Jungle Cruise he did the Spielus Minimus. He'd go, "Ladies and gentlemen, welcome aboard the World Famous Jungle Cruise. Let's all sit back and listen to the animals." And that was it! He'd put the mic down and never talk again.

George Trullinger, 1970s–1980s

There was a skipper who did the "Spielus Minimus." He got suspended for it.

Sue Barnaby, 1980s–1990s

After they are working there for a while, many skippers begin to realize that the strict rules about following the script are more of a guideline.

I slowly began to realize that skippers did whatever they wanted to do on their boats. I rode other skippers' boats just for fun and realized that nobody was following the script. I heard one scripted joke per tour, and that's when I realized that I can say whatever I want to as long as it was funny. There were some managers and leads that tried to stamp out any kind of creativity just because they thought it could be dangerous if a guest heard it. But I didn't think I was doing anything other than being funny so what was the harm? And literally everyone else was doing it. This was maybe three or four months into my career at Jungle Cruise. I didn't do it to be mean or to be rebellious, but I kept doing it because I thought it was better than the material that they had given me. There were many jokes in the script that were funny and I did all of those, but about eighty percent of the jokes in that script just fell flat. There is a balance because there are guests who want to hear nostalgia, the old jokes, and then there are people who want to hear surprising new things.

I knew how to balance what I think is funny with what the guests think it's funny. I'd argue about it with Trevor, another skipper. "Who are you doing comedy for? Is it for you or for the guests?" It's both. It has to be entertaining to you so you can put yourself into it. It has to be entertaining for the audience; there's 40 of them and only one of you. Sometimes if there was a joke that I didn't think was funny but the audience loved time and time again, I would do it. For example, the backside of water. I'm not going to do a joke like it's a jackass routine where the jokes are only funny to people later.

So when I'm in the boat I will imitate Robin Williams and Jim Carrey and other popular comedians so people get a wider range of what they might find funny. It might be a cop-out to do that. It might be reaching for the lowest common denominator to do that, but the point is for them to have a good time on my boat, It's not a place for me to hone my Andy Kaufman routine. It's for them to enjoy. I think that's what made me different. I was willing to make the guests laugh. I would do anything to make them laugh even if it was something that I didn't like or I didn't necessarily think was funny. The point was to entertain them. So I tried to find a balance between people that only do jokes funny to them and those that would do anything to get their boat to laugh.

I liked getting the audience to like me, I like making people laugh. And that fueled every trip to try something new, to try to be my best at it. The other reason was meeting people at the Jungle Cruise who I wanted to impress. There're other people there who I thought were funnier than I was. These guys made me crack up and I thought I needed to be as funny as they were, so that when I approach the dock I can make them laugh more than the guests in my boat. It was important to me to impress my fellow skippers more than the guests some of the time.

Joey Hurley, 2000s

My character for the Jungle Cruise was a very flirtatious children's show host. I'd always talk with the kids, but if their grandmother was there I'd flirt with her. Once this elderly lady got mad because I was flirting with her and she was a married woman.

Kevin Lively, 2010s

The most interesting thing about Jerad as a Skipper wasn't that he was funny; he was. But he was an actor, and he approached the World Famous Jungle Cruise like any other acting job. That's why he and I clicked. He'd sit down before an early morning shift and say,. "I'm going to work on an accent today. So make sure I stick with it." But he wouldn't tell me what it was. I'd have to wait until he pulled up at the dock when I was there. Southern twangs, a nasally Boston accent. It was the strangest roulette designed to make him a better actor.

Whitney Drake, 2000s

My spiel changed dramatically during the first three weeks. I quickly learned what wasn't working and if it didn't work I would drop it. I would drop it and move on, and try to find something else that would work. I don't remember what my spiel was like when I first started; all I remember is I don't like doing jokes that all the other skippers are doing. I wanted to be more of an individual. Some guests frequent Jungle Cruise often, and they knew the spiel as well as some of the skippers so they would steal the punchlines. That always frustrated me. It would drive me crazy. I didn't know how to write comedy at that time. So what I first tried to do was create a spiel that was more rhetorical so they wouldn't have the opportunity to heckle. Many of the jokes on the script are written as questions which just encourages people to yell out things. The joke used to be, "Do you know why tigers have stripes? Because they don't want to be spotted." And I changed it to, "The reason tigers have stripes is because they don't want to be spotted."

When I started out I was like a machine gun, trying to do every joke I possibly could at every scene. Dead time to me was just terrifying. So I would fill it with jokes. I began to realize that by doing that I was walking over the laughs. I realized the reason they weren't laughing at this joke is because they were still trying to process the last joke. That's when I began to cut out a lot of material. Now I do maybe one joke or two jokes per scene, at the most. That really helped me with both my writing and my timing.

Kipp even wrote some jokes for Jingle Cruise, the annual Christmas overlay at the attraction. However, not all of his jokes met with official approval.

I did a Donner Party joke that isn't on the script. At the veldt they had these roof decorations, Santa and his sleigh, and they were scattered everywhere. One of the reindeer is up with the lions, so I'd say, "Look, there is Dasher, and Dancer, and oh look, the lions are having a Donner party." It gets a great laugh. And the next year it was put in the OG (Operation Guidelines): "No Donner Party jokes."

Kipp Hart, 2000s–2010s

The hardest part is the ad libs at the dock. Out in the jungle you have those visual cues to help you remember what to say. Learning how to ad lib was an important part. I remember there was a really long list of cannibal jokes, just one after another. You had to go on somebody else's boat to learn them. I would ride other boats and pick stuff up.

Fred Martin, 1980s

I didn't like that we didn't have as much creative input and control as I thought we were going to have. When I started I thought it was going to be a little more lenient because my experience in the 90s when I was a teenager going there was that it was a lot more fun. It felt like the skippers were having a lot more fun. That's why I was excited to go there.

I thought that skippers would have a lot more input when it came to their spiel and a lot more freedom. I never got in trouble, even though I did stuff on my own and I improvised and did a lot of things that were just me. I had managers ride my boat and I did it anyway. I never got in trouble for it because I didn't do anything that was inappropriate for the era it was supposed to be in. I came from a background of doing improv and theater and I really thought that the comedy piece would be bigger. I just thought our characters formed more naturally on our own.

Jen Chavez, 2010s

One lead said that being in the hippo pool at the moment when the skipper fires his pistol is the dramatic high point of the Jungle Cruise.

Sometimes when you would go to fire your gun, the ammo didn't work, so I'd just yell, "Boom! Boom!" then I'd turn to the guests and say, "The hippos don't know the difference."

Ron Robledo, 1980s

The hippos were fun, pulling out a gun was fun. They don't get to do that at Storybook. People were always surprised when the gun went off, especially those not paying attention. It's so iconic, it's part of Jungle Cruise DNA.

Kevin Lively, 2010s

For reasons that were never made clear, in 1999 Disneyland's Jungle Cruise skippers had their guns taken away. Some say it was political correctness, others said that the guns were simply too much of a hassle, but for whatever reason, they were gone. What happened to this dramatic moment in the years (2000–2005) that the guns were gone?

I worked the last night that we had guns. I have the last blanks that were fired on that last trip.

We were never told the reason that the guns were taken away. There were a lot of rumors going around. People said, "It's an animal cruelty issue, it's a gun safety issue," but we never got an official company position. Anyway, they came back because getting rid of them was stupid. I think the managers knew why, but I doubt the lead team knew. At the park you are told to "do" and not to question. We think somebody really high up decided they didn't like guns and that was that. At that time they removed guns from all across the park except for the Frontierland shooting gallery. It was great when they came back because it was way more fun. The guns were a fun element that we missed when they were gone.

Matt Nerrie, 2000s

One of the great struggles of the no-gun era was finding something funny to replace the guns. What some skippers used to do was when they came to the S curve was tell the guests that they were looking for two baby hippos. At the first turn in the S they'd yell, "Found one!" and then the boat jerks to the other side, "Found the other one!" One skipper would say, "One time a Gorilla snatched a kid from the boat and I rescued him with my gun...." He would then look in vain for the gun and then say, "Well, I guess that kid had to die."

At the hippo pool when we had guns there was one skipper who would tell everyone to look at the hippos, then he'd yell, "Give me your wallets!" and when they looked back he was pointing the gun at the guests and telling them, "No, really, give me your wallets."

Chris Ramirez, 2000s

I missed the guns when they were gone. I loved hearing the two shots from the Jungle Cruise. Guests didn't even notice it, it just blended in with the rest of the noise of the entrance to the park. I loved hearing the gun shots from the parking lot. In Florida their guns have a button and it just makes a gun noise over the speakers, it's just awful and the skippers there don't know any different.

Fred Martin, 1980s

And then one day the guns came back just as mysteriously as they had disappeared.

I was working Jungle Cruise in the summer of 2004 when a couple of skippers came running in and said they had just talked to then Disney CEO Michael Eisner. He was touring the park and stopped to have lunch at the Inn Between, the backstage cast member restaurant. While there he visited with people at other tables and happened upon these skippers. After chatting for a bit, Eisner said, "One day I'd love to join you in the Jungle Cruise and shoot at some hippos." One of my friends replied, "They took the guns away." Eisner asked why, and the skipper said that they didn't know the reason. Eisner then turned to one of his staff and said, "Get their guns back!" A few months later it was announced the guns would return and everyone but the hippos have been happy ever since.

David John Marley, 2000s

Every skipper has their favorite joke. Usually it's not something from the script, but something they came up with.

You'd come out of the jungle and see the Tahitian Terrace and there'd be women doing the hula dance. And you were supposed to be quiet while the show was going on. So if I knew a show was going on, I'd do the backside of water joke and as we passed the dancing girls I'd say, "And there it is ladies and gentlemen, the backside of...never mind," because you could see them shaking their hips at us. That always got a good laugh.

Ron Robledo, 1980s

Trader Sam was the best comedic partner you could ever have. He doesn't talk back, he just takes your abuse. That is a lot of fun, especially if you're stalled at Sam because they're pulling off a boat or something; then you have the perfect Laurel to your Hardy. He just stands there like a doofus. I like to have a staring contest. I'd say, "Sam, staring contest, you and me, go!" and just stare as long as I could, saying, "I got this, I got this" into the mic.

Kevin Lively, 2010s

I used to introduce myself as Lotta Top. I used jokes from other skippers that worked. I was more sarcastic. Not warm and fuzzy.

Sue Barnaby, 1980s–1990s

A favorite I did came as we left the gorilla camp. You turn the corner heading toward Schweitzer Falls and the entire jungle just opens up to you and it's beautiful. When I got to that point I'd say, "Well, as they say in the jungle, 'safari, so goodie.'" I think that was the most skipper moment that anyone could possibly have. Enjoying that view and that joke.

Mike Pucher, 2000s

I don't know who created this, I didn't, but I loved to do the whole "scene behind" gag. At the dock you check out your boat and if the guests look like they're going to be difficult and not listen, then you did this version where you drive through the jungle and you do your regular spiel, but one scene behind where you are so nothing matches up. It was great. Basically, I would start at the butterflies in the rain forest and start my load spiel there. In the Cambodian shrine I would talk about the Indy queue. I kept going from there, one scene behind the entire way.

The guests who got it loved it. There were so many people there, especially during the day in the summer who were not paying attention. I liked doing it more in the summer. Nobody wanted to be there and the guests are talking to themselves. You were just gunning it around the jungle as fast as you could. I would usually do it if there was another skipper on the boat, or if my friends were visiting I would be all, "Check this out, people won't even notice."

Leo Romo, 2000s

I heard a variation of the "scene behind" gag, where you pretend that it is your first day and you have the script written on note cards and then you drop the cards and put them back in the wrong order.

Trevor Kelly, 2000s

Every time I left the dock I would ask guests about their day and then I'd tell them about what I was going to do later on that night, like laundry, and how I was working on this great ham that has been cooking for 8 hours. I kept bringing up the ham and how I couldn't wait to get home and eat it. I then brought it up again at the squirter and then at the gorilla camp and then when we got to the gorilla with the ham I'd start yelling, "No, no! My ham!"

Kriztina Varga, 2000s

I also liked to use a joke that a skipper named Ritt came up with at the king cobras. "Over there you have two king cobras. Do you notice anything about these cobras? Look at them, they're all drunk, they can't even stand up straight." Because the snakes were all wobbly.

Trevor Kelly, 2000s

Ritt had the best bit. At night he would enter the hippo pool and slow the boat to a crawl and do the Velociraptor spiel from *Jurassic Park*. It went, "There is always one staring at you. And that is when they attack. Not from the front, but from the sides, the ones you didn't even know were there. The point is that you are very much alive when they begin to eat you." And then he'd roar off. He did the creepiest voice, too. He made kids cry.

Chris Ramirez, 2000s

What is the difference between a good and bad boat?

Yelling into the mic. The mic has a speaker, you don't need to yell. If you just speak normally, people are going to hear you, so don't try to blow out the speakers. Don't try to cram in as many jokes as you can. When you do that, you're not worrying about the comedic timing. You need to give a joke time to land; comedic pauses are everything. Repetitive vocal inflection can kill an entire trip. People should focus on having one really good joke per scene. The script is funny. I think it's people who are just trying to get through their shift instead of doing their job. They act like the guests do not matter. That's what makes a bad boat.

A good skipper engages their guests, is a great storyteller. Their guests will leave the boat happier than when they got on it. It's your job as a skipper, that if you are having a bad day, you keep that in your head and you don't let it impact your guests.

Joshua Sudock, 2000s

I did a trip in 4 minutes, 33 seconds. It was during my second summer. I was spieling the entire time, I ran the squirter, no one got wet. The guests had a blast.

Matt Nerrie, 2000s

A skipper named Adam decided to beat the record for the longest trip and I was in the boat behind him. What I didn't realize is that I needed just as much material as he needed. So I ran through every clean joke that I knew. I don't think Adam broke the record. He got within a minute, but the record was like 30 minutes for a single trip.

Leo Romo, 2000s

I thought of a way to raise morale, I was going to see how many spiels I could do in a row. They made a big deal out of it. They posted up signs saying, "Can he do it? How many trips will he take?" So the idea was that I was going to stay in the boat the entire day, never get out, and see how many spiels I could do. The idea that as I pulled my boat up to the dock, I would hop out and get into the boat being loaded and take it out. But supervisors said no because it was too dangerous and I would slip and fall into the water, so they said I had to stay in one boat all day. So I get there on the big day and I have a towel around my neck and I get into the boat and start doing trips and skippers would run up to me with water or a snack while I was at the dock. It was really fun. I ended up doing 44 trips. I never left the boat, never took a break, it was an 8-hour shift.

The next summer a guy named David decided to break my record, which is exactly what I wanted to happen. I wanted this to become a competition. So he did 46 trips in 8 hours. It was really fun, and it wasn't that hard. Your mind was set that you are going to spiel all day, you get a nice break between unload and load, it's a couple of minutes. When you're doing it you become a bit of a celebrity so that gives you a boost of energy.

Jeff Rhosds, 1970s–1980s

There was a skipper named Tom who was a U.S. Navy vet who could get away with saying the most offensive things to guests and cast members. I could hear him from Main Street because he would just scream into the mic. He was older than us, in his late 40s. He used to yell at the guests in the upstairs part of the queue. He'd say, "Hey, why are you up there? The ride is down here! You're stupid!" He asked Asian guests where they were from. If they said China, he'd say, "My shoes are from China!" or "My TV is from Taiwan."

Chris Ramirez, 2000s

There were some skippers who created a trip for their guests that was totally unique, for better or worse.

There was a skipper named Rick, he was there for a year at most, but had the funniest trip I had ever been on. What he did was, he never faced the guests and he did this very pre-recorded sounding spiel. Then he would pause it, turn and interact with the guests, then face forward again. So from a skipper perspective it was amazing because he had a character, he had it mapped out really well, and he knew when to jump out of the recording. He had a very popular boat.

Benny LeMaster, 1990s–2000s

I did an entire tour as the Mad Hatter. It was the normal tour, but I did the Mad Hatter voice [from the *Alice in Wonderland* cartoon] the entire time. After 7 minutes of that, this one lady was just done. Thankfully, Benny was the lead that night because she got off the boat and started yelling at him and pointing at me. He totally dismissed her. He came over to me and said, "Look, that lady is very angry so I'm pretending like I'm yelling at you, so act like I'm giving you a good talking to."

Trevor Kelly, 2000s

Some skippers took the idea of a fantasy-based jungle spiel even further.

Jerad didn't always stick to the script. His pride and joy was the Dr Seuss-style script that he did only once; it was too draining. But he sat and worked on that, messaging me with rhymes now and them to see if he couldn't hammer out something amazing. I wish I remembered it all, or that I'd been able to record it. He lost the sheet with the lines during a move after he left Disneyland, but he loved that he'd been able to do it.

Whitney Drake, 2000s

One night we did the "Puppet Tour" where we got hangers from backstage, put them around my wrists, and two skippers puppeteered me while Leo drove and spieled and I just badly mouthed the words. They'd have me wildly point at stuff. It was really fun, but the guests were sick of it after about two minutes and now we had to go through the entire jungle doing the spiel. We used to do really weird tours at night.

Trevor Kelly, 2000s

When I got bored or had a group that wasn't into it, I'd do a tour I called the "Pun Killer" where I would give the most literal interpretation of the Jungle Cruise's puns. At the Indian elephant pool, instead of saying, "It's okay to take photos, they all have their trunks on," I'd say, "It's okay to take photos, they are all dressed appropriately." At the rhinos, instead of saying "That rhino will get his point across, in the end," I'd say, "That rhino is about to impale that guy." It always made me laugh, which often caused guests to stare at me, which made me love it more.

David John Marley, 2000s

There was this one guy when he was at load, he would pretend like he was putting a cassette tape in a player, and he would play different songs. So he would pretend to put one in, and then he would sing this song from Pirates on the microphone, stop it, and then say, "Whoops, sorry, wrong tape." Then he pretended to put in another tape. He did all of this over the PA while the boat was loading. It was pretty funny.

Kipp Hart, 2000s–2010s

There was a skipper named Mitchell and if he was working you had gold. He was the only one I ever saw who successfully pulled off the sock joke. It was a joke as you went through the temple that was like, "On your right you can see four king cobra snakes, let's go ahead and count them, 1, 2, 3," then you'd look down at your feet and scream, "Ah, my socks! They're matching for the first time in weeks!" The way he was able to play it was great. He would hop up and pull up his pant legs to show off his socks.

Kevin Lively, 2010s

Disneyland is a carefully constructed alternative reality. It's a show and skippers are the only ones allowed to break the fourth wall, to let guests peek behind the curtain, as it were, to see what these particular cast members were thinking.

I always felt the Jungle Cruise skippers were the only ones allowed to break the fourth wall of Disneyland. Skippers are the Han Solo of Disneyland. We were allowed to wink and nod at the guests. We were the only ones who were allowed to be sarcastic. You can make fun of the long lines or the price of a churro, the things that guests are actually thinking, but no one else can say. I always thought that if you said it with a wink and were not too obvious about it, you can get away with comments like that. But we of course took it too far.

Joey Hurley, 2000s

I don't know how to Jungle got away with that, or why it works so well there. I think it might be because there's this sense of isolation and privacy in the jungle, because you're not surrounded by this audience, you're trapped and alone with these guests. So it's night, it's dark, you've kind of escaped the madness of Disneyland with these guests. And I think the guests kind of see you as more of a friend who's telling them something sarcastic about Disney and not a cast member being sarcastic about their job.

Mike Pucher, 2000s

Our jokes related to the fact that the guests were having this very stuffy experience at Disneyland and it was time to let loose a little bit. You're with your family, you've had a tough day, and we understand that. I'm gonna try to make you laugh, whatever it takes. I joke about it because I know what it's like to come to Disneyland as a guest, I know what it's like to be there when it's very hot. How can I possibly pretend that your experience at Disneyland has been perfect? That is the experience that they sell to you, but of course there're always things going wrong. I always saw it as an opportunity to show the guests that you were a real person, too. For example, a joke that says, "There is something you don't see every day, but I do." That can be an extremely funny joke if said perfectly. You don't even need to add anything to it; if you say it perfectly, it's a perfect joke. I think that one joke sums up being a skipper 100%. It makes the guests realize that we're humans and we have lives, too. And I think that always connects you to the audience if you say it the right way.

Joey Hurley, 2000s

One of the most valuable skills a skipper learns is how to read his audience. How to figure out what kind of jokes each particular boatload of guests is going to enjoy.

Think about the dock jokes a skipper does as guests are being loaded onto the boat. Dock jokes are where you feel out the crowd and figure out what is going to land, what is going to work for you. What kind of delivery works best for the people on this boat? Who am I not getting? Who do I have to work on? And who can I use? I try to understand where they are coming from.

Joshua Sudock, 2000s

Being able to read a crowd of people while working at Jungle Cruise has helped my public speaking skills immensely. It takes about 4–6 seconds to have people loading onto your boat and that is the amount of time you have to judge the crowd and connect with them. You learn to read body language, grouping, how to change your style if the first joke doesn't land well. They have to learn that their role is to sit back and enjoy the ride, which you have to teach them as well.

Michael Libby, 2000s

There is one joke that hardly any skipper can avoid, the infamous backside of water joke. Skippers come to hate it, but guests love it, and nearly every skipper, at some point in their career, has tried to come up with something that would replace it, but to no use.

I wrote a joke that I've heard other skippers use. I would talk about rear ends. Walt Disney did a lot of butt jokes in his cartoons. And so as I approached the backside of water I'd say, "I'm sorry, folks, this is a little inappropriate, you might want to cover your children's eyes, this waterfall is showing us its backside." It lasted for a bit, but everyone wants to hear the backside of water joke.

Fred Martin, 1980s

I was determined to do something new at the famous backside of water, I hated that it was the one joke that we always had to do. At night you could do all kinds of jokes. I used to flash the lights and do a Jungle Cruise version of Fantasmic. But during the daytime, you were stuck with the backside of water. I had one joke that I loved that was universally hated by guests. As we approached the waterfall, I'd do the same set up as the old joke, "Here it is, folks, the thing you've all been waiting for, the one, the only..." and then I'd point to a boat that was on the other side of the waterfall and say, "There it is, folks, the boat with the really funny skipper!" I loved it, but I don't think it ever got a single laugh. The backside of water defeated me.

David John Marley, 2000s

CHAPTER SIX

<><><><><><><><><><><><><><><><><><><><><><><><><><><><><><><><><><><><><><><><><><><><><>

FUN ON THE DOCK

The boat wasn't the only place where the skippers let loose. While working a dock position, or waiting to hop into a boat, skippers would routinely create havoc on the dock, usually the exit dock. As you will see, for many skippers their entire exit spiel was designed to crack up his fellow skippers, not necessarily the guests. Many times the guests had no idea what was going on.

The unload dock was the place where a new skipper could prove to their coworkers that they were funny. Besides the skippers helping unload the boat, you could be heard by everyone hanging out at the shipping office. As a result, there was an especially intense pressure to be funny. Compounding this pressure was the fact that your audience of skippers had already heard every dock joke there was, so there was a desire to break the boundaries in order to get a laugh.

Working load and unload is where you got to see who was on their game, who really cared about being there. People who didn't care just stood there or did a basic joke. Good skippers would bounce jokes off of you and there was a good back and forth. That's how you could tell who the funny people were.

Chris Ramirez, 2000s

My favorite thing as a skipper and lead was the dock jokes. That was my favorite part. Skippers were notorious for trying out new material on skippers and guests. They would sit backstage and come up with new jokes and run out and do them. It was also a challenge to see who you could make laugh. I knew that my Disney career had peaked when I made a lead named Gerry fall over laughing. I would put clean water in my mouth and I would lay on the dock and pretend to drink water from the jungle with my hands as a boat pulled up from Trader Sam. The skipper would yell,

"Benny, don't drink that water!" and then I would stand up, spit out the water, then dramatically pass out. I just laid there and made guests step over my body. And the first time I did it, Gerry almost fell over laughing.

Benny LeMaster, 1990s–2000s

After the Indy conversion the Jungle Cruise still had the original boats for a few years, but now they were themed to the late 1930s. These first boats had these nice cushions, and you had to remove the ones by the doors before unloading. One night a friend and I were bored, so instead of leaving the cushions in their side holders for the loading crew, we hid them all around the boat, under the canopy, behind the engine. My favorite place to stick them was in some of the prop luggage and the top of the boats. We thought it was funny, but the load crew got pissed, as did the lead, so we had to stop.

David John Marley, 2000s

On hot days we threw water at each other, and as the time went by it would become increasingly dangerous. We would have cups of water and first we would just throw them at your pants, or on your shirt. Then we would start throwing it in skippers' faces. And then it would be thrown in their face as they're pulling the boat up to unload and spieling to guests. And then we'd throw it at their crotch as they spieled to guests. That was really fun.

We came up with another joke where we were always thrusting our hips at the exit dock. A lead saw us and said you can't thrust your hips at the guests, so we started doing it backwards and yelled "bow chicka bow wow."

Joey Hurley, 2000s

Back in the 1990s there used to be this big thick rope that came down from the artificial tree that hung over Aladdin's Oasis. From the walkway back to boat storage you could use a hook to grab the rope then skippers would swing out in front of an oncoming boat and then back to the walkway. It was incredibly important that the skipper only swing out once, then hop off the rope. This was because the rope dragged in the water, and since it was centered over the river, if you didn't hop off after the one swing, you'd get stuck. One day the lead allowed a bunch of skippers to swing on the rope and they took turns terrifying oncoming boats. Each time the lead would warn them to only swing once. This one skipper refused to listen and instead of hopping off, tried to extend the trip to a second swing. Unfortunately for him, the rope came to a dead stop, leaving him suspended above the river. He begged for help, for someone to reach out with the hook to bring him in, but no one did. Finally, the lead walked over, pointed to him, then pointed down to the water. The skipper let go, crawled out of the water, and headed to costuming to get changed.

David John Marley, 2000s

I loved how we could say pretty much anything in the shipping office. The guests never seemed to notice what was going on in there.

Heather Wilkins, 2000s

When Tarzan's Treehouse opened they had a couple of hot guys dressed like Tarzan do walkarounds. Some of the 40- and 50-something women would just harass them. One night, Todd was the lead and these women came up and were asking about Tarzan as they got into a boat. We told them that we'd look for him while they were out. We took the lead and put a mop on his head and gave him a spear, a real spear that was on the dock, and found a sheet to wrap around him like a loin cloth. Then we had him stand on a box. When the boat returned the skipper figured out what was going on. He said, "Ladies, there he is! Tarzan!" and then hits him with a spotlight. The lead stood their stone faced, then said, "Hi, my name is Tarzan, come see my treehouse." Everybody laughed and the ladies took pictures with him.

Kaz Liput, 2000s

Many of the best dock jokes were the simple ones.

Everybody would bring their A game to the unload jokes. One of the best unload spiels was a skipper named Casey who would say, "And now as you exit the boat, please enjoy the calming sounds of the ocean." and then he would make sounds like the waves crashing on the beach, a fog horn, and the guests would just awkwardly walk off of the boat.

Trevor Kelly, 2000s

We did this one joke at the exit dock. You would hold a rock in your hand and show it to the skipper as the boat pulled up. And you'd say, "Hey, skipper, look at this rock." And the skipper would say, "That is the second-largest rock I've ever seen." And then I would say, "Oh, really, what was the biggest rock you've ever seen?" And he'd say, "You don't want to know." And we would laugh and laugh and we thought that was the funniest joke ever.

Joey Hurley, 2000s

There was a skipper named Mitch and whenever you saw him at unload you could have fun with him. You could do the dancing native girls joke. Or you'd say, "There, folks, is Skipper Mitch, and the great thing about Mitch is that anything goes," and then Mitch would break into the song "Anything Goes" in Chinese like in the beginning of *Indiana Jones and the Temple of Doom*. Or he'd attempt it. It was always a matter of who you had. Some people wanted to play along, others did not. The people who didn't do anything could also be funny because you'd say, "And to help you out of the boat today are these two beautiful dancing girls," and they'd just be standing there.

Kevin Lively, 2010s

Guest cell phones that are recovered from the bottom of the river were a frequent source of jokes.

In the shipping office we have a collection of cell phones that we had fished out of the river. As a boat pulled up to the exit dock you'd tell the skipper, "Hey, there's a phone call from your mom." And as you walk toward the boat holding the phone you would drop it and then accidentally step on it. Then you would kick the pieces into the river. The guests would always freak out about that.

Joey Hurley, 2000s

Guests were constantly dropping their phones into the river. It seemed like we got a couple of them each week. We'd try to fish them out with our pool nets, but couldn't always find them. When we did, they were usually covered in mud from the river, and we'd rest them on a beam in the Shipping Office as a kind of Hall of Shame. One night I was at unload and would pretend to be talking on a phone when a boat pulled up. The skipper would say, "David, you can't talk on your phone while you're working!" and I would apologize and throw the phone in the water. It always freaked people out.

David John Marley, 2000s

We did this 1-800-COLLECT bit where I would take a phone from out of the shipping office, one of the phones that people dropped in the water and we later fished out. I'd be pretending to talk on the phone as a boat pulled up, so already I'm super professional. Adam would say, "Hey man, you gotta use 1-800-COLLECT," and he'd repeat the script from the commercial. When he'd finish I'd say, "Well, then why am I using this stupid thing?" and I'd throw the phone to the ground and smash it and then throw the pieces into the jungle. The audience was always real quiet after that.

Trevor Kelly, 2000s

Adam and his stupid 1-800-COLLECT commercials. They would re-create the commercial word for word. He got a guest complaint because a guest said they didn't understand what collect calls had to do with the jungle.

Chris Ramirez, 2000s

In the world of stand-up comedy, prop comedy is considered the lowest way to get a laugh, at the Jungle Cruise this technique was taken to extraordinary lengths.

There was a game we would play with the guests who are in the queue. The game was called sink or float. A skipper named Eric invented the game. He would do it whenever there were no boats at the dock. He'd introduce himself, and say, "Hey, everybody, let's play sink or float!" He would then take random items from the shipping office and have the guests guess if this item would sink or float when he dropped it in the river. He'd always throw it in the river and the guests always laughed. He would throw whatever he could find in the shipping office, like toys, old cell phones, pencils, and pens.

Joey Hurley, 2000s

Joey had one bit with an umbrella that someone had left and Joey jumped off the rope pretending to be Mary Poppins and he just crashed to the floor.

Once we set up a crate and put two boards in front of it to form an X. We then took two ropes coming out of the crate and tied them to two smaller pieces of wood and we called it our Xbox. The boat would pull up to the dock and we'd say, "Hang on, we're almost done playing our Xbox," and nobody laughed. We'd then do this song and dance to celebrate the fact that the bit didn't work. My favorite thing to do when the jokes didn't work was to sing and dance until people weren't entertained anymore.

Trevor Kelly, 2000s

Some nights I would take a water bottle with a sports top and stand at the edge of the dock and position myself so that as a boat came around the corner, it would look like I was peeing into the river. When people would freak out, I would turn and pretend like I didn't know why they were freaking out. Taking something normal and making it seem obscene in such a family-oriented place was the most fun.

Matt Neire, 2000s

The spare skipper joke. We had a chest on the dock, a trunk that used to open. So you'd get a small skipper and put them in there. When a boat pulled up the skipper would say, "Hey, there are supposed to be two of you. What's going on?" You'd say, "My partner went to lunch, but don't worry, we have a spare skipper." Then you would open up the crate and they would pretend to inflate.

There was also the Tiki Room ending where someone would be on the catwalk and you'd shine a spotlight on them and say, "Wake up, Jose" and tap a stick on his foot and he would do the introduction to the Tiki Room.

Chris Ramirez, 2000s

When things got slow at night, skippers would create elaborate entertainment for the guests as they exited the attraction.

We did this Michael Jackson bit. Trevor and Adam would get on the boats on the catwalk and shine the spotlight at the dock and they would turn off all of the lights on the dock. As the boat came from around Trader Sam they would yell, "Ladies and gentlemen, Michael Jackson!" Then they would point the lights at me and I would do a Michael Jackson dance on the exit dock.

Joey Hurley, 2000s

We did this bit we called the Pinocchio show, where we took these big tow ropes and threw them over the walkway. I put my arms through the ropes and we did this big puppet marionette show.

Joey Hurley, 2000s

There were nights when it was only me and Joey at unload and this one lead would let us do whatever we wanted. Once we went backstage and got two tow ropes, linked them together, swung over the second story of the exit queue, and we were swinging on the ropes out toward the boats as they came to unload. Once we did the Indiana Jones bit at the end of the ride with the rolling ball. I'd be hanging from the rope and yell, "Hey, get a light on up here," and the skipper on the boat would hit me with the flashlight. Meanwhile, Joey would roll a wooden barrel toward the boat and I'd yell, "Back up, back up." It never occurred to us what would happen if we lost control of the barrel and it hit the boat or fell into the river.

Another time we had an epic exit joke ready, but a skipper named Kevin ruined it. Last boat of the night, Kevin comes around the corner and we had set up the cannon battle from Pirates. We had the lights set up, we all knew our lines. We completely re-created the scene; we even had a girl upstairs to yell, "Don't be chicken!" But Kevin comes around the corner like nothing happened. He ignored everything, just did his regular spiel and stopped the boat. He had no reaction. Kevin just never acknowledged dock jokes.

Trevor Kelly, 2000s

One skipper, Dwayne, would sing "I Will Survive." This was a joke that skippers knew to help with. As you came around from Trader Sam you'd see Dwayne sitting on the walkway from backstage looking all sad, dangling his feet over the water. The skipper would say, "Hey, Dwayne, what's wrong?" and he would say, "You don't want to hear it." So the skipper would egg on the boat of guests and beg him to tell us what was wrong. Then Dwayne would make his way to the exit dock, where the two unloaders were standing, backs to the dock, collars turned up. Then Dwayne would yell "Hit it!" and he'd get a spotlight. And he'd begin to sing "I Will Survive" complete with choreography. It was great.

Kaz Liput, 2000s

There is a narrow catwalk between the dock and the jungle beyond. Skippers would sometimes use this location for comedy.

A male and female skipper rolled up their pants and hopped on the spur sline, wore straw hats, and were fishing. They used the props that were laying around. I told my boat, "Say hello to Tom and Becky Thatcher."

Chris Ramirez, 2000s

Once we fished this Nemo plush toy that had fallen into the river and I took a bamboo pole and some string. I went and sat on a chair at the spur line. Then as boats would pull up they'd ask me what I was doing and I'd say, "I'm finding Nemo!" I'd pull the toy out of the water and yell, "I found him!"

Joshua Sudock, 2000s

For years the true test of whether a skipper was funny was based on what they said as the guests exited their boat.

This is not good at all, but you know how people would get to the dock and do the spiels from other attractions? I used to do the spiel from the end of the Haunted Mansion as the exit dock. Well, one time I did it and then said, "But of course, there is always my way," and then I jumped out of the window and onto the dock. Leaving no skipper in the boat. The look on the skippers' faces was classic. Thankfully, the lead wasn't at the dock. The guests had no idea what we were doing.

Leo Romo, 2000s

A skipper named Ritt came up with this trick that I quickly adopted. If you had a good boat you stopped at Trader Sam and prepped them on what to do when you get to the dock. He'd say, "Management has been watching me because they don't think I'm that funny, so I'd like it if you'd help me out. When I pull up to the dock I'm going to say something weird and I want you all to laugh and clap and jump up, like it was the funniest thing you've ever heard in your entire life. Okay?" So I'd pull up to the dock and say, "And despite what Hitler did, I think fascism is on the rise again." The boat went nuts! I did it for three boats in a row, with different lines, like, "I think in the future human heads will be replaced with kazoos." And I remember that two of the three times there was the same manager on the dock and she came up and asked me what I was doing to get such a great reaction. Ritt came up with some great things to make management leave him alone.

Trevor Kelly, 2000s

When I was doing my National Geographic tour and I knew that nobody was listening to me on the dock, just to make sure they weren't listening as they exited the boat I would give advice to kids like, "When you go to prison make sure you stab the biggest person that you see. The proper way to stab someone is to hold the blade horizontal so it doesn't get stuck on their rib cage." The guests wouldn't react and the skippers on the dock would just be laughing hysterically.

Trevor Kelly, 2000s

Jerad and I would do the "Scooby Doo" ending. He'd have this hat pulled over his head, and I'd say, "And in the back is Jerad and...wait a second, that isn't Jerad! It's old man Withers from the Haunted Amusement park!" Then Jared would cackle and throw the hat into the air and yell, "I would have gotten away with it if it hadn't been for you meddling kids." The entire boat would always just stare blankly at us.

Chris Ramirez, 2000s

Occasionally a skipper is forced to ad lib while waiting for the boat ahead of them to finish unloading.

After the cruise is done and you're approaching unload there can be lots of downtime and it can be awkward and you'd better have some filler jokes to pass the time. So one thing I did to make it fun was to flip it so instead of it being awkward for me, I made it awkward for the guests. I'd segue into how we had bonded as a family and I'm going to miss them all. I'd say, "I'm gonna miss you, and you, and especially you." And at that point I'd pick out someone near the front of the boat, usually an elderly person works best, and then I would just gaze at them with googly eyes for as long as I could.

Anonymous, 2010s

CHAPTER SEVEN

‹‹‹

JUNGLE AFTER DARK

Most Disneyland guests only ride the Jungle Cruise once during their visit, and that one trip is usually during the daytime. One of the best-kept secrets at the park is that the Jungle Cruise is actually two different attractions. It has a day version and a nighttime version. Most skippers claim to like working the nights at Jungle Cruise the best. I think it's best to let them explain why.

My second summer I worked nights and I thought that was really a lot of fun and you could play with the lighting and it added an entire new dimension to the boats. You could turn the running lights off and be in total darkness and then use your spotlight. Or fire the gun in the darkness and it would light up the boat and always get a reaction. You had a chance to act a little more and have more fun with the people in your boats. I really enjoyed working nights. Days were fun. too, but they were different kinds of experiences.

My show in the hippo pool was totally different at night. You could build suspense and tell people they had to be quiet or the hippos would turn the boat over. Then you'd yell, "There's one!" and "Bang! Bang!" then turn on the lights and you were surrounded by hippos. People saw things they didn't expect and there was a different element of suspense at night. Sometimes there was some crazy business going on with a young couple in the back.

Alan Coats, 1960s

I loved doing the Jungle Cruise at night. We had spotlights and they were very good, they were the big hot lights, and you'd pull the trigger and they were as bright as can be but they were hot, so you didn't keep them on very long. Because they were so bright instead of shining them on the gorillas I would shine them on the water and let the light reflect up. I thought it made the gorillas look better than just hitting them with this blinding light.

Fred Martin, 1980s

If it's evening and you don't have lots of people in your boat and you're at the dancing natives and you do a joke that bombs, then I would say, "Oh, you didn't like that joke, how about this one?" and I would throw the boat into reverse and then move forward and try another joke. Usually just putting the boat into reverse would get a big laugh. If they didn't really laugh at the second joke, I'd stop the boat again and say, "Nothing? Really? I'm here until midnight," and then I'd act like I was going to back up again and they'd laugh.

Ron Robledo, 1980s

Sometimes after park closing there would be a ton of people hanging out at the dock and sometimes we'd take a trip through the jungle and tell scary stories.

Leo Romo, 2000s

I took the *Sesame Street* ""Mah Na Mah Na" song where I would do the National Geographic tour, then shut off the lights and do the song between the scenes. The guests couldn't see anything.

Trevor Kelly, 2000s

Sometimes on a night time deadhead I would stand on the bow and adjust the throttle with my foot. It felt like you were floating through the jungle. It was so beautiful and calm. Disneyland would be packed on a summer night, and I'd be totally alone in this beautiful jungle garden.

David John Marley, 2000s

I love working nights at Jungle Cruise because they were less crowded and more relaxed. I think if I had to choose one thing I like most about working at Jungle Cruise it was working a night shift. You would have so much more fun at night. I mean during the day, it didn't matter if you were the most off-the-script skipper there was, you knew that everybody was going to come together during the day to try to hit those numbers. There were no pranks during the day, you couldn't mess around during then; having a day shift was pretty serious business. You still had fun, but everybody took the job of keeping the boats running very seriously. We prided ourselves on having a short line, on being able to get people through. Because the guests didn't enjoy themselves as much if they had to wait a long time for the Jungle Cruise. You would see that in your boats. But at night they would pull a few boats off at the river so you can go a bit slower. If you had really good veldt jokes, you can spend more time out there. But during the day you had to keep the spacing even. With eight boats on the river you can't customize the trip as much. At night you can customize your pace a little more. You tended to have fewer kids on the boat, so you'd be more successful with sarcastic jokes. The guests also usually tended to be tired, they usually had had their fill of Disney by that time of night, so the jokes that came at the expense of Disney really killed.

Mike Pucher, 2000s

Working nights was the best. It was cool; people thought the ride was closed, so the line was short. The guests were very receptive to the types of jokes I wanted to do. People during the day, when it's all hot they're tired and just trying to get on as many rides as they can.

Leo Romo, 2000s

A fun thing to do was night tours when you only had two people on your boat. You could just drop the mic and talk to them. The jungle is so beautiful at night, you can bounce the spotlight off of the water to get that cool ripple effect. I wish they would teach that more. At nighttime it is so romantic.

Kevin Lively, 2010s

One of the most common nighttime activities at Jungle Cruise was becoming a "real skipper." Becoming a real skipper required peeing in the river, usually at night. For obvious reasons, most of the skippers that I interviewed wanted this part kept anonymous.

They said you hadn't made your bones at Jungle Cruise until you have peed in the river.

Terry Eaton, 1970s–1980s

I closed most nights and on the way out, we'd always go by the skull canoe and pee into the river. Every night. You close the ride, then pee in the river.

Matt Nerrie, 2000s

There was this one lazy female skipper who was a notorious maxer, and on my last day I wanted to be in the boat all day. This lazy skipper loved it because she hated working. I took a bunch of deadheads and a veteran skipper went with me and was giving me a real hard time for never having peed in the river. So I stood on the bow and peed, and some landed on the bow. And when I get back to the dock she comes up, kneels in my pee and tells me she is going to max, and asks if it was okay.

Anonymous, 2000s

There was this one guy who just refused to pee in the river. So one night a couple of skippers and I decided to make it happen. It was hot, and we were all drinking lots of water. Whenever he asked permission to leave to dock to pee, the lead would say no. This went on and on and eventually he asked why. The lead said he could only go pee if he peed in the river. He refused for another 20 minutes and the park was closed. After everything was tied off we walked him over to the hippo pool and about four of us peed into the river.

Anonymous, 2000s

I knew a few female skippers that were "real skippers." They'd go up to the top of the falls, drop their pants and pee into the pool above the waterfall.

Anonymous, 2010s

I'm on a deadhead and I have to pee. So I thought I could take advantage of the situation. So when I left the dock I took off, I drove that boat as fast as I could to the Nile. I was trying to put as much distance between me and the boat behind me. This is before the gorilla camp added the explosion. So I turn up the Nile, and I put the boat at a nice slow speed to go up the river, and I'm standing in the front door and I'm just peeing in the Nile. I wasn't going very fast, it was at night, and then suddenly this boat comes tearing around the corner, full speed with lights blazing! And I'm standing in the doorway peeing into the river. I don't know how they caught me because I had been going full throttle. So I jumped back into the boat and just pushed the throttle all the way forward and got out of there. That was the only time I peed in the jungle. I know most people go pee by the python so they can compare.

Anonymous, 2000s

CHAPTER EIGHT

SKIPPERS PRANK SKIPPERS

The Jungle Cruise is staffed mostly by young people who are paid to be entertainers. They work hard, but get bored easily, and then chaos ensues. There are mainly two types of pranks that regularly happen at Jungle Cruise. The first are pranks that they pull on each other for fun, and the second type is the hazing of rookies. One old-time skipper called it "hazing out the suck," by which he meant hassling rookies until they learned how to do their job better.

Sometimes the guests don't even realize that they are pawns in a prank war between bored skippers. One of the greatest things that the Jungle Cruise can do for guests is to give them a fun experience that is totally unique to them, and often that means guests getting involved in a prank. As you will see, when the guests join in on the fun, the regular magic of Disneyland is amplified.

One evening we were driving the boats and it was very quiet. Bob Carbonell and I loaded up two .38s, the blank pistols, and went out to the jungle in the village area and hid behind the pepper tree. When Don Weir came around and fired at the natives and yelled at them, we fired back and scared the hell out of him. It took him by surprise. He was so unnerved that he fell to his knees. A guest had to bring the boat back to the dock.

William Sullivan, 1950s

When you get guys like that together they're going to start pulling pranks on each other. You always had to watch your back because you didn't know who was going to do what to you if you were not paying attention.

You know how there are two types of ammunition, the regular ammo and the breakdown ammo, and the breakdown is a lot louder. We would take a skipper's gun when he didn't notice it and switch out the ammo so that every other shot was a breakdown. So the first shot would be normal and the second shot would be super loud, freaking out the skipper.

It was a real locker room. At the Jungle Cruise it was just a lot of pranks we pulled on each other that we probably wouldn't have done if there were women around. Our favorite was to try to take a cup of water and pour it on the guy's crotch without him noticing, to make it look like he peed his pants. There were times where we did that and the skipper would get on the boat and realize it looked like he peed his pants, and then all the guests saw it, too. Sometimes you would walk by another skipper and pretend to slip and then try to pull his pants down as you fell. You just hoped that they had put on underwear that morning.

Terry Eaton, 1970s–1980s

I used to have this little toy plastic boat. There's a spot at the veldt where the water at the shore made a perfect little dock for it. I used to drive my boat by and think that it was a perfect spot, so one day I brought a little plastic toy boat and I'd run out between boats and put it out there and tie it off, like it was Storybook Land Canal Boat. I'd wait to see how long it would stay out there before someone noticed it and it got taken away.

Jeff Rhoads, 1970s–1980s

We would also take any really hot girls and have them sit at the back of the boat as far from the skipper as possible. Also, if there were little kids that were acting really wild, we would make sure they sat in the front of the boat.

Terry Eaton, 1970s–1980s

One time I told a kid I'd give him a dollar if he went to the skipper on the boat and kicked him in the shin. The kid ran up, kicked the skipper as hard as he could, and then ran back to me for his dollar. I paid up. The skipper saw the whole thing and thought it was funny. I would do that whenever I was having a boring day and I was friends with the skipper on the boat. I almost always had a bunch of dollar bills in my wallet just so I could do it.

There was a guy at that was always betting me $5 that I couldn't do something. He bet me $5 that I couldn't run the squirter without getting any guests wet. Sometimes I made it, sometimes I didn't.

Terry Eaton, 1970s–1980s

By the end of the night the big wooden counter in the shipping office was dirty after a day of sweaty hands and ammo boxes that had been sitting in bilge water all day. One night we put together a bunch of money, over

$100, to dare a skipper. We had him lick from one side of the shipping office desk to the other, and he did it. There is so much skipper pee in that water.

David John Marley, 2000s

In 1977 somebody once foolishly left a five-gallon jug of concentrated liquid soap in the back of boat storage, and it inadvertently got dumped into the water and turned the entire river into a bubble bath. It shut down the ride. I remember that first, at the little water cascades, you'd notice a little soapy foam coming down and then Schweitzer Falls was starting to get a little frothy, and the next thing you know the whole jungle is just getting flooded and it made its way to the dock. So they called maintenance, and I guess this sort of thing happened regularly enough because they came out with these two big bottles of stuff and dumped it in. It was a defoaming agent and it went away pretty quickly and things went back to normal. It was almost like they were waiting for it to happen.

Jeff Rhosds, 1970s–1980s

When I was there we had a classic black Mickey Mouse plush that people would hide out in the jungle. He would end up in a variety of places. This one guy was notorious for hiding it random places. He was really strait-laced and followed the rules, but this was his one rebellion. The best place he got it was into one of the backpacks of the guys on the trapped safari and you could see its little legs bounce up and down as the rhino charged. We were always looking for the Mickey.

I had been told that one of the original monkeys from 1955 was still out there in the jungle. Skippers claimed that it was moved around the jungle, but I never saw it. I think they called it Bobo. Skippers would randomly claim to have seen Bobo, who was supposedly mossy green since it had been in the jungle for 30 years at that point. I never saw it.

Fred Martin, 1980s

We did a Dominguez switch move to a guy on his last day. You would clear out all of the boats on the catwalk, and so when a skipper comes round the corner from Trader Sam on his last boat, you send them back into the jungle again. He can't pull up to the dock and he has to do it all over. One guy who worked there hated being on a boat and he got so angry when we did that to him. The guests always thought it was the funniest thing because they knew it was something unusual and they could see the frustration on their skipper's face. When it happened to me I was totally into it.

Fred Martin, 1980s

One time I was on a boat with guests and a bunch of skippers were out on safari, and I'm into the veldt, and when you're at the veldt, the guests are busy looking at the animals and you're looking at the guests so you're looking toward the back of the boat. There's this overhang of bushes and I look across the guests and in the skiff there are two skippers who were mooning me. None of the guests could see it because their attention was focused in the other direction and I had a hard time keeping it together.

Fred Martin, 1980s

I remember there was one summer where I went to dinner with two skippers and after dinner we went out and bought a bunch of rubber ducks. We thought it would be funny to randomly throw them into the jungle river. But we decided to be subtle. So we threw ducks into the river over the course of the next week. Skippers were trying to figure out where these rubber ducks were coming from. I then went online and ordered a couple dozen rubber ducks off eBay. And for the rest of that summer every couple days one of us would throw a duck into the river. The three of us were sworn to secrecy; we didn't tell anybody else about it for years. We would ride each other's boats but sit in the back and then subtly drop the duck into the river, usually in the veldt, or we'd chuck them off the dock when no one else was looking. No one made a big point about it, but I kept hearing conversations between skippers trying to figure out where these ducks are coming from. And then a lead found one and she became convinced that it was something that somebody had thrown into the jungle on their last day years ago and it had been stuck out there in the jungle. She considered it her prize possession because she got this guy's duck that he threw out on his last day. I never had the heart to tell her the truth.

Mike Pucher, 2000s

In training you were taught that if the lights at Trader Sam's shield are flashing, you are supposed to stop there and not move forward until the flashing stops and you hear, "Move it up, skip!" One night we got bored and chose a random skipper to flash the lights on. We weren't moving any boats, which is the normal reason to flash the lights. We just wanted to hassle him. I think we kept him there for five minutes until he began to creep forward and saw us all laughing.

David John Marley, 2000s

One day I got to the shipping office to begin my shift and found a note for me. It said, "Call Mike," and gave his extension. I dutifully called the number, only to hear a woman answer saying, "Michael Eisner's office." I panicked, yelped, and hung up. Once my heart stopped pounding, I found the stack of "while you were out" memos and left the same prank for another skipper.

David John Marley, 2000s

I did this one night several years ago. The dock was filled with mostly new skippers who didn't know me really well, which made it even better. It was about 7 o'clock at night and the boat pulled up. While the skipper was loading his gun I told him, "By the way, I know you're new, but it's after 7pm and you cannot fire the gun anymore because of Anaheim's noise abatement law." He looked at me and said, "Really?" and I said, "Yeah, after 7 o'clock we're not allowed to fire guns." I told every skipper that came in the same story. So for an hour and a half there was no shooting in the hippo pool. Eventually the lead gets back to the dock and one of the skippers asked him about it and he just said, "What?" And I got called out on it.

Kipp Hart, 2000s–2010s

I was there for a female skipper's final night and one of the things she did was take a pair of bright pink panties and hang them from the clothesline that's on the second floor of the boathouse. I had an opening shift the next day, and for the first and only time in my career I walked into work with the opening lead, Gerry. We were chatting and he was telling us jungle stories and as we walked onto the dock, he began to give us orders, "Pull on a boat!" and "Do the animation check!" and without seeming to look up or even pause in his list of commands, "And somebody take those panties down." He then walked off to the Adventureland office to get the morning paperwork. I have no idea how he saw them so quickly and why he didn't react. That was funnier than the prank itself.

David John Marley, 2000s

There was one summer where there were a couple of skippers that liked to go into the jungle and untie the skiff in the elephant pool. They thought it was funny to shut the ride down. So one time I came into the Indian elephant bathing pool and there are all the elephants and the skiff floating around. I said, "These elephants enjoy bathing in groups and boating." By the end of that summer, facilities workers had installed a steel cable to keep the skiff from floating away. That solved the problem.

Mike Pucher, 2000s

It is human nature to break into groups and cliques. At the Jungle Cruise there was a single dividing line between skippers and it was if other skippers thought you were funny or not. Skippers would haze a rookie to see how they reacted. The ones who kept their cool were usually admitted into the club.

Sometimes when you were working at the load position at dock and you had a guest that smelled really bad you would try to get him to sit as close to the skipper as possible. We did that, especially if the next skipper was going to be a rookie.

Terry Eaton, 1970s–1980s

I remember when I came back in April 1990 for my second summer at Jungle Cruise. They had hired a bunch of new guys while I was gone and one of them called me rookie. And as I turned toward them somebody came to my defense before I could say a single thing. He said, "He's no rookie." And I realized that I was part of the experienced group of skippers now.

Fred Martin, 1980s

It was most of the guys that did the pranks. They would do things like stand at Schweitzer Falls and dump water on the new skippers. They tried to do that to me, but I was on to them. They took us out in the jungle on a boat, and there was a skipper hiding up above the falls. During training, Joy and I made it very clear that they would have the wrath of both of us on them if they tried to get us wet. We said we'd be mad if they messed up our hair. So they didn't do it.

Sue Barnaby, 1980s–1990s

I got harassed a lot during my first month at Jungle Cruise, but in a loving way.

Benny LeMaster, 1990s–2000s

I once saw a lead hang a guy by his ankles over the river. It was back when hazing was really bad.

Kaz Liput, 2000s

There was a guy we worked with that we always called him "rookie." Even after he had been there a year, we kept calling him that.

Leo Romo, 2000s

I remember one time I was hanging out in the shipping office, telling jokes with the other skippers and this new guy walked up and tried to join in.

A veteran interrupted him and said, "You're not funny, shut up," and then handed him a set up and told him to go pull on a boat.

Anonymous, 1990s

This one skipper called me the "new girl" for over four months. The old-school people tried to make the new-school people feel worthless, which was stupid because we were so much funnier than they were. They had this whole bitter attitude but us new people didn't care and we all became close friends because we were teased by the old-school skippers.

Kriztina Varga, 2000s

I had a roommate that was an annual passholder and a pin trader and I begged him not to tell anyone he worked with that he was those things when he was trained at Jungle Cruise.

Kaz Liput, 2000s

As you leave the Indian elephant bathing pool there is an elephant that looks like it's going to squirt the boat. He rises once and squirts water from his trunk, then drops back into the water, as if to reload, before rising back up. The second time he never squirts water, but the skipper is supposed to make the boat think they are about to get soaked.

There was a prank I liked to play on rookies. On a new skipper's first day I went into Bertha's cave and found the reset button for the squirter and waited for her. I peered through this little hole in the rock wall so I could see her boat approach. As expected, the elephant raised its head and shot out water then sunk back down. Before it could rise up a second time I hit the reset button, causing the elephant to start the cycle all over again, and spray the boat with water. I waited in the dark cave for ten minutes and hit the boat a second time. She was horrified, guests were getting soaked, and nobody could hear me laughing. When she came around for a third time it was just her and a lead in the boat. I didn't touch anything, just watched as the elephant did its normal cycle. I heard the lead explain, "You see, the elephant goes up twice, the first time he shoots out water, the second time he doesn't." The rookie was exasperated and swore up and down that the elephant was squirting twice in a row. The lead was very gentle and tried to figure out how she was messing up. I wanted to wait around and hit her boat again, but my lunch break was over and I had to run back to the dock. I never told anyone the truth.   *David John Marley, 2000s*

I remember one time we went into Bertha's cave and used the squirter to hit guests. We turned it on manual and just blasted people as boats went by. Because back then it was like a firehose. You can really line it up, it was like shooting ducks in a shooting gallery. People would be screaming it was so much fun. The skipper's reactions were the best part, because they're always terrified.

Anonymous, 2000s

We got a new skipper named Jeff at the squirter. He was brand new, it was maybe his third day, and the squirter was broken, and so Gerry had shut it off. We told Jeff that the sensor on the squirter was not responding like normal, so if it doesn't come up right away just wait, because it will. If you start to go before the squirter starts you will get your entire boat wet. We were running four boats and three came back and we sent them out and finally in comes Jeff and says, "You guys suck."

Chris Ramirez, 2000s

My trainer told me that there is no set time for a trip. But I quickly learned that if I took my sweet time I would literally be pushed through the jungle. A boat would hit me and push me forward. A skipper named Matt did that to me. I was taking too long.

Andy McGuire, 2000s

For decades the most important rule at Jungle Cruise was the old phrase, "What happen in the jungle, stays in the jungle."

There are many rules that are not in the books, but need to be learned when you are a Jungle Cruise skipper. The most important was, "What happens in the jungle, stays in the jungle," and if you start ratting people out you will disappear very quickly. They will make quick work of you. You will be gone. I always liked that. I hated writing statements. At Indy, people were always writing statements on each other for the silliest of things.

Andy McGuire, 2000s

I was on a deadhead just cruising through. I saw a pair of Mickey Mouse ears floating in the water, so I grab them. I was trying to figure out what I can do with it, and I get to the skull canoe and I think, "If I can get it on those skulls, that would be epic." I couldn't reach the front of the boat, and as I pulled the boat up I noticed the tail of the boat kicks out right toward the canoe; you're only about two feet away. So I stopped the boat, leaned over, and put the Mickey Mouse ears on one of the skulls, and then I left.

I get back to the dock, and I was thinking this would be pretty cool. The skipper in the next boat behind me, doing their deadhead, starts yelling, "Hey, somebody put a Mickey ears on one of the skulls." It didn't last two minutes, and so they got taken off about 30 minutes afterwards.

So the old rule "what happens in the jungle stays in the jungle" doesn't really exist anymore. Back in 2004 those Mickey Mouse ears would've stayed there all day.

Kipp Hart, 2000s–2010s

There are three classic pranks that have happened for years at the Jungle Cruise. The first is called Light's Out and usually happens to the last boat of the night. The second is called Jungle Police and is a skipper getting arrested by a boatload of skippers who have been waiting for him. The third of the famous pranks is not so much a prank as it is a way to enforce the rules. It's called Jungle Justice. First up is the Lights Out prank, where all the lights and animation are shut off while the last boat of the night is still in the jungle. The skipper then returns to the dock only to find that everyone is gone. Jungle Cruise policy is that a boat cannot approach the dock unless there are skippers there ready to help unload guests, so the skipper is stuck until the pranksters think the skipper has suffered enough.

We once did the Lights Out prank and made a skipper unload an entire boat by himself. We turned off all the lights, all the sound, all the animation. All of us, and the lead, hid in the upstairs queue. He gets on the mic and said "C'mon, guys, c'mon! I know you're there!" and nobody went down to help him. He sat in the boat for a couple of minutes and called for us. Finally he pulled the boat up and unloaded the entire boat from the front door. And then we came down laughing and he just looked at us and yelled, "You guys suck!" and stormed off the dock.

Chris Ramirez, 2000s

I got cross trained into the Jungle Cruise during a hiring freeze, so they hadn't seen a new skipper in a long time. On our first shift, me and the other new trainee were told to take the "Nighttime Animation Trip" and I knew it wasn't a thing, but we went. When got to the African veldt they turned all the power off. So we drove in the darkness with no animation. We stopped at Trader Sam because they had moved the track switches so we'd derail. The other guy began to freak out. He hopped onto the island then came back. Nobody ever came out, so I had to back up around the entire jungle back to the dock and they were all laughing at us.

Benny LeMaster, 1990s–2000s

There was one skipper, however, who was far too clever to fall for a prank like Light's Out. He turned the tables and pranked the pranksters.

We pranked Ritt on a night shift. Often times when the last skipper was out they would shut everything down to hassle them. So we do this to Ritt. We shut down all the animation and lights and Ritt comes toward the dock and says, "Well, I guess they've all gone home, we'll have to sleep in the jungle tonight," and then he backed up the boat beyond Trader Sam, back into the jungle. We didn't know what was going on, so we all come out of hiding. He was back there for a few minutes, then the boat starts to slowly drift toward the dock. Ritt was gone. So we hop on the boat and stop it and unload the guests and we asked the guests about where their skipper had gone and they said that he told them he couldn't take it anymore and he was going to live in the jungle and he got out of the boat. So we tie off the boat, shut everything down, and were preparing to go to the island to look for him when Ritt comes walking through the queue. He had switched jackets with a guest, and we all had no idea. The best part was the lead's face, because she thought we were going to prank him and he beat us all.

Amanda Case, 2000s

The successful execution of Jungle Police takes planning. A proper victim skipper has to be picked out without them knowing it. And you need a group of foolhardy skippers who are not afraid to climb from boat to boat out in the hippo pool in the middle of the night.

During Keoni's first night shift it was really slow, so we decide to do Jungle Police. We took some red-and-blue gels from the Aladdin show and we taped them on the lights of a boat and moved backwards into the hippo pool. As Keoni enters the pool, we hit the lights and start yelling, "Pull the boat over, your skipper is not funny! This is the jungle police." We tied the boats off. We tied up Keoni and put him in our boat. Benny took over the boat and when his boat got to the dock, Keoni was tied to a post at the exit dock.

Heather Wilkins, 2000s

I had been a part of several Jungle Police pranks, but had never been the one to replace the skipper. So once we decided to hit Mark's boat, we waited for him in the hippo pool. We hit the lights, did the siren, the whole thing, then after Mark was removed, they introduced me as the new skipper as the boat roared off into the night. I said hello, apologized for Mark, and restarted the tour. I always considered myself pretty funny, so I thought they would love me instantly, but they didn't. They didn't seem to like me at all. I did all my best jokes and act outs, but they were clearly not happy with me. I sped up the boat and got back to the dock, and there was Mark tied up to a pole like he was supposed to be. Afterwards, he told me that he'd had one of his best trips ever, and that they laughed at every joke he did.

David John Marley, 2000s

We did it all the time if it was a slow night. Once we did it and we should have been fired. We stopped Brandon's boat in the hippo pool. We tied him up, put him on our boat, and just drove away and left a boat full of guests alone in the jungle darkness. We left them there for like 30 seconds and then raced back and the guests were all still just sitting there. Nobody did anything.

Leo Romo, 2000s

Once we tried Jungle Police during the day, but we made it like a train robbery. A skipper named Joey worked at Big Thunder Mountain and he had the handkerchief so he put it on and we pretended to rob the boat and steal the skipper.

Kaz Liput, 2000s

We did Jungle Police one night that was very ineffective. The skipper that was getting arrested was resisting arrest; he kept backing up and we couldn't get to him. So we tried to get him. I'm surprised we didn't derail because we kept backing up fast through the hippo pool. But we never caught him.

Kipp Hart, 2000s–2010s

It is a fairly common, perhaps overly common practice at Disneyland to complain to managers and write a statement about one's fellow cast members. The writing of statements has historically been frowned upon at Jungle Cruise. Skippers liked to handle things on their own. So if there was a skipper who was not pulling their weight, their fellow skippers would deal with it. The biggest sin a skipper can commit against another skipper is to "max" on their break. If you take a longer break that you are supposed to, then your boat partner ends up doing too many trips in a row. It is rude and what most maxers don't realize is that it's easy to punish the wrongdoers. And this is when Jungle Justice happens.

We had this thing called Jungle Justice. If everybody was true to their break times, you only had to do three trips an hour. But if your partner maxes on his break, the first time you warn him, then if it happens again, if it becomes habitual, or you purposefully bump around him, or if you're in a loading position and you've got some rookie who thinks he's going to max out on his break, you'd give a signal to the guy at rear load and they would shove as many people as they could onto your boat, way more than they were supposed to. You bump around them until it's about their sixth time doing a trip and you don't even let them have a drink of water. Then they get all apologetic and you ask them, "Now, how long are breaks?"

George Trullinger, 1970s–1980s

There was a skipper I'll call Teddy who had been regularly maxing on his rotation, and Jungle Justice had been called for. I was in the shipping office during several of the times the hapless skipper came back to the dock and he demanded to know where his bump was. One time his boat partner was hiding in the shipping office behind my legs as he came to the dock. Teddy would complain and I would just look at him and say, "Move it up, Skip." After six or seven trips in a row he brought the boat back to the dock and said, "I'm sorry, okay? I'm sorry! I'll never max again." With that I yelled for Teddy's boat partner, who came skipping around the corner and into the boat. Teddy got the message.

David John Marley, 2000s

Jungle Justice isn't there anymore, nobody knows how to do it, and as a result so many people max on their boat partners. It's ridiculous, it's just awful. We used to be self-governing, and it was great. I never maxed, but I was able to be a part of Jungle Justice on some skippers, and it's very satisfying. You know after spending an hour and 15 minutes in the boat it's just wearing on them, and they keep asking, "What's going on?" until they figure it out. It's a beautiful thing to watch. I forgot how delightful it was.

Anonymous, 2010s

CHAPTER NINE

<><><><><><><><><><><><><><><><><><><><><><><><><><><><><><><><><><><><><><><><>

SKIPPERS PRANK GUESTS

If there is one thing that skippers enjoyed more than pranking each other, it was pranking the guests who came to Disneyland.

I thought I could jazz this ride up. One of the things I did was that most people had no idea that the boat was on a track. So I tried really hard to make it look like I was driving the boat. I had loosened the nut that held the steering wheel on and as we approached Schweitzer Falls I leaned back and the wheel fell off and I'd scream that we were going to hit the waterfall. I'd pretend that I was ready to jump for the shore and half the boat was ready to go with me. Then I'd laugh and tell them that we were on a track.

Missing the falls was always fun, people loved seeing the animals. Parents would sometimes grab their kids. They liked the animals very much. People knew that they weren't real, but maybe for the first 30 seconds they would be tricked.

Warren Asa, 1955

We used to mess around the queue ropes all of the time. This was before the boathouse and so the ropes just went back and forth underneath a triangular thatch roof. If you had a nice group of people coming into the queue and you wanted to make it a bit longer so you can fit more people, all it took was moving one rope and you could mess everything up. But we enjoyed pulling the ropes and making it into a little loop and seeing how many times guests would walk in a circle before they realized what's going on.

Fred Martin, 1980s

When an annual passholder would come up and tell you what jokes they wanted to hear, "I wanna hear the backside of water jokes and I wanna this joke and that joke," I would do the National Geographic tour with no jokes.

Trevor Kelly, 2000s

I think the most successful prank I was ever involved with was called "Breaktime." You'd be out of the jungle in your boat and somebody would announce over the PA system, "Attention in the jungle, it is now breaktime." If you had been given the heads up, you'd take a cup of water or a magazine with you. At that point you would stop your boat, look at your guests, and say "I'm sorry, folks, but it's my breaktime."

The bit didn't work as well if you weren't by one of the PA speakers or if a skipper decided not to play along and kept driving their boat and came into your show scene. But when it worked, it was golden. The best it ever worked for me was when I was going down the Nile one night and I was just by the second elephant and out of the derail zone. There is a PA speaker right there so guests heard the announcement. When I stopped the boat they all laughed really hard. I shut off the exterior lights and turned on the interior lights and that's when guests began to realize that I was serious. So I picked up my cup of water and began chit-chatting with two of the guests who were sitting in the front of the boat. They seemed really surprised that I was drinking a cup of water and talking to them about television shows. It usually lasted no more than 60 seconds before the PA would announce the break was over. I'd fire the boat up, pick up the mic, and say "worst union ever."And the guests laughed really hard.

Mike Pucher, 2000s

I had a full boat and there was a group of five guys, four of whom had girls with them. The one single guy in the group kept yelling out punch-lines to my jokes and was being a jerk. As we passed the gorilla camp, he started to yell out old Jungle Cruise jokes that he'd heard before. So I said, "Do any of you find it surprising that the one guy doing all the yelling is also the only one without a girlfriend." The boy melted into the seat as his friends, and all the other guests, roared in laughter. I almost felt bad for him, but it did finally shut him up.

David John Marley, 2000s

I once took a trip with a bunch of dead kids on it. It was late at night and Fantasmic was going on so the line was dead and these kids show up. Maybe five little kids, they were all under 10 years old. And there was nobody in line so I just went with just these kids. We were chatting and I said, "Do you kids wanna do something fun?" and they were into it. I told them all that I was going to park the boat at the backside of water and everyone just pretend to be dead, slump over the railings and what not. I turned on the inside lights and I had the boat just slowly drift under the waterfall as another boat came by and I just started screaming, "They're dead! They're all dead! AAHHH" and the other skipper just stared at me and the guests said nothing and just kept going. Then later on I think, "What if one of those kids had fallen into the water because some of them were really hanging over the railings. What would I have told management? I would have just said that the kid was drunk.

Trevor Kelly, 2000s

Once I blew through the squirter with a boat full of guests on accident. The squirter shoots water out hard! It hit me in the sternum and it hurt. Thankfully, the boat was mostly empty. On really hot days I would ask guests if they wanted to get wet, then I would run the squirter.

Kriztina Varga, 2000s

There was this Asian tour group, about 60 people. A few skippers and I rerouted the ropes so they ended up going on Indiana Jones. They went up the stairs, across the boathouse, and down the back stairs into Indy. I got into a boat and saw them all standing at the exit to Indy looking confused.

Anonymous, 2000s

We were really bad with feminine protection. We used to get those really big Kotex pads and write our names on them in lipstick and then wear them like name tags. We took some tampons and we tied them on the fishing lines and then we threw those behind our boats as we drove around the jungle. This one male skipper noticed what was going on and started yelling, "Oh, no, the water level is going down." It was just stupid crap, but it made us laugh. Sometimes the guests would notice, sometimes they wouldn't. I'm not sure why we found feminine protection so funny. We just did.

Sue Barnaby, 1980s–1990s

One day a rather large-breasted woman wearing an American flag bikini was in line. When I spotted her I walked into the shipping office, grabbed the boathouse PA, and began to say the Pledge of Allegiance. Soon the entire queue was joining in what they thought was a spontaneous patriotic moment. Meanwhile, every skipper was laughing.

David John Marley, 2000s

Once I came into the Indian elephant bathing pool and I saw a skipper in the shower with Bertha wearing only his boxer shorts and he had a bar of soap and was going to town. What could you say? I just laughed and laughed.

Andy McGuire, 2000s

I used to do this one joke with cameras. Back before everyone had digital cameras, I kept a roll of exposed film in my jacket. Guests would give you their camera so you could take a family photo, and as I grabbed their camera I would palm this roll of exposed film in my hand. I would say, "Ready? Okay, 1, 2, 3," and then I'd drop the roll of film and it looked like I just ruined their entire vacation. People would totally freak out, but then they would laugh really hard.

Joshua Sudock, 2000s

The family of the tween will always cherish the time you spent busting his chops.

I once had a pre-teen girl try to read a copy of *Twilight* on my boat. That was the last time she ever did that. I don't remember the jokes that I did, but I spent the entire time messing with her. It's the elephant in the room, everyone on the boat could see her and knew what she was doing. She was sitting right next to me and when you sit up near the front you are a part of the show, so you just own it. Every one likes to pick on teenagers because they are teenagers and they have it coming.

Kevin Lively, 2010s

Some skippers got their guests to go along with a prank.

The only really good pranks I could come up with was when it was a slower day, I would get my whole boat to play dead at Schweitzer Falls. I would stay at Schweitzer and I would convince my crew to play dead so that the approaching boat would come up on us and it would look like a boat full of dead people. It was really funny. I would also do the sleeping boat when we approached the dock. I would get the whole crew to pretend they were sleeping.

Jen Chavez, 2010s

There is a spot in the Jungle Cruise that is truly unique for any Disney theme park. It's where the river runs next to the queue for the Indiana Jones and the Temple of the Forbidden Eye attraction. The scene was designed to look as if your boat had left the rain forest and came upon the dig site of Indiana Jones. You could see the beautiful temple and all the excavation equipment, and the hundreds of guests waiting in line as well. Unfortunately for Disney, those guests proved too ripe of a target for most skippers. Just about every skipper did jokes about the guests waiting in line. However, the one incident that really brought management wrath down upon skippers was when a skipper did the "Monkey See, Monkey Do" joke to an African-American family, who immediately went to City Hall and threatened to sue the park.

My favorite joke, it wasn't the best joke, but it always worked, before they blocked off the Indy queue was the "World's Most Popular Bathroom." You asked guests leaving Indy, "Sir, Sir, what did you think of it?" and this one time I did it and a guy yelled back, "I crapped my pants!" He didn't know the set up for a joke.

Trevor Kelly, 2000s

Indy was closed due to a technical problem, and as usual the Jungle Cruise was filled with people killing time waiting for it to reopen. I had had a couple of boats in a row filled with sweaty and tired guests who were just killing time until Indy re-opened. It had taken its toll on me. As I approached the Indy queue, the attraction was re-opened and the boat full of guests saw hundreds of people walking into the temple. This happened right as I hit a punch line. Instead of hearing laughter I saw the entire boat look toward Indy and let out a collective groan. I had had enough so I stopped the boat and said, "Look at that line. It's getting longer and longer, and you're just sitting here. What a bummer! That line is going to be at least 45 minutes long by the time you get off this boat." I sat there until another boat came out of the rain forest and I was forced to move. The guests on the boat were not amused and it was then that I realized that now they all hated me and I had to entertain them for another seven minutes.

David John Marley, 2000s

CHAPTER TEN

<><><><><><><><><><><><><><><><><><><><><><><><><><><><><><><><><><><><><><><><><><><>

BAD NEIGHBORS

The Jungle Cruise is the only attraction at Disneyland where a barrier had to be put up to keep cast members from hassling guests. Disneyland has all sorts of visual barriers to keep guests from seeing what happens behind the scenes, but the space between the Jungle Cruise and the Indiana Jones attraction was meant to be wide open, to look as if your boat could pull up to a dock at the Lost Delta to help with the expedition. As it turned out, the dream of Disney Imagineers was foiled by skippers who passed the Indy queue and saw a target too tempting to resist. They could see too many people waiting in line, people exiting the Indy attraction, and they were within shouting distance. How could anyone resist?

It wasn't just guests waiting at Indy who had to deal with rowdy skippers. A one point just about every area in the park has had to deal with skippers who thought they could take the jungle with them wherever they went. Let's start with those areas that were closest to the Jungle Cruise itself and see how skippers interacted with the larger world of Disneyland around them.

The Tahitian Terrace was a dinner and show set up against the Jungle Cruise as a beautiful backdrop. The show featured hula girls, drummers, and a fire dancer. The Tahitian Terrace was also the first attraction set up close to the jungle.

What was fun was my second summer the Tahitian Terrace had opened and as we approached the dock we would say, "Now here comes the most dangerous part of our journey, California and those terrible freeways," and over this you'd hear some beautiful Tahitian drums and music. It was fun to bring people out of the jungle into this beautiful Tahitian environment.

It didn't change the attraction, it just changed what you heard at the end. The whole environment of Adventureland changed. I thought the music was so exciting and you just couldn't help but get with the rhythm of that. It was a pretty good show, the dinner was okay, and the show was fun and it was an improvement over the original restaurant that had been there. We would take our breaks on the balcony above the bazaar. There was a row of chairs up there and we would take our 30-minute lunch and if the show was going we could enjoy the music. Or if there wasn't a show we would hang out and talk.

Alan Coats, 1960s

The skippers and the performers at the Tahitian Terrace tended to get along very nicely. This was, perhaps, largely due to the fact that the Jungle Cruise at the time was staffed by men only, so this was one of the only places a skipper would regularly see a female.

They walked on stage from boat storage in the back where we were. They were all very pretty single ladies and we were all single guys, so we did our best to try and impress them.

We weren't supposed to make any noise when we came in if their show was going on. I would warn my guests before we pulled up to the dock that we had to be quiet, and at night we were to turn off the boat's outside lights. The guests always understood.

The Tahitian Terrace had these guys who did a fire dance. So one day a skipper took one of the small brooms, hiked up his pants, lit the broom on fire, and began to twirl it around. I pull my boat up to the dock and there he is doing the same dance as the guys are doing on stage right next-door. Eventually the lead came back and was really mad that his broom was burned, but we played dumb and told him that we didn't know how it happened.

Terry Eaton, 1970s–1980s

That place had a waterfall that would part so the dancers could walk onstage. The controls for that and the fire were backstage. We used to randomly walk by and open and close the waterfall.

They were kind of on the snobby side. They made us promise to turn our lights off between Trader Sam and the dock if they were doing a show. If you didn't, they'd get really mad. The guy who was the fire dancer was really cool. So were the drummer guys.

Jeff Rhoads, 1970s—1980s

In the 1990s the Tahitian Terrace was closed and a few years later became Aladdin's Oasis, a children's show. Unlike its predecessor, Aladdin's Oasis didn't have a smooth relationship with the Jungle Cruise. Disneyland Show Director Diane Doyle, creator of this and many other popular Disney theme park shows, presents her non-skipper point of view.

The show was called Aladdin's Story Tale Adventures. We did a two-week test of the show and it ran for 18 years. Those two sites (Jungle Cruise and Aladdin's Oasis) were built too close to each other; they were so close, too close. There is literally five feet between the water and the back of the stage. The smell of the river, and it was so smelly, would waft into the show sometimes. We had to share a walkway. We loved bantering with the skippers, it was like dealing with frat boys, that's what we used to call them. However, skippers were doing their last turn before they got back to the dock and this is where they did all the birthday songs or their big finale. It's about having a good finish there, but that spot was literally right behind our stage and it was too loud. Our show only had three performers and our audience couldn't hear the show.

Diane Doyle, Disneyland Show Director

By all accounts the skippers and performers at Aladdin's Oasis generally got along because, according to Doyle, "actors and skippers are made from the same DNA." However, it was the meetings between the Aladdin's Oasis stage manager and the skippers that didn't go smoothly.

So one day I sent my stage manager over there to see if they could calm things down a bit. She would march over there, all 5'3" and 90lbs of her, and she would storm over and yell for the skippers to be quiet. The skippers would make all kinds of noise backstage on purpose. My actors started getting so angry about the noise.

Diane Doyle, Disneyland Show Director

The constant battles with Aladdin's Oasis were a huge issue. Part of my struggle was that I was a skipper at the time as well as a lead, so I was guilty of screaming as loud as I could into the microphone outside of their show. The birth of my whale joke came from my desire to annoy Aladdin's Oasis. I thought, "How can I make a loud annoying sound right here for as long as I can?" The joke worked and got its own traction and might have inspired Dory talking to the whale in *Finding Nemo*. The three actors, Aladdin, Jasmine, and the Story Teller didn't care; they didn't hear the noise of the boats. We shared a break room with them. It was the stage managers that took issue with us. They were so passive-aggressive, they always called, they never came over. I never met anyone over there but the actors; the managers would just call, and I thought that wasn't cool. If you're really that concerned, come over here and talk with me.

Benny LeMaster, 1990s–2000s

Another funny story is when Benny did the whale joke and the phone was ringing louder than ever, while Benny was wailing away. It would always be, "Could you keep it down, we're doing a show."

Andy McGuire, 2000s

The stage manager would call over because they couldn't leave during the show.

Diane Doyle, Disneyland Show Director

You knew if they had a show going because they'd have all their stage lights up. That's when the skippers would encourage each other to make as much noise as they could.

Anonymous, 1990s.

And slowly things began to escalate.

One day a skipper stole the lamp when it was backstage so Aladdin couldn't bring it on stage. Jasmine and the Genie were trying to improvise while Aladdin searched for the lamp. We didn't know that the skippers had stolen it.

Diane Doyle, Disneyland Show Director

This tension hit a peak in July 2003 when a skipper named Trevor Kelly pulled the greatest prank in Jungle Cruise history. It might actually be one of the best pranks ever pulled by a cast member in the entire history of Disneyland.

We heard about how these old-time skippers back in the 1970s did these amazing pranks and nobody did them anymore because they were afraid that Disney would just crush them. The movie *Ocean's 11* had come out around this time and we were inspired by the fact that if there were enough people involved it would work out great and we'd not get caught.

I remember we were at Norm's Restaurant with a bunch of skippers and we begin to plan this thing like a heist. The initial idea came about because the Aladdin's Oasis Show would constantly complain about the jungle boat spieling as we came toward the dock and they wanted us to be silent. Our argument was, "We were here first and we will be here long after your show gets cancelled," so we thought of a way to mess with them.

We went to Main Street and scoped out where we thought the security cameras might be. We then figured out the safest route to blend in was to go through all of the shops. I went into work dressed as Indiana Jones, walked backstage, ran up the ramp to the Cave of Wonders, and on my exit I had a Dickies jacket, sunglasses, and a baseball cap lined up along the route to Coke Corner. Joey Hurley was sitting at the break table, so what I did was, I ran into the show, I had listened to it a bunch of times so I knew when they were all going to be on stage and the lamp was available. I had also been to the show so I knew where the lamp was stored. It was kept in this podium off to the left of the stage.

So I ran up, ran over to the podium, grabbed the lamp, and yelled, "This belongs in a museum!" I ran back out, and ditched the lamp under the ramp. I did that so I could maybe come back later and get it or if I got caught at least I wasn't stealing anything, I was just disturbing the peace. I took off the jacket and gave it to Joey, who put it in a locker.

Let me preface the story by saying that when I got to work everyone was backstage because they knew what I was going to do. The lead that day was Gerry. If it was any other lead, they would have been fine with it, but Gerry would have shut it down fast. I remember that because a skipper saw me, and I had butterflies really bad and she looked at me and said, "This is not right," and she stormed off to go tell Gerry. So I knew I had to go.

I threw my jacket to Joey and put on my civilian clothing, walked out to Coke Corner and saw a skipper named Adam there with his girlfriend. He was dressed just like Indiana Jones, too, and had bought food before the prank so he had a time-stamped receipt to prove that it wasn't him pulling the prank. I gave him a wave to let him know to be on the lookout for security and made my way through the stores down Main Street. And, I kid you not, as I walked out the main gate, the Indiana Jones theme music was playing. It was a peak moment of my life. I made it out without any hint of disturbance. I heard it took a while for security to get there.

The lamp was under the ramp for a long time, then somebody found it and put it in the upstairs queue at Jungle Cruise for a while. It was up there for a decent amount of time and then it disappeared. For about a year it was there in the Jungle Cruise queue and now I don't know where it is.

I pulled the prank on the final day of my two-week notice. Before then, however, people knew I had something planned, and they were nervous about what I was going to do on my last day. So they had the lead keep me off the Jungle Cruise boats as much as possible. He sent me to treehouse and said, "Oh, we're giving you a break on your last day," and whenever I made it into a boat he got mad, like he thought I was going to do something.

Near the end of my shift that night everyone started showing up for my last trip. I was still on the fence about doing the Indy prank. Management came down right before I took my last trip and said, "He's not allowed to do a last trip, everybody go home." So I thought, "Forget these people, I'm doing the prank." It is literally Disney's fault that the prank happened.

Security never even went that way (down Main Street) as far as I know. They knew that it was me because I got a call a week later. Some manager called and told me that they had footage of the prank. I told them that I'd like to see their footage because theirs was probably in color and mine was shot in black and white. And that was it. They had nothing on me.

Trevor Kelly, 2000s

We were all worried that Gerry was going to come back there. I was waiting and waiting back there for it to happen, but my break was over and I had to get back into a boat. Security was looking for Trevor in the jungle. They thought that he had run into the jungle to hide out. I remember seeing uniformed security talking on their radios on the high ridge [by the backside of water] and they were looking for him. All the skippers knew that he had already made it out of the park.

Leo Romo, 2000s

After a while, once I relaxed, then the skippers relaxed and became more respectful of the other show going on. In the park you have to be respectful of the other performers because things are so close. With cast members it's all about playing in the sandbox and getting along and how it makes you a stronger team member.

Diane Doyle, Disneyland Show Director

During the 2000s the Jungle Cruise and Indy cast members wore the same costumes. This made it easy to pull people from one attraction to the other. Sadly for skippers, it was usually Indy leads that were calling the Jungle Cruise looking for more help, and not the other way around.

Indy was awful. There was a time when they cross trained us all, maybe half of the Jungle Cruise skippers. It got to the point that when they wanted to pull you to Indy you'd check out the sheet and find someone with less seniority and tell the lead to send them instead.

Chris Ramirez, 2000s

Any event happening in Adventureland was an open target for skippers.

I remember when we had a guy dressed as Indiana Jones out in Adventureland doing his "Summer of Hidden Mysteries." There were some really cool guys performing Indy who would play along with you and others that were jerks and didn't want to have fun. They had the "Random Acts of Indy" and they would have little stunt show moments throughout Adventureland, such as Indy getting into a fist fight with someone above Tropical Imports. He'd come on stage through Aladdin's Oasis and onto the exit dock area, and you'd see him walking out and if it was a good Indy you'd yell, "Hey, Dr. Jones, are we still having that quiz?" and he'd yell back, "Yeah, Michelson chapters 5 thru 12." One Indy asked where I'd gotten that question from, so he went back and watched the first movie and saw that Indy was a college professor. I had a jerk Indy who yelled back, "Yeah, and you're going to fail!" We would do that and he'd be having a fight up by the Adventureland office, and one time it was happening while Jungle Cruise was closed so I was standing at the entrance watching the fight and I started yelling, "That's my professor!" It was great having something different that you were able to play off of. Originally they made the villian that Indy fought a girl, but people got mad that he punched a girl so they had to change that.

Kevin Lively, 2010s

For decades Jungle Cruise skippers had the reputation as the rowdiest cast members at Disneyland. Here is some proof to back up that claim.

There was a period of time when the costumes worn by cast members in Tomorrowland looked very similar to the ones worn by employees at Taco Bell. They had the same color scheme. One day I had a very long day of training new skippers, At the end of the day about 10 skippers were all waiting for the shuttle van to take us back to K lot. As was the custom with the skippers when the shuttle arrived, we all sat in the back together. I was sitting with my trainees and I noticed a Tomorrowland trainer and his trainees come up the steps of the van. I had watched them in line and they were clearly very excited to be at Disneyland. We always thought the Tomorrowland people were a little arrogant. So as they walked up the steps into the van where everybody could see them I yelled out, "Yeah, I'll have two soft tacos, a cheese quesadilla, an order of nachos, and a large Coke." Everybody on the van started laughing, and I watched the trainer's shoulders slump in defeat as he took a seat in the front of the van. To make matters worse, one of the skippers in our group yelled out "Westside, bitches!" Then all of the skippers started to chant "Jungle Cruise! Jungle Cruise!" as the van pulled away. And that is why people hated us.

David John Marley, 2000s

Once there was a bunch of a skippers sitting in the back of the tram, and we were waiting for some other skippers to get on board. Some guys from Space Mountain came on the tram and tried to sit in the back and I just said, "There's no space back here." And everybody laughed.

Kipp Hart, 2000s–2010s

Somehow it was discovered that you could call Walt Disney World in Florida and even transfer calls there from our phone in the shipping office. During the summer of 2003, most of the time that City Hall called to find out our wait time, they were transferred to the Jungle Cruise in Florida. As a result the sign on Main Street said the wait for Jungle Cruise was 45 minutes when it was usually just 10. Management eventually caught on and they blocked our phone from being able to transfer calls.

We used to call other attractions and pretend to be from City Hall. We liked to call Autopia and tell them that we had guests doing a scavenger hunt and we needed them to count how many red cars they had running. Once the lead protested that he was understaffed. I replied, "I don't care what your situation is, you need to call me back in ten minutes with the number!" and then I hung up. At the time a skipper was dating a guy from City Hall, and one day he stopped by to ask if we were calling other attractions and pretending to be City Hall. I tried to play dumb, but we all couldn't stop laughing.

David John Marley, 2000s

I worked Big Thunder Mountain Railroad a handful of times. Whenever they'd pull me to Thunder, I'd take my time going there, so they stopped pulling me. They'd say, "We need you right now," and I'd show up 30–40 minutes later. I'd stop and get something to eat, then go change costumes and slowly walk over there. Then once I was there I would usually break down the ride. There was this computer system that I think was called Fred and it would warn you when the ride was close to breaking down so you could start doing stuff, but I didn't know what stuff to do. So I'd just sit up there as the ride warned me and I slowly watched it shut the entire ride down.

Trevor Kelly, 2000s

They wanted to train me on Star Tours, but I just called in sick. I got trained on the rockets, the Astro Orbiter. I got trained and I worked there one time and I told them I would never work there again, I would just call in sick. I hated it so much. It was just pushing a button and sitting there.

Kriztina Varga, 2000s

I only knew Jungle Cruise. Whenever I saw cross–training on my schedule, I'd just call out. I didn't want to work a push-button ride.

Leo Romo, 2000s

Skippers were very territorial and protective of the Jungle Cruise. Heaven forbid you try to "cross the rocks" which means walking from boat storage to the dock where guests could see you. I once saw a skipper on a boat full of guests yell, "Don't cross the rocks!" to a Disneyland security guard. I'd seen other skippers physically block cast members not in jungle costumes who were trying to get backstage.

David John Marley, 2000s

The people who do primarily work Jungle Cruise, I do notice their enthusiasm. They bring it with them. There are certain attractions where the cast members are not as pleasant. But when skippers go to those attractions, they bring their silliness and fun with them. And they make a boring shift into something fun. I have noticed that.

Anonymous, 2010s

Every skipper knows that when they are at another attraction they are probably going to be reminded at some point that,"This isn't the Jungle Cruise." This tended to be a common warning given out whether a skipper had done something or not.

Skippers are not taken seriously outside of the Jungle Cruise. Also, skippers would wonder why you wanted to leave the jungle. Why did you want to learn another attraction? I always came back because I kept getting thrown off these other attractions. I wanted to learn Mansion or Pirates and they said, "No, you'll just hurt yourself." So I stayed at Jungle Cruise. I think there is an element of awe because this person is a Jungle Cruise skipper.

Eventually, Jessica left to work at Guest Relations at City Hall, a world away from the Jungle Cruise.

I could not be as funny. They wanted me to become a tour guide right off the bat. But I didn't want to do that anymore. You couldn't be funny because their whole tour is scripted.

Jessica Harris–Lopez, 1990s–2000s

At the Jungle Cruise the skipper has so much to do with the attraction that it comes in their personalities. I loved working Jungle Cruise because of how dry and sarcastic you could be. I loved to tell the worst, cheesiest jokes on the script, and I would tell them as cheesy as I could, and then when it flopped I would explain the joke to the guests. I loved working with people on other rides, but you didn't get to see their personality come through like you did at Jungle Cruise. Working Main Street vehicles you had that interaction, but your persona has to be 1890s, you are the gateway to Disneyland so you have to be super Disney. At Pirates, you're mostly doing load and dispatch, you don't get much interaction with the guests, especially after they brought in the automated spiel. Skippers embraced their ride and ran with it.

Ben Case, 2000s

I worked Main Street vehicles, and they were very concerned about having another skipper working there. You had to narrate on the omnibus. At Jungle Cruise I mostly stayed on script because, I enjoyed giving the classic experience. There was one lead at vehicles that was really worried that I was going to go off script. I remember the lead telling me, "Don't forget, this isn't Jungle Cruise." He said it to me very sternly, it clearly wasn't a joke.

Mike Pucher, 2000s

The only time I got in trouble was when I was assigned to steam trains. I was in training. We are on the train and we got to Tomorrowland and I was supposed to say something, but I just said something off the top of my head, I don't even remember what I said, but I remember hearing the people on the train laughing. One of the leads walked right over to me and said, "This isn't the Jungle Cruise." It took me down a notch, because I was just trying get people to enjoy themselves. It's a little strait-laced at steam trains. I only did three shifts there and then told them I didn't want to do it anymore.

Kipp Hart, 2000s–2010s

I was working at the monorail and I made a joke one time over the PA. It wasn't even a Jungle Cruise joke. Guests laughed, and a lead came over to me and said, "I know you work Jungle Cruise, but this isn't Jungle Cruise, so lay off the jokes."

People from other areas of the park hated it when skippers would come over. It had to do with personalities. I behaved myself in Tomorrowland; the managers were good. When I went over I had to change my mindset. I saw a Tomorrowland lead one day and we were working the monorail and Downtown Disney and the line was huge, so I looked at the lead and deadpanned, "We're gonna need a bigger boat," and he just stared at me. He didn't get that it was a reference to *Jaws*. There were some people there that just did not understand jokes. You had to put on a different face, a serious face, when you were in Tomorrowland.

Chris Ramirez, 2000s

This simple statement from popular skipper Joey Hurley sums up perfectly how many skippers, and cast members for that matter, view the differences between the east and west sections of the park.

The westside had pirates and swashbuckling adventures and wildness. The east side had attractions that ran on time. They had spaceships and they tucked their shirts in and knew they had a job to do and had to be efficient. On the westside it was all about leaning on things and having a good time.

There certainly is a difference between skippers and the rest of the park. But it has changed and evolved. I think the generation of skippers from 1995, when they first let women work at Jungle Cruise, to about 2004 was the last one where skippers were different from other cast members. Now everybody is sarcastic and everybody makes jokes; it doesn't even matter what land you are in. You'll be on Splash Mountain and hear the cast members make a snarky comment, where that kind of thing used to be reserved for skippers only. Now at Disneyland everyone is more loose, not everyone is so uptight. People are no longer afraid to say something disparaging against the company.

Joey Hurley, 2000s

Skipper and 2003 "Adventureland Trainer of the Year" Kaz Liput recalls working at Storybook Land and how she added her own Jungle Cruise touch to this otherwise sedate attraction.

It's hard to not want to get into Jungle Cruise mode, but it's a very different atmosphere. For me I made the best of it by adding voices, telling stories, and adding a couple little jokes here and there. They had a lead and two managers ride my boat soon after I'd gotten signed off and I thought I was in trouble and I did my regular bit, but I dropped one joke. At Cinderella Castle I'd say, "And that's where she lived with her prince, happily every after, and got a master's degree. Dream big, girls." I imitated the Genie when we got to Agrabah. Afterwards, they came up to me, and I was sure I was getting fired, and they said, "Wow, they were right, your boat is really good!" I was glad I didn't get fired.

Kaz Liput, 2000s

The extended roles that skippers played changed over time. For some decades, Walt Disney's Enchanted Tiki Room and the Swiss Family Robinson/Tarzan's Treehouse were totally separate from the Jungle Cruise, and at other times they were part of a skipper's regular rotation. Starting in the 1990s, the Tiki Room was regularly staffed by skippers. Some were there for an entire shift, some went over to give the regular cast member a break. Since the Tiki Room became a second home to skippers, it became the scene of chaos as well.

One time I had a shift at the Tiki Room and I spent the entire shift building a fake skipper who was asleep in the break room. I used any pieces of costume that I could find. It looked like this guy was asleep in the Tiki break room/office. Someone came to give me a break and they poked at the dummy, trying to wake him up, and the dummy collapsed on the floor and the guy freaked out.

Trevor Kelly, 2000s

They came to us one year and said if you get enough counts at Tiki the money will be there for a rehab of the Tiki Room. The Imagineers told us this and management was with them. So me and two other skippers decided to make sure that the guest counts at Tiki were high. One thing we did was block off the entrance to Adventureland and funnel everyone through the Tiki Room turnstiles and out the exit. We would do a vaudeville routine and promise air conditioning. We blocked people's paths and made them go through the turnstiles and ran them out of the exit. It worked because there were three of us that worked Tiki all of the time. We forced guests to use the Tiki Room as a walkway.

Sometimes things don't disappoint you. We would give backdoor passes to attractions to the Dole Whip girls and they'd give us Dole Whip for free. Tiki was fun.

Chris Ramirez, 2000s

CHAPTER ELEVEN

WOMEN ON THE DOCK

American women got the right to vote in 1920. There were female congressmen, governors, and Supreme Court justices before Disneyland allowed women to pilot the dark and dangerous waters of the Jungle Cruise. This delay wasn't the fault of any women; some had tried for years to get trained there. It was Sue Barnaby, a 15-year Disneyland veteran, a woman who knew all the skippers and got along with them, who broke the gender barrier. As it turned out, she was the perfect person to be the first female skipper at the World Famous Jungle Cruise.

Before Barnaby changed things, many attractions at the park were not gender neutral. It wasn't just the Jungle Cruise that was men only, the *Mark Twain* and *Columbia* were also male-only terrain, and the Storybook Land attraction was exclusively female. Bringing women to the dock revived that old argument about whether or not women are as funny as men. The brave women who took to the Jungle Cruise proved that they could hold their own.

Back in my day it was only men at the Jungle Cruise and only women at the Storybook Land Canal Boats. I thought it was fine that women are at Jungle Cruise, I think they should be there.

Alan Coats, 1960s

Disneyland had tried to put women on Jungle Cruise before, with limited success.

In the 1970s they had four girls that they trained, but I don't think they were given a chance to succeed, because at the time it was very sexist, it was seen as a guy's thing. I don't think they were even given the chance to be funny and if they tried to be funny they were shot down.

Sue Barnaby, 1980s–1990s

I thought it was cool that it was only men at the Jungle Cruise. I thought it was the only way it could be. We all saw Humphrey Bogart as the archetype of the skipper. Having grown up in Anaheim and going to Disneyland on a regular basis, a skipper was the male pinnacle of greatness. I came in there with the picture of that's what you would become. Here is what I found interesting about that period of time. There were very few women. There were a couple of girls on Big Thunder, there was one pregnant lady who worked Tiki. A couple of the girls also did the treehouse. But the whole of Adventureland and Frontierland were all guys. It was a vast wasteland of no girls except for the brave ones that would hang out with us, and they got all of our attention. So when a girl did come around, it was magical.

Fred Martin, 1980s

Sue Barnaby worked at Disneyland for 17 years, but it is the two years she spent at Jungle Cruise that have made her famous.

I know that I opened the flood gates at Jungle Cruise, but I was only really there for a little over a year.

We used to joke about it during the 1980s. We used to tell the guys who worked there that they should let women be skippers cause we were just as funny as they were. We did ask the managers a few times, but they said no. It was really a boy's club back then.

I was Adventureland/Frontierland only and that sucked for girls because when Big Thunder would go down for a rehab we didn't get any hours. As it was, we only worked weekends and some evenings because we were in school. But when Thunder went down there were no hours. The only things available were the Tiki Room, the treehouse, and the shooting galleries, and that was it. Jungle Cruise was open, but it was all guys. There was one year when we were going to have to file a grievance, so six of us were shipped out. Two went to Storybook Land, two went to America Sings, and two of us went to Rocket Jets. I went to Rocket Jets for three weeks. We called it the Skillet in the Sky because it was hotter than hell and you had to wear that jumpsuit.

Sue and some other female cast members appeared in a home-made movie that skippers filmed at the park called "Jungle Cruise Movie" in 1982. Even though they couldn't work the attraction, they still got Jungle Cruise costumes and appeared as skippers.

I think the Jungle Cruise Movie was made in 1982 and parts of it are really hysterical. That was Karen, Sharon, Arlene, and myself, the women who wanted to go over and work at the Jungle Cruise. For me, one of the funniest parts was Karen in the skiff when she gets the wrong boat and heads off into the jungle. It was just a small blurb, but it was just us girls who didn't want to work at the shooting gallery so we came over to the Jungle Cruise to work. We went into the Polaroid shop and took a picture. We got Jungle Cruise shirts, our own shorts, and we had jungle scarves and a Jungle Cruise hat. I think we had to borrow the clothes from the guys; somebody had to sign it out for us and then we could borrow it.

While they were making this movie we asked management why we couldn't work Jungle Cruise. They told us we couldn't. It was some old-school managers, including a woman, who said no. We really did want to learn it back then, so we kept trying. That's why I didn't believe it when I asked again in the 90s and I got trained the next day. I was thinking, "Really? that's all it took? All I had to do was go to Florida and notice they had women and tell you guys?" No one asked how long women had been there or anything.

The moment when Barnaby finally did break the gender barrier at Jungle Cruise was so sudden it took her by surprise.

I took a trip to Walt Disney World in 1994 or 95 with a few cast member friends, and we noticed that the Jungle Cruise there had female skippers. And I thought, "What the hell is this?" This is right during the time when the Indiana Jones attraction opened and I got stuck on the opening crew. I didn't want to be on the opening crew. It was the time when Disney would take the A-level cast members and have them open the new attractions. I hated working Indy; it was miserable and loud. So when I came back from Florida I went to the managers and said, "If there are female skippers in Florida, why can't there be female skippers here?" A manager named Joe is the one who did it. I'm not sure how he did it, but it went up to Disneyland president Paul Pressler who said okay. The very next day I got a call: "You're going to be trained tomorrow." So I told him I wanted my friend Joy to be trained with me, and she was really pissed at me, but I told her not to worry, it was going to be fun.

It was funny because we didn't know what to wear. We ended up getting an Adventureland merchandising costume; it had culottes and it was just ugly, it was the worst costume ever, so we tried to make our own ensemble because that one was hideous. On our second day we wore Indiana Jones costumes, and that is how that whole thing started. I just did it as a dare and the next thing you know I was thinking, "Oh crap, I'm being trained."

The old timers would say that they didn't need women working at Jungle Cruise, because they're not as funny as men. It was just a dare, and I did it. I remember that once the word got out, every newspaper, all the media, were at the park. I was off that day so they called me at home and said, "You need to get down here because they are here to interview you." So

I had to frantically get ready and rush down there. I remember getting interviewed by some morning show. It was so bizarre. I was on the front page of the paper; it was my 15 minutes of fame. I had a friend who was living in Germany and she found a blurb in the paper about me. So it made international news. I found it all surprising because why should all this attention pour on me when they already had female skippers at the Florida Jungle Cruise? I was amazed that it was suddenly such a big news story.

I don't think people were actually that surprised. A few guests would say, "Oh, a woman!" For the most part, I didn't see any hesitancy from any of the guests, none of them said they wanted a male skipper. I didn't notice it, anyway. Maybe that's because when I did it, it was a new thing, a novelty.

I remember on my very first trip a kid got on my boat and he said, "What? A female skipper?" And my trainer was looking at me, so I just looked at the little boy and said, "Well, at least if we get lost, I'll stop and ask for directions, you smart ass." That was before social media, so you could get away with saying things like that. His dad thought it was funny.

And what about the fellow female that Sue dragged along to Jungle Cruise?

She had been there for a couple of years, and the only reason that she agreed to do it with me was because she wanted to work at Dave Crockett Explorer Canoes, she wanted to be a lead at Canoes, and that opened the door for her. She was the first woman to work at Canoes. She hated me for dragging her to the Jungle Cruise.

Sue Barnaby, 1980s–1990s

Nowadays women are a regular feature on the Jungle Cruise dock, but that oesn't mean it still isn't a boys' club at times.

It was still a boys' club in 1998, but us ladies, we brought our own, having to compete with the male skippers and everything. I had over 100 guest compliments, so I was doing something right. I was being myself and being funny.

Jessica Harris–Lopez, 1990s–2000s

I'd heard that it was an old boys club, but I never felt left out. I always felt like I was part of the team. It was like getting 20 big brothers who were really nice. Plus, I only have brothers so the environment seemed normal to me.

Karen Vogelvang, 2000s

Being a female skipper was tough because there was still a wall and a line. I think it will always be there because the nature of the attraction and the nature of genders. When I started in 1999 it was heavier. Not just from cast members but from guests, who didn't want women skippers. People would complain if I did a dry spiel that I was a bitch and I got complaints. So I created a ditzy character and it went over like gangbusters. Guests loved it. I would do silly call-backs. At the gorilla camp I would do the "Jeep turned over" joke and just lose it. I would laugh and laugh and the boat would stare at me, then I'd calm down and motion with my hand and say, "It was upside down." Then I would lose it when I got to the skull canoe and said the joke about it being "a dangerous place to be-headed." So I'd laugh and laugh and slowly die, then look at the boat, do the same hand gesture, and say, "It was upside down." It had nothing to do with the skull canoe, but it worked.

So there's that fraternal order from the crew and also the guests. Not everyone was like that. The girls that came in who were gorgeous were not treated the same as the ones who came in and were really funny. It was a different thing. They would treat the hot girls the way they treated women they wanted to ask out on a date. They'd be nice to the cute girls, then mock them behind their back. The girls that were funny, the men were wary of you. There was certainly a sense that they would accept you if you rose to the challenge.

Kaz Liput, 2000s

Some girls were really mean to me. There was a strange competition between the women there. That is why [my best friend] Allison and I gravitated toward each other immediately because we both thought those chicks were just evil. I don't know, it was a weird competition thing. Women that are funny, there is just something about that.

Kriztina Varga, 2000s

I did the "bitter skipper" trip. I thought why can the guys do it and the girls can't? So I'd be sarcastic. I made sure that I'd connect with the guests. At the attacking natives I'd say, "There is something you don't see everyday, but I do...you got kids, you know what I'm talking about." Stuff like that to connect them to the jokes. Make everything relatable to the guests and you can be as sarcastic as you like. Or I'd act like a mom and make fun of teenagers.

A skipper named Natalie and I would do "twin skippers" where we would take turns spieling during a trip and say things like, "Well, Natalie, you don't say?" and throw it back and forth. It was so fun. I did Skipper Barbie. It was based on the Barbie tour guide from *Toy Story 2*, where everything was happy.

Jessica Harris–Lopez, 1990s–2000s

Because of who I am, the sassy thing didn't work for me, so I started to do this thing, mostly to annoy Kaz, where I was the Skipper Barbie who played dumb. I didn't get my own jokes. I was just totally stupid. I was an airhead. If I did a sassy tour, people would say I was bitchy and complain, so I switched and guests loved it.

My brother Andy and I did the same joke at the veldt about the zebra. I did it where I believed that the zebra was asleep and I'd say, "Look it's so cute, isn't it wonderful," and if I did it sarcastically like men, I'd get complaints. The more "legally blonde" I went with it, the more laughs I would get.

Karen Vogelvang, 2000s

I had to do the same thing as Karen. I heard people laughing at some female skippers who were sarcastic and I tried it and people hated me, so I went back to being silly and dumb.

Kristin McGuire, 2000s

If a joke doesn't work, you try something else. There are certain jokes that women could just not do. Some female skippers I worked with would do a perfect boat and guests would walk over to me and complain and say, "That girl is a bitch." It's sad because you can take the same spiel and if a woman does it people will get pissed off.

Andy McGuire, 2000s

Girls could tell the exact same joke as a guy and still get complaints. Especially if the girl was cute or too sarcastic. We had funny girls and we loved our funny girls.

Chris Ramirez, 2000s

You kind of had to be one of the boys. If you were a girlie girl, I don't think you'd last that long. Even though it was co-ed it was still manly and testosterone driven, although we'd put up with quite a bit if you were pretty.

Andy McGuire, 2000s

One night I was lead and standing in the shipping office when this female guest walks up to me all red faced, points at her female skipper, and yells, "Fire that bitch!" The skipper, who was brand new, was horrified, so I waved at her to move it up, then I talked to the lady. It turns out the skipper had been doing all the scripted jokes like she was supposed to, but this lady thought she was just being bitchy.

David John Marley, 2000s

Although women began working at the Jungle Cruise in 1995, the first pregnant skipper didn't hit the dock until 2013. In fact, Jen Chavez, who already had two young sons at home, realized that she was pregnant for the third time while driving a boat through the jungle.

The night before that shift I had been really sick on a parade shift. I'd had a really bad headache and found myself throwing up and they actually sent me home. The next morning I was feeling kinda bad, but I had to do my Jungle Cruise shift; I was excited about it. I remember feeling kinda not myself, feeling bad. I went out on my first run of the shift and we turned the corner and something about turning the corner into the elephant pool and the motion of the boat while I was talking and I didn't know what to do because I knew I was going to throw up and it was a full boat of people. I tried to distract them by saying, "Look at those elephants over there," and turned my head to throw up into the river while they were looking, but I was really bad doing that. There was no hiding it. I thought, "This is really weird. Why am I so sick? No one else is sick in my family. Oh god, I can't be pregnant!" and it clicked in my brain that this was a possibility. So I pulled back around to the dock and I looked at the lead and said, "I need to get out the boat right now; I just threw up." He said, "Oh, my god, do you want to do a deadhead?" So I did a deadhead and I remember driving around the river all by myself thinking, "I think I'm really pregnant" I was excited but actually really freaked out because my baby was still a baby and the other one was just two. I went home after that because I was really sick and I threw up another time, but it was backstage. They sent me home again. And then I had two days off after that where I did the test and confirmed it.

Being pregnant sent me into a panic because I was so happy and I was loving Jungle Cruise so much and I didn't want them find a reason to fire me because I hadn't passed my probation period yet, so I thought I should hold on to this little secret for as long as I can, which was very hard because I was so sick and making up excuses was rough. On my "Congratulations, you've earned your ears day!" when the managers pulled me up on stage and told me that I'd made it past probation, I said, "That's great, can we talk?" And she said, "Are you leaving?" Her face got panicked and I was said, "No, I'm not leaving, I don't want to leave. I just wanna let you guys know I'm expecting." She was really happy and supportive. She was relieved that I wasn't leaving, which was nice, and she was just told me, "Whatever you need and just communicate with us and we'll make sure you're always comfortable and accommodated." It was a really cool experience and it wasn't negative or as scary as I thought it was going to be, especially at Jungle because I wasn't sure how it was going to go being pregnant.

Life was rough for the first-ever pregnant skipper, but Chavez was tougher, and her fellow skippers and Disneyland management were very supportive.

The first couple months were rough because I had a condition where I either vomited or had the urge to vomit twenty-four hours a day for almost twelve weeks and they actually took me off work for a month right at the beginning. Disney was really cool about it and let me come back when I was ready, so I took some time off to get better. Coming back was hard because I still easily got sick, but the other skippers were so awesome about it. They learned from the look on my face that I was going to throw up and they all knew to send me to the back. I really wanted to work Jungle Cruise until I couldn't work anymore. The managers were worried, but I told them, "I will tell you guys if I don't think I can do it anymore, but I really think it's my third time around and I think I can do it." And they were fine with that.

The one problem Chavez encountered was the costume. Adventureland managers contradicted each other and the Costuming Department had their own ideas.

One manager told me I could wear my shirt untucked and another manager saw me with my shirt untucked and told me I couldn't do that. So I started wearing a jacket but then it started getting warm when it was approaching the summer and I thought, "I can't do this, I'm gonna die." I finally went upstairs to the manager's office and said, "Look, we need to figure out a costume." The girls wanted me to wear a dress, and I'm not going to wear a dress. I went to go check it out and it was like an overalls with a skirt and it was just weird. It was designed for Indy, I believe, but there was no way I could step in and out of boats or go on safari and do any of that with a dress on. It didn't make sense for me, so we had to find something different. They sent me to costuming and costuming didn't know what to do and they told me where the maternity section was and I went and checked out what they had and they actually had some khaki maternity pants and a little white baby-doll shirt and I thought I could wear with my hat. Costuming called the managers and the managers said, "Well, if you say its okay, we'll say its okay," and costuming said, "Yeah, it's okay." And that was my makeshift costume.

Chavez worked at Jungle Cruise until right before she gave birth. Being in the boat became increasingly difficult as her pregnancy progressed.

It was funny the reaction people would give me because they would see this big pregnant girl loading people in and out of boats and just doing all the work everyone else was doing. Guests would say, "I don't wan't you to help me out of the boat, I want to help you get out of the boat," and I had to tell them, "No, it's okay, I'm totally fine." It was the summer, so there were times when I would get really tired and it was really hot. But everyone was good about it. The skippers were making sure I had enough water and taking my breaks and everyone was very cool. It was a different experience. No one was stretching out their breaks or anything because they knew they had to take care of me. So it was nice.

Jen Chavez, 2010s

Thanks to Sue and Joy, and the funny women that came after them, women were a success at the Jungle Cruise, even though resistance remained for years.

The older skippers were bitter and they hated us for coming in. A lot of the old-timers would say, "I dunno, women at the Jungle Cruise, it's not right." And I'd say, "Sorry. I just wanted off Indy." Seriously, that's all I wanted."

Sue Barnaby, 1980s–1990s

One morning, because of shift changes and people calling in sick, the dock was all guys. We noticed it was an all-guy crew and the lead said, "Yeah, it's like it should be."

Chris Ramirez, 2000s

I had people not want to get on my boat when I would pull up because I was a girl. They'd say, "Oh, we'll wait for a boy." The great thing is the skips listen to them and they'd say, "You can get back in line completely or you can go on her boat because she's great." The male skippers really supported the girls that were there. I would have guys just come sit next to me and they'd say, "You'd better be funny. I've been on this ride a hundred times and I know what the good jokes are, so you better be funny." They were dead serious. So I'd say, "Well, I'll be funnier than the way your mom dresses you."

Jen Chavez, 2010s

We had one afternoon where it was raining really hard and we were discussing the reasons why girls didn't get respect from guests at the Jungle Cruise. A bunch of big bamboo had fallen in the river because it was raining and also really windy. It was a cold, miserable day. Guys from horticulture showed up and said they needed a couple of volunteers to go with them to get the bamboo. It was raining, the wind was blowing, and it was freezing. So they wanted to take a couple of boats and the skiff. We were riding in the skiff which had no motor or any way to steer it. There were six of us riding on the back of a boat. We came around the corner of Schweitzer Falls and realized that we are going to hit it and there is nothing we can do. We finally get back to the shipping office and all of the girls working that day were huddled together in the shipping office. We looked at them and said, "That's why women don't get respect at the Jungle Cruise." Every guy went, maybe eight of us, and we were soaked and muddy and had so much fun.

Chris Ramirez, 2000s

I kind of miss the time when there was stuff that guys did and stuff that girls did. I totally understand why it has to be the way it is; everything changes. Disneyland was selling a show, like being in a movie, and it isn't like that anymore, so that idea is lost. I think the sets and scenery of the park are fantastic, but the human element isn't as good. Plus, today the park is so crowded that the experience is just totally different.

Jeff Rhoads, 1970s–1980s

When I was working load I would occasionally get guests who would tell me that they didn't want a female skipper. About 90% of the time it was a young woman who made the request. I would try to get them to take the boat, but they rarely did. I'd just have them wait for a guy.

David John Marley, 2000s

I might know why women don't like having a female skipper. They are going there to score with these hot male skippers. But in this day and age, half of them could be gay, or they could get a female skipper.

Sue Barnaby, 1980s–1990s

The hardest I ever laughed at the Jungle Cruise was in the boat of a skipper named Helen. We were approaching Trader Sam, who wasn't working. When she said, "There is Trader Sam, the head salesman of the jungle," this guest yelled out, "He's broken!" Helen paused and said in this dry but sad voice said, "He's not broken, he's just...disillusioned." The ad lib combined with her delivery was too much for me and I laughed until she had to turn around because I was making her break character.

David John Marley, 2000s

CHAPTER TWELVE

RUNNING THE MADHOUSE

The Jungle Cruise is a rough place to be a lead. The tension of being a lead at Disneyland is that you are still technically a ride operator like everyone else, and will have to work with these people at Jungle Cruise and other attractions. I think that is a good tension, because it keeps a lead from being too power crazy since they still have to work with these people. At least, that is how it's supposed to work. Being a lead at Jungle Cruise is tough because you can never be sure when something will go wrong or even what might go wrong. The leads are stuck between the expectations of management and the wild ideas of their fellow skippers.

Jungle is the world of grey. There are no rules, only guidelines.

Andy McGuire, 2000s

I always heard that the job of the day lead was to keep the Jungle Cruise running, and the job of the night lead was to keep the skippers out of the trees.

Mike Pucher, 2000s

Out of all the places where I worked as a lead at Disneyland, the Jungle Cruise was the hardest. It was the hardest because you had to convince the guys that the rotation you put them in was a good one, that it was okay to take that boat even though the Maggie may have a better microphone. Everybody there had their own pet peeves and foibles, and you had to deal with trying to orchestrate all of that. In my opinion, as a skipper your guests are the customers and it's your job to make them happy. As a lead, the skippers are your customers and it's your job to make them happy. So, as a lead, if you made your customers, the skippers, happy, they in turn would make the guests happy.

It was really hard sometimes with all of the personality clashes. The complaints are always stuff like, "I don't want to work with him in that boat, he's a jerk," or "Why do I have to work unload, I always work unload." You had to put up with all of that stuff. You had to be careful not to play favorites or even be perceived as playing favorites because then somebody would run up to management and complain to them. I enjoyed it.

I also had to write the performance reviews of the skippers and you had to learn how to balance the positive and negative aspects. They sent me to a class on how to do performance appraisal writing as a part of Disney University. I invented the "Performance Appraisal Wheel" for management. The idea was that you start with a positive, then you hit the negative points, then end on the positive. When you have a hundred or more appraisals to write, it's hard to come up with unique things to say. So I made this wheel out of card stock with little windows and you'd move the wheel and open the window up to help you. For example, you'd line it up to dock safety, positive or negative, and it would give you a little phrase to use. Then one day somebody found it and complained and they told me that if anyone found out about the wheel we'd be in so much trouble because we were supposed to be so serious and this made it seem like we were all making things up.

Jeff Rhoads, 1970s–1980s

When I worked there a guy named Don was the head lead. He was a scruffy old dude who used to work for the California Highway Patrol. He wore mirrored sunglasses that barely met the Disney Look. He used those glasses as a mask between him and the kids working the ride. He was 60 years old and just as gruff as could be. He'd always be warning us about keeping 18 inches between the boats. You'd hear him say, "18 inches, guy," in his gravelly voice. He called everybody "guy"; everyone else used the term "skip," but to him you were just "guy." And everybody was afraid of him. He was like that one high school teacher that everybody was afraid of. But here's the deal with Don; once you got to know him, once you got on his good side, you could really tell that he liked you. He was like that character Curly in the movie *City Slickers*. He was way too tough for many of us, but once he liked you, you knew that you were in.

I remember one thing that Don used to do. Sometimes he would get on your boat and say, "It's time to check the animation," and he would go out for a smoke. He just wanted you to keep him out of view of other boats so that he could have a cigarette break.

Fred Martin, 1980s

Benny LeMaster perhaps best exemplifies the tension between being a skipper and a lead.

I had to have the most patience with skippers, and part of that was that I had to negotiate my skipper hat and my scheduler/lead hat. There would be parties and it was not uncommon that after scheduling closed at midnight, a skipper would call in sick and then pass the phone around and the opening Jungle Cruise crew would all call in sick. It was rough because I was at those parties sometimes and sometimes I was the opening scheduler, so I would have to deal with this in the morning. I'd walk around the party getting people to pick up shifts and negotiating with people at the party while I was drinking with them.

Benny LeMaster, 1990s–2000s

I loved being a lead. If there was a role I was born to do, it was being a lead at Jungle Cruise. Being a working lead at Jungle Cruise can be a bit like being a babysitter. The creative, youthful enthusiasm can get overwhelming. When all that energy is focused and shared right, there is nothing like it anywhere else at the resort. It's a different focus. They are a creative bunch who just want to entertain. So keeping them within Disney spiel guidelines is a challenge, but it makes the Jungle Cruise what it is. The attraction generates more guest compliments than anything else.

David Schoenwetter, 1990s–2000s

I was a lead there and things were going great. And I was getting comfortable in my job, feeling like I had an office at the top of Adventureland. You're in charge of the Jungle Cruise, the Tiki Room, the treehouse, and you think it's a big deal. You're walking around feeling great. Being a lead at Jungle Cruise is kind of like being the Mister Rogers of Adventureland; you just walk around and ask people, "How are you doing today? Are you having a good day? Me, too!"

Michael Libby, 2000s

When I was being trained as a lead at Jungle Cruise, I was told that you have to circle like a shark. You're constantly moving. You start at load, check the load rotations, walk back, split the line, check the break sheet, walk to unload, check the unload rotations, check the special assistance line, fix the strollers, adjust the wait time, fix the ropes, come back, check your counts, and then do it again.

David Schoenwetter, 1990s–2000s

Guests had to go all the way to City Hall and fill out a form to complain to get someone suspended, because the leads always had your back. The leads would say to the angry guest, "Oh, really? Well, I'll take care of that." You have to look at the context of the complaint; sometimes they are really baseless, and you have to take that into account. Some managers and leads don't know how to do that.

Sue Barnaby, 1980s–1990s

The primary difference was that at Jungle Cruise I held a lot of secrets. I didn't have secrets at the other attractions that I worked, but there were secrets at Jungle Cruise and they were about the rules the skippers were breaking. There were certain managers that let things fly because the person was a skipper. My attitude was, "Do what you will, but do not tarnish the image of the attraction."

Benny LeMaster, 1990s–2000s

I would love coming in during the morning and setting up the schedule for the day—who was going where, who wanted an ER (early release), or whatever. From the lead's perspective, you are playing a game of Tetris. Disneyland staffs for so many units of Jungle Cruise and the lead tries to adjust those units based on guest demand and skipper needs. So if it's a quiet day and the attraction is fully staffed, you would try to ER as many people as you could. But then you had to worry about how that would impact rotations and turning a 3 man into a 4 man. Setting up in the morning is like doing a crossword puzzle.

Every single skipper has something to say when they show up. They never just took a set up and got a boat. They always had some story to tell or some interaction. Even the ones that came in really hungover. They all had to talk about something.

Sometimes you are having a great count and a trainer would show up and want to take a deadhead and that would kill your numbers. A skipper once asked me, "What's so hard about being a lead here, it's just standing around and tapping your pencil." I would tell them, "We're not paid the big bucks for what happens moment to moment, we are paid the big bucks for what could happen." Our quick response.

Michael Libby, 2000s

It wasn't uncommon that all of the westside leads would all have dinner together at the same time, from noon to one o'clock, at the Westside Diner. I remember it happened a couple of times that while we were on lunch we'd have a brown out, where the power dipped and came back up. Suddenly, fifteen leads and trainers would all pause in the middle of eating, then all turn up our radios to listen for the call to hear which attractions had been effected by the power surge. And usually it meant that only the Jungle Cruise kept running, so I stayed behind as everyone else went running back to their attractions, and picked at everyone's food. I'd then go back to Jungle Cruise and extend the line to get ready for more guests. That was a common occurrence for Jungle Cruise; we were off the power grid in a different way than other attractions, like Indy, where they had to do a full evacuation of the ride then restart it. That could be an hour-long process, but we just kept running along. So with that came an inherent chillness with being a skipper and being a lead; the pressures are very different than those on other attractions.

Benny LeMaster, 1990s–2000s

My first foreman [lead] at Jungle Cruise was a guy named Jack and he would tell somebody to get in the skiff. He would have that guy drive and he would stand in the front of the skiff holding onto the rope. And he'd bring a gun with him and shoot spiders. You would just hear this "pop pop pop" as he drove around the jungle shooting at spiders. That was his big thing to do.

Jeff Rhoads, 1970s–1980s

I liked being a lead, keeping track of everything and making sure that everyone is getting their break. Being a lead at Jungle Cruise was different than being a lead at other places because you had to keep track of boats. Taking them on and taking them off, keeping track of when your crew was coming and going, rotations, guest complaints. I don't remember the Jungle Cruise ever getting a complaint. I don't think we did, except for problems like derailments or engine breakdowns. It was fun, I liked it. When it got really hot I let people keep water on the boat. I know you're not supposed to drink onstage, but it was over 100 degrees. I know you could drink in the shipping office, but I let them keep water on their boat.

Sue Barnaby, 1980s–1990s

There is this sort of ritualistic upbringing at Jungle Cruise. I was passed the keys when I became a lead. Gerry brought me into the office to sign this book that all the leads signed. It was very meaningful to me.

Michael Libby, 2000s

Andy McGuire was one of the more popular leads and I asked him why he thought he was so well liked by his fellow skippers.

I think because I allowed fun to happen. I believed in setting up the day and letting things happen. As long as they didn't burn the place down, I was happy. I don't think I was popular, but I was available, so I hung out with Jungle Cruise people after work. I was accessible, more of a friend to them. I was also the youngest, by far. Scott was 4 years older than me, Brent was 2 years older than him, and Gerry was ancient (his 30s). I was 19 when I became a lead.

When an outsider [non-skipper] is told, "Now you're in control," everyone knows that it's going to be a train wreck and that's what it was. I don't think they intentionally messed things up. Part of the chaos is Disney's own fault. The way you become an emerging leader is through a project. To have a project, you have to change something. FastPass was a project, CDS was a project. Someone thought they could do better than the four-man rotations that we had been using for 50 years. Well, you can't, and you're dumb. They try and it fails.

Andy McGuire, 2000s

At one point I was the C Lead. That was 2007 or 2008 to 2010. I was the night lead a lot, so I tried to get back to what I loved about the Jungle Cruise and how it had been. You have to go from eight boats to six. And you do it with newer cast members who don't know the attraction as well. Sunday nights were easy, but Saturday nights were bad. I had to learn how to ramp down the attraction. When I came back to work Jungle Cruise all of the time, I had to relearn the four man and how rotations worked.

Kristin McGuire, 2000–2010s

It was tough because the managers wanted you to kind of be a dictator and be on people, but the Jungle Cruise lends itself toward letting the chaos happen. So I found myself being the goalie, where I was deflecting all the pucks shot at us from management, and letting the skippers do their thing. Most of my time as a lead was being told to leave. For example, a skipper named Matt would come up to me and say, "You need to take a walk and check the treehouse." So I would go and check the treehouse and shenanigans would happen while I was gone. I was told to leave a lot. I think it was good; you should have fun where you are working. If the cast members are having fun, the guests would have fun, too; it would spill over.

Let's be real, what is Jungle Cruise? You drive a boat, it's really safe. We never sacrificed the guest's fun for our own amusement. We would use them, but it would never be at their expense. The Jungle Police prank is a good example; where else is something that unique going to happen? Then they come back to the dock and their first skipper is tied up with heavy ropes to a post. They would go home and tell their family about it. That was my lead experience, stepping back, letting everyone have a good time because I knew that would translate into a happy experience for the guests.

Andy McGuire, 2000s

Different managers came to Adventureland and they had a different attitude as well.

You had a different management team from when Andy was there. He was there with guys who you could talk to and explain things and they'd be okay with it. My managers were more focused on micromanaging. They wanted to see our time sheet and rotations. It's one of the reasons that I didn't want to be a lead at Jungle Cruise anymore. I don't care about counts, I want the ride to practice efficiency, if we got a 2000 count that was good, but I really wanted happy guests.

Kristin McGuire, 2000–2010s

When I left it seems like the ones who became leads after me didn't understand their role. I set things up and let the day unfold. When you allow people who are creative the opportunity to be creative, amazing things can happen.

Andy McGuire, 2000s

They moved in leads who had other goals. The old leads cared about the Jungle Cruise and how it ran and were happy to let the Jungle Cruise be the Jungle Cruise. The ones that came in after that were focused on becoming emerging leaders and moving toward management, so they needed to prove that they can make changes.

Kristin McGuire, 2000–2010s

Whenever you hear shots you just sit and wait to hear how many and then you react. It was always something different.

Kevin Lively, 2010s

My personal favorite lead story is once I walked into the shipping office and a lead was stapling netting to the "drive-thru window" where guests walked by. I asked him why he was doing that and he said, "It cuts down on the guest interaction."

Chris Ramirez, 2000s

A lead rode my boat once. He told me that was the funniest trip he's ever had and then told me never to do it again. That is my all-time favorite quote from a manager at Disneyland. I asked him what was wrong with what I was doing? And he said it just wasn't LOG [in keeping with operational guidelines].

Joey Hurley, 2000s

We stole some jokes from Florida. A bunch of skippers had visited there and one guy pulls up to the dock and says, "Thanks for visiting Disneyland, where all of your dreams can come true, except short lines and cheap food." And the lead comes out of the shipping office, stands on the bow, and says, "Don't ever say that again."

Chris Ramirez, 2000s

Gerry kept a tight rein on things, but still allowed us to be free. I thought he was the perfect mix of what a Jungle Cruise lead should be. He kept the operation going, he kept the counts up, and he would call you out on your spiel if you were doing something wrong. He'd tell you right there at the dock in front of everybody, which was perfect. You never took that personally, because he did it to everybody.

Kipp Hart, 2000s–2010s

This is the story of my best day ever at Jungle Cruise. I had a shift that started at 11am. Around 8am I got a phone call from Frank, the lead scheduler for Adventureland. He asked if I could come in early that day, which is a pretty common call to get from Disneyland. I told him yes, and he said, "Thanks, please get here as quickly as you can. Hurry." Now this particular guy was always laid back, so if I was smarter I would have noticed his tone and asked what was going on. Sadly, I didn't ask. I took a shower, had breakfast, then headed over. I arrived at about 9:10, the park had been open for just a few minutes.

As I'm walking backstage by Space Mountain, I pass an Adventureland manager who was heading in the opposite direction. As we pass each other she said, "Thank you so much for coming in! This is so helpful! I'll be over later to see how you're doing." Not once in all my years at Disneyland had a manager said that to me when I had agreed to come in early. Stupidly, I didn't put her comments and Frank's together or I would have realized that something odd was going on.

I finally get to the dock and I'm standing in the shipping office looking at the rotation sheet to see where I'm working, but I can't find my name. As

I'm looking, a skipper I'll call Fred came walking up to me and said, "Dave, this is crap! Total crap! You're a nice guy, and this has nothing to do with you, but this is crap!" and he storms away.

At this point, I finally realize that something is wrong, so I call Frank and tell him that I can't find the lead and my name isn't on the rotation sheet. It was only then that Frank tells me that I'm the lead for the day. I never had any training on being a lead, but I guess they thought after three years there I was ready. Thankfully, most of the skippers working that day were veterans, and had set up the rotations already. My only problem was Fred. He refused to work any position, but just kept complaining to everyone on the dock that he should be the lead since he had the most seniority. I talked with him several times, but he was just too amped up to do anything. I asked him if he'd like to go home or work Indy, since it was clear that he sure as hell wasn't going to work Jungle Cruise. He had already wasted 20 minutes looking for a manager to complain to. So I called Frank and we sent Fred to Indy. He thanked me, told me again that I was a "nice guy," but that the entire situation was "crap."

That was my first 45 minutes of being a lead at Jungle Cruise.

Since I was mostly terrified all day, I didn't leave the dock once. I tried to make a quick run to the bathroom, but as I was walking towards the catwalk to get to backstage, I heard 3 shots ring out, which means a boat has broken down. That took maybe 30 minutes to fix. Crisis averted, now I could pee. As I tried to leave the dock for a second time, another 3 shots rang out.

After that I just stayed on the dock until my shift was over. I never took a break, never touched my lunch pail. It was a busy summer day and I had 8 boats on the river, which is the maximum. Indy called and asked for people, but I didn't have any to spare. It was a crazy day, but nobody died, so I considered it a success.

I got to be an emergency lead a few more times after that, but at least I had a warning ahead of time.

David John Marley, 2000s

There was a weird dynamic because you are their co-worker and suddenly you are telling them what to do. I was always uncomfortable with that. That is normal lead stuff, but at Jungle Cruise everyone is like family so it was all amplified, "Oh, good, now I get to tell my brother what to do." I just remember it being awkward. I think I spent most of my time trying to make the rotation sheet. I did more stints as an emergency lead in the morning than I did scheduled lead shifts.

Kevin Lively, 2010s

I never wanted to be a lead because I didn't want this to become a job. It really changes your role when you're lead, now you're a babysitter. I don't mind being a mentor, but I'd rather do that on my own.

Kipp Hart, 2000s–2010s

I found that being a night lead was a lot more difficult than working the day shift. The day time could be chaos and was always really busy, but at night, especially in the summer, is the time when boats might run out of fuel or break down. For me, the biggest concern was letting people go home early. As the night lead you are slowly closing the attraction as the day draws to a close, and sometimes it got so slow you could send people home early if they wanted. I was always worried that I'd send people home early, then we'd get a rush of guests after Fantasmic or fireworks. Or maybe Indy would break down and guests would come over to us.

David John Marley, 2000s

‹‹‹

CHAPTER THIRTEEN

FUN WITH MANAGEMENT

Being a manager at Disneyland has to be one of the world's great thankless jobs. You have to deal with angry guests and cast members who are often just out of high school and more intent on having fun than doing a good job. There are so many problems that guests will personally blame on a manager when it wasn't their fault and there was nothing they could have done to prevent the problem. All of those problems seem to be amplified for the managers of Adventureland. These managers had the misfortune to work with skippers, who saw themselves as professional smart asses.

The managers looked at our fun as a liability, which it probably was.

Chris Ramirez, 2000s

We hardly ever saw our manager, a Hollywood type who wore suits and ties. The man who ran it day to day was a tough guy, a real dock worker guy, who would give us tips and warn us about how to drive our boats so we didn't derail. One time I got in trouble with him because I was firing my gun too much at the hippos and the crocodiles. They sent out a rescue boat. He was on the boat saying "Don't worry, we'll get you unstuck." I told him that I already broke free, and he wanted to know why I kept shooting the gun so much.

Warren Asa, 1955

They had an internship program for new managers so we always tried to find out who the new intern was so that we could hassle them. Management was never too bad. Every once in a while you would get a manager who came in and tried to put their foot down, but eventually they would relax.

There was this one manager that none of us liked. He was a total hard nose named Joe Petaluga. If I had cast members on my boat, I did a special joke just for them. When we got to the dancing natives, I would tell everybody that I can speak their language, and then I would say, "Petaluga, Petaluga, Petaluga." The cast members always laugh really hard, and the guests never knew what was going on.

Terry Eaton, 1970s–1980s

So we go down to the Pit [the Westside Diner, a cast member-only restaurant below New Orleans Square]. I set my hat on the table and then I get in line for the buffet. When I get back, Adventureland manager Glen Hicks is there and he's wearing a shirt and tie. And someone had taken a Denver omelette and put it in the crease of my straw jungle hat. So I see this and I pretend to be all mad and I slam my tray down on the table. I looked at Hicks and yell, "And you wonder why the morale sucks around here!" and I took the omelette and started eating it like the Cookie Monster. So he gets up to leave and the entire Pit is cracking up. He didn't know what to make of us.

George Trullinger, 1970s–1980s

As a manager, I knew that a skipper connects directly with about 1,300 guests per day. Knowing this, I tried to get people to connect with the guests, stick to the spiel, and stick to the Disney guidelines. And if you're going to go off script, at least keep it to the theme. The opportunity gets even bigger during peak periods. I would see that Fantasmic was about to end and the park was busy so I would go pull on a boat for a half hour and help keep the wait time short. Other times I would take a couple of trips for a cast member that was having a bad day. It was good for them and good for me. When I hopped into a boat with a skipper who looked tired, I considered it training them on how to get laughs. I liked being a lead because I was trying to find that balance between guests, skippers, and company shareholders.

David Schoenwetter, 1990s–2000s

The first time I worked there was when the Narrations Department was around and run by a former skipper and very funny guy named Bruce Kimbrell. One day he got on my boat with a handful of plain-clothes Disney people and asked if he could take my boat. I said sure and asked if I could join them. He kindly allowed me to. He loaded the boat with guests and proceeded to give one of the best tours I'd ever seen. He then did the now famous joke where instead of being afraid of the attacking natives, you stop the boat, yell at them, and tell them to get back down and attack the boat behind you. He stopped the boat and yelled, then said "Get back down!" As soon as he said it, they did it. It was the funniest thing I had ever seen. When we got to the dock he explained to me how the trick worked. You had to time it exactly right. I tried it, it worked, and then I told every skipper on the dock. When I came back to Disneyland years later, it was on the script.

David John Marley, 2000s

I was doing something at Schweitzer Falls and the front guide came off at the Nile, so it was my fault. Two deadheads come out on either side of the boat. A manager and a skipper arrive and the manager takes the J-hook to "check" the rear guide and then he derailed the back guide. He called it in as a double derail and that he had no idea how it had happened. I never got in trouble for it. This one manager never let a skipper get a bad rap. He realized that the Jungle Cruise skippers were the cool kids, so he let us get away with all kinds of stuff.

Benny LeMaster, 1990s–2000s

There was a manager and she once told me that she'd never let me become a lead because I was incompetent. I had signed her off on her training at Jungle Cruise, even though she double derailed a boat while she was being trained. I told the lead that I was done training her and she needed a fourth day [which usually was done with a new trainer]. I didn't want to be responsible for signing her off, and she held it against me. It led to this constant clash. So one day I bumped a boat that was empty. The boat was pulling up to load and I was in no man's and I thought the boat was going on a deadhead and I wasn't paying attention and I bumped it. A lead saw it happen and reported it to that one manager and that was it, they took my trainer status away.

Jessica Harris Lopez, 1990s–2000s

One of the great benefits of working the Jungle Cruise is that you also get to learn the Tiki Room. It's such a fun place and it's such a classic. It could be hard to get Tiki shifts because those always went to people with seniority. I was keenly aware that the 40th anniversary of the Tiki Room was coming up. No one else seemed to notice or even care. Disneyland celebrated the anniversary, but they did it a few months after the actual date. I had to execute a three-way shift change to get Tiki that day. I think the two people who were supposed to work there didn't know it was the anniversary of Tiki; they could just sense my excitement.

So the night of the twenty second I stayed up late making a stupid hat. I think I even called it the stupid hat. I took a straw hat and I taped a balloon on it and some Tiki birds. I was aware of how dumb it was, but

I wore the stupid hat to work. At the end of my shift, an Adventureland manager came up and said, "I heard about your hat," and then he handed me a handful of Mousecar Moolah, those reward tokens. That was kind of a big deal, because you usually only got one at a time. Then he said, "That is an amazing hat, don't ever wear it again." I laughed, because I was clearly never going to wear it again.

Mike Pucher, 2000s

One time a manager named Paul got into my boat and said "deadhead," so off we go. He lays down on the center crate and tells me to warn him if we see another boat. At the backside of water I see a boat coming from the attacking natives, so I start singing the "Kali Ma" song from the Indiana Jones movie, and Paul slowly rises up like a zombie and marches around the boat. The other skipper just stared at us and drove his boat away without saying a word.

Chris Ramirez, 2000s

The skippers had used boat storage as a break room for years, maybe decades. During the summer of 2004 a manager decided that we couldn't sit there anymore, since it was by a fire hydrant. He told us to use the little break room shack behind Walt's apartment like everyone else. He had our chairs taken away and put up a sign that said to keep the area clear. Skippers stole chairs from Coke Corner and used them, and he kept putting them back. One day I stopped by Disneyland as it was closing and I was wearing a suit since I had been teaching at Cal State Fullerton earlier that day. I took a skipper and we walked to Mickey's Toontown and each of us took a couple of chairs and walked with them back to the Jungle Cruise. We just strolled down the main path, past the Matterhorn and Sleeping Beauty Castle, carrying chairs, and since I had a suit and a name tag on, nobody dared to stop me. The chairs remained there for the rest of my time at Disneyland.

David John Marley, 2000s

I remember when Jungle Cruise won "Attraction of the Year" back to back in 2002 and 2003. We were all really proud of that. I remember seeing how other attractions got backstage BBQ parties and things like that when they won. The only thing we got from Adventureland management was a memo stating that if we went off script we could be terminated. That was our thank you. I was so pissed I wrote a letter and hand delivered a copy to each manager. I told them that I know they bragged about us winning these awards to their superiors, so why didn't a single manager congratulate us? All they did was criticize us. It really killed morale in 2003.

Anonymous, 2000s

When we would hang out in boat storage for our breaks we would always be silly when we answered the phone. One day it rings and I say, "Bob's Brick and Tile, we'll lay anything!" and I hear them yell, "Who is this?" and it was a manager, so I replied, "No habla Ingles," and hung up the phone.

Kaz Liput, 2000s

Once there was a manager who wanted to keep skippers from going off script, so he found a copy of the "black list" of jokes that were never, ever supposed to be done. His logic was that if skippers see these jokes, they will know not to do them. When I got to the dock one day and saw the list, I immediately walked up to his office. I told him that giving funny people a long list of jokes and them telling them not to do them was a recipe for disaster. Instead, he should tell skippers that if a joke wasn't on the script, then they couldn't do it. He didn't listen, as more and more skippers, myself included, began to add these banned jokes to our trips. About a week later he called me up to his office and admitted his mistake.

David John Marley, 2000s

Nobody rode the Jungle Cruise in the morning. When the park opened everyone just ran by us and into Indy. So we knew how much time we had before guests would start to show up. Those of us who smoked would stand in the shipping office and smoke. Then one day here comes a manager and I was in mid smoke, so I flicked my cigarette into a puddle in the shipping office but I missed and the cig landed against the wood and was smoldering as the manager gave us her morning update talk. All the skippers were staring at the cig, worried that it would ignite the whole boathouse.

Chris Ramirez, 2000s

When land locking happened, a manager at Adventureland who hated me moved me to Tomorrowland so I would be stuck there. I ran into Jim Lake and I told him about how I wanted to be at Adventureland. He moved me back, and that manager was not happy that I had thwarted him. Two days later another manager walked into the shipping office, slapped my folder down on the table, and said, "Well, I guess you're staying," and walked away. I was fired not long after that.

Chris Ramirez, 2000s

I worked there for years and only knew Jungle Cruise and Tiki Room and refused to work anywhere else. I only wanted to work the Jungle Cruise. The Adventureland managers kept trying to convince me to get trained at Indy, but it was clear that everyone hated to work there, so I said no. This went on for months, and one day a manager said, "What if training at Indy showed up on your schedule? What would you do?" So I looked at him and said with a big smile, "I'd probably have a panic attack or something and fail the KA [knowledge assessment exam]." He just looked at me and then said, "You'd really do that, wouldn't you?" I never went to Indy.

Anonymous, 1990s

There was a female manager that had big frizzy hair and a skipper gave her the nickname "Poof" to show this exploding hair. She wasn't very nice to us, so if a skipper saw her coming toward the dock they'd yell "poof!" as a warning.

Anonymous, 2000s

When management came from attractions or elsewhere in the park, they knew what was going on. Then Disney did all those change ups and new managers came from outside Disneyland and they were not prepared to do the job. They were butt kissers who were skilled at corporate management and didn't know about the theme park business and many of them didn't care to learn it. Disney kept rotating managers so much. Like Chinese Checkers, they moved people all around the park. Every manager was so focused on keeping their job that they couldn't really do their job. That was the end of the sense of teamwork.

Kaz Liput, 2000s

Managers in the Attractions Department at Disneyland are regularly moved around every couple of years. In the mid 2000s a new group of managers arrived who seemed bound and determined to crush the wild spirit of the Jungle Cruise. One of these managers was given the nickname the "Enemy of Fun." It seems that almost every skipper who worked with him had a story to tell.

I had no personal beef against him. It was required for skippers to be at odds with management. As I was leaving work one day, I remember remarking to a skipper about a bad interaction I had with him and I ended the story with, "That guy is the Enemy of Fun." Apparently that name got traction and quickly spread. The name of the Jungle Cruise softball team that year was "Enemies of Fun." One thing you learn at Jungle Cruise was when to keep your mouth shut. When the term "Enemy of Fun" caught on, I kept my mouth shut. I'm pretty sure to this day that nobody knows that I coined the nickname.

Anonymous, 2000s

I was considering putting in my two weeks. I had started a company so I didn't need to work at Disneyland anymore. What got me to quit that day was a friend of mine named Adam was really excited. He had applied to be trainer and he thought that he was going to get it. Everyone thought he would get it. Then this manager we named the "Enemy of Fun" comes on the dock and walks over to Adam while he is loading guests onto a boat and over his shoulder starts giving him his feedback about his interview. He was telling Adam why he didn't get to be trainer, and Adam looked crushed and he was still loading guests. That did it for me. So as the manager walked by, I said, "You idiot! How could you give someone their feedback like that in front of guests while he's working? You know that no one likes you here in the Jungle Cruise and we call you the Enemy of Fun. You are an awful person." Then I turned and walked away and went backstage.

So after my break I get back into a boat and when I come back from a trip another manager was there waiting for me. "We need to talk." She takes me upstairs and explains that I'm getting fired, which I knew was going to happen. I explained the story to her, and she says that she has to walk me out, and she may deny saying this, but as we were walking backstage she said, "Between you and me, that was amazing, that guy had it coming." I wish I could have had a last trip or something, but later someone from another part of the park heard about what I did. Years later I met people from Splash Mountain who had heard about me yelling at the manager.

Leo Romo, 2000s

There was the week when the Enemy of Fun decided to create junior skippers. When he realized that managers couldn't drive boats he came down and said, "We're going to do junior skippers," and we were supposed to give them a hat and little Tiki shirt and let them drive.

Andy McGuire, 2000s

One day the Enemy of Fun came to the dock with a little straw hat and told us that on every rotation through the jungle, a skipper was to pick a kid to be a "junior skipper." This kid was to be brought to the front of the boat to drive, and he or she would wear the hat. No one seemed excited about that. After he left, the lead said, "Why not just put a sign on the hat that says 'Free Lice." Then he walked to the edge of the dock and said, "Tell you what, let's play sink or float," and into the river it went.

Anonymous, 2000s

We had a boat break down on the dock and we had to get it back to boat storage, but all the boats were out in the jungle, so we couldn't tow it backwards. So we got a bunch of guys and we pushed the boat the length of the dock as fast as we could and hoped it would make it most the way back to boat storage. It got close, so we threw the skipper in the boat a tow rope and a bunch of us pulled the boat back into boat storage. We were really tired; the guests in line clapped. And as we stood there catching our breath, the Enemy of Fun walked by the dock and said, "Hey, you guys, stop standing there and get to work." A guest heard him and said, "Who was that jerk?"

David John Marley, 2000s

I got punched on the dock once by a guest. I was loading people, grabbing them by the elbow as we were supposed to. I grabbed this one lady by the elbow. She had severe OCD and she turned around and punched me and my head hit the rail on the boat and she yelled, "You can't touch me!" and her husband said, "I used to work at Six Flags, I know you are not allowed to touch people." I was dazed and I sent the boat off and told the lead, who got the manager. I explained what happened and the manager asked if I wanted to press charges. I said no, that I didn't want to ruin their day, but I'd like them to know that they can't go around hitting people. Maybe we can put the fear of God into them.

He talks to the guests and then comes back to me and said, "My problem isn't that they hit you, my problem is that you didn't say you were sorry." And I told him, "I was doing my job! And if I say I'm sorry that's an admission of guilt and he could sue Disney," and the manager said, "Well, you are still getting a written notice because you should have apologized." So he has me fill out a statement and I got written up for it. I should have gone to my union rep, but I didn't. I was leaving the company soon anyway and I didn't want to press charges, so I didn't care. He was a nice guy, but was totally wrong on that situation.

Joshua Sudock, 2000s

It wasn't just Adventureland managers who had a rough time with skippers; anyone in authority was going to have a hard time getting them to behave.

I was sitting in boat storage having a cigarette and unbeknownst to me out comes a bunch of people. All I see are suits walking by me as I'm reading my newspaper and I just yell out, "Don't cross the rocks!" And then I look up and see Disneyland's president, Paul Pressler, and vice president, Cynthia Harris, and Cynthia was very nice and said, "Well, thank you, we'll go through Aladdin's Oasis then." So they all changed course and went through Aladdin's Oasis. I was terrified.

Chris Ramirez, 2000s

Once I was sitting in boat storage smoking, literally right under a sign that read "No Smoking," but underneath it someone had written "Skippers Exempt." So one day I'm smoking and reading the newspaper and someone walks up to me and says, "Excuse me, but the sign says no smoking," and without even looking up I tap the sign and say, "The sign also says 'Skippers Exempt,' so leave me alone." He then introduced himself as the fire marshall. I felt like such an idiot.

Kaz Liput, 2000s

CHAPTER FOURTEEN

GUESTS

The average guest spends more time with a Jungle Cruise skipper than with any other cast member. It is usually 8–10 minutes of close interaction, so a skipper can and does have a big impact on a guest's day. Guests are a constant source of entertainment for Disneyland's cast members. Some guests seem to check their brains at the entrance to the park. Skippers have seen it all.

I used to get the most random questions. Once I was literally standing under the sign that said Jungle River Cruise and a woman came up to me and asked, "Where is the Jungle Cruise?" and I felt like saying "See that rocket ship in Tomorrowland, it's over there."

Once I was driving a boat through the rain forrest and a guest asked me, "Is this real rain?" and it was a totally sunny day. People would ask you the silliest things, but you had to be nice. I never had a major problem on a boat where someone got out of control or got sick. I can remember having a great time, no hecklers. Everybody was there to have a good time, it was Disneyland.

I remember one time a guest tried to give me a tip. I was working unload and a supervisor was standing there and this guests hand me a $5 bill and thanks me for the great trip. So I had to explain that we are not allowed to accept tips. I wasn't going to take the money right in front of Ron Dominguez. I think I told him to spend the money on his family.

Alan Coats, 1960

When I could connect with the guests on my boat and crack them up, it was the greatest feeling in the world. The idea was that I could make guests happier when they left than when they got on my boat.

Joshua Sudock, 2000s

Like most skippers, I think the thing I hated most was when you had a boatload of guests that just sat there and didn't do anything. Guests that just stare at you and you wonder if the microphone is on or if they even speak English. Those were the times when you think, "This ride can't be over fast enough."

Terry Eaton, 1970s–1980s

If you have a good crowd, you're not working.

Ron Robledo, 1980s

I was there when a guest jumped off the back of the Jungle Cruise boat in the hippo pool. He stood up and said, "Don't' worry, I'll save you!" and dove in. They arrested him because he was super high and they followed his wet footprints.

Amanda Case, 2000s

I had somebody jump off my boat once. We were in the hippo pool and this guy yells out, "We're not safe!" and he jumps into the water and runs into the jungle. I remember calling it in and the lead was stunned.

I had a moment where I was sure that I was going to get fired, that I'd gone to far. I was just doing my normal spiel, it wasn't a great boat, but above average and people were laughing, but there was this one lady in the back who'd yell out, "I heard that one." Then later she yelled, "You're not funny." I said, "Well, you're fat!" and everybody laughed and she said nothing. I think because everyone was looking at her, even her friend, and they were laughing. I just knew that she was going to go straight to City Hall and complain. They got off at the dock and they walked right by the lead and I never heard anything.

Leo Romo, 2000s

While I was on the boat, a guest asked me where was the best place to see the fireworks. I said, "Up...look up."

David John Marley, 2000s

One time as we passed by the dancing natives a young boy said, "Look, Mommy. Indians," and his mother corrected him and said, "No, son, those are Native Americans."

Joey Hurley, 2000s

Once when I was lead, a middle-aged white lady and her early 20s daughter exited the boat and came right to me at the shipping office. They were in tears. The lady explained that she worked with "rain forest peoples" and that the skipper saying "dancing natives" was hurtful to her. I tried to explain Disneyland's intention, but she wanted to officially complain to a manager about them, so I sent her to City Hall. Why waste a manager's time?

David John Marley, 2000s

My trick to getting people off of the boat quickly was to do lots of puns. The "bread" spiel was great at making people flee. It wasn't flashy, it worked for me. I liked to stand there and do my puns.

Andy McGuire, 2000s

One time I forgot to do the backside of water joke. As a guest was exiting the boat, he said, "Hey, you didn't do the back side of water joke, you're supposed to do that." So I apologized and told him I forgot. And he said, "You have to do that joke because it's a classic one, everybody loves that one." And so I said, "Sir, at one time everyone loved slavery, too."

Joey Hurley, 2000s

One of the big no-no's at Jungle Cruise was touching guests. If you weren't helping somebody get into a boat, you're never allowed to touch a guest. One day I was on a trip through the jungle. We had just passed the gorilla camp and there was a lady who was loudly talking on her phone. She had answered the phone in the Indian elephant bathing pool and kept talking and talking for about two minutes. Normally when this happened, I would just make a lot of noise over the speaker to ruin their phone call, but this time making noise did nothing to stop her. So before we got to Schweitzer Falls, I leaned over grabbed her phone and said into it, "I'm sorry this person is having a wonderful time at Disneyland so you'll just have to call back later." Then I hung up the phone handed it to her and said, "Put that away." And she put it away and everybody laughed. I forgot that we weren't supposed to do stuff like that to guests.

For some reason everybody at Jungle Cruise was obsessed with mullets. That is the hairstyle usually found on men that is short in the front and long in the back. At Disneyland, you see lots of interesting people from around the world and we saw plenty of mullets. It got to the point that if you saw a really good mullet you would call out over the boathouse PA "Code M" and all the skippers on the dock would try to find the mullet. Eventually a game developed where skippers would try to touch a person's mullet.

You got a point for every mullet that you touched. A skipper named Benny was amazing at this. He would walk over to a guy with a mullet and say, "Excuse me, you have something on your shoulder," and brush it off so he could touch the mullet. After Facebook became popular, it was common for skippers to post pictures of mullets they saw at the park.

I never understood how guests could lose walkie-talkies at Disneyland. If you had one, why don't you just call for the other one? We took lost walkie-talkies and set them on the desk of the shipping office, volume way up, so we could hear if anyone tried to find them. Sometimes we would pick it up and announce, "Hello, if you lost a walkie-talkie, it's waiting for you at the Jungle Cruise." One night someone came over the air and began to cuss and say, "Get off this channel, this is our channel!" He was so aggressive that I told him that I was another park guest and I refused to change channels. He eventually got so angry that he challenged me to a fight. So I told him to meet me at the bridge in front of Sleeping Beauty Castle right after the fireworks. I told him I was wearing all khakis. I hope he didn't go punch a random guest.

David John Marley, 2000s

Jen Chavez got to have her young boys ride through the Jungle Cruise on her boat. What did they think of seeing their mommy as a skipper?

They thought it was weird, and they tried to talk to me the whole time. Charlie was maybe one-ish and Isaac was three. Isaac just kept talking to me. I made it cool, I guess. I worked with it because he's very talkative. It was like any kid who just wants to talk to you the whole time you're out. They sit right next to you and they're just full of questions. It was cute.

Jen Chavez, 2010s

For a while there was this popular haircut in southern California where men pretty much shaved their head except for a patch at their forehead, the size of a candy bar, that they kept. A little kid got on the boat with that haircut and without thinking I said, "Hey, look, that kid went for a $7 haircut, but only had $6.50." Everyone laughed, his mother really laughed, and his dad, who had his back to me and clearly didn't hear the joke, had the exact same haircut. I though the mom was going to hurt herself because she was laughing so hard and her husband had no idea what was going on.

David John Marley, 2000s

Sometimes if we are in a good mood we would let little kids drive the boat. The only problem was eventually you would forget they were there, and you come to a corner and muscle memory would take over and you go to grab and spin the wheel, and you would slam their little hands between the wheel and the deck, and crack their hands.

Joey Hurley, 2000s

It only happened to me once where it was confirmed that nobody on the boat spoke English, so I just said "peanut butter and jelly" and they would wildly applaud. I sang "The Circle of Life" at the lion scene. When we got back to the dock they went nuts. They were so entertained. Another time I almost had a non-English boat when a skipper purposely loaded two English-speaking people. I was so mad.

Trevor Kelly, 2000s

If it looked like a boat was going to be all non-English speakers and I was at load, I would try to find two English speakers and wedge them into the boat. I thought it was so funny.

David John Marley, 2000s

Once when I was brand new I had a talent agent give me her card and say she wanted to sign me. I was flattered and I asked a couple of veteran skippers if that was unusual. One guy said that it happens all the time, so I tossed her card. Turns out, that never happens! I'm still pissed about that.

Kaz Liput, 2000s

Being able to read your audience and adjust your jokes correctly is the key to being a great skipper. This is a story of how I did that terribly wrong. I had watched the TV show *Family Guy* the night before and they did this great joke about the Republican party while the show's main character rode around on an elephant. I foolishly decided to try out the joke at Jungle Cruise.

The next day I had a large group of African-Americans on my boat, and figuring that they are more than likely Democrats, I decided to do the joke. As we drove past an elephant on the Nile I said the *Family Guy* joke, which went, "There are one of the two symbols of the Republican party, the other symbol is a middle-aged white man who is threatened by change." The boat roared with laughter, they loved the joke, and at that moment I thought, "They didn't laugh because they are black, they laughed because I'm so funny." That was one of the stupidest thoughts I ever had, and my arrogance quickly burned me.

The next boat was a regular mix of people, though mostly white. So at the Nile I did the same joke and as I finished the laughs were not as good and I see a middle-aged white guy stand up in the back of boat. I couldn't hear what he was saying, but he was red faced, yelling, and shaking his fist at me. All I heard him say over the roar of the engine was "blah blah blah Republican!" At that moment I knew that I was fired. I realized that I had 5 minutes left in the tour, and I spent those 5 minutes trying to get him and his family to laugh. They seemed happy by the time we got back to the dock, and thankfully they didn't complain.

David John Marley, 2000s

Disneyland has a whole set of code words that cast members use to communicate with each other, without having to let guests know what is going on. At the Jungle Cruise, skippers created a wide range of unofficial secret codes that came and went over the years. As you might expect, most of these secret codes had to do with attractive girls and unusual guests, and were not approved by Disney.

We had codes that we used at the Jungle Cruise so guests wouldn't know what we were talking about. Most of these codes dealt with genitals because we were horny college kids. Many of these existed before we got there. One code was "watch your hands." That meant there was a woman on your boat that had large breasts. You would say "watch your hands" and do kind of the jazz hands thing and that was a signal to the other skippers to make sure you look for the lady. Most people thought it was us telling people not to get their hands stuck between the boat dock.

There was also a courtesy. A courtesy is an attractive woman. You would put your hand into a C shape and yell out "Courtesy!" It came from the idea of a courtesy trip before you took your lunch break. You would do a courtesy trip so your partner wouldn't have to be in the boat that long. And eventually it just got to be known as a hot girl. Female skippers had a similar thing; they would say "Herman called" and a Herman was a good-looking man. So a female skipper would say to another, "Your uncle Herman called."

Joey Hurley, 2000s

I once had a guest who was angry that I didn't spiel in Spanish because I was denying my heritage. He got right in my face and asked, "What's your last name?" When I answered him [with Smith or Jones], he turned sort of white and backed out of the boat.

Anonymous, 2010s

This little girl got on the boat and she had a birthday button on. I remember it vividly, her name was Sasha. And I said, "Hi, Sasha, today is your birthday? How are old are you?" and she said, "I'm nine." I said, "Oh, really.

You and I have a lot in common; when I was nine, I was a girl, too." And as soon as I said it I thought, "What the hell am I doing?"

Kipp Hart, 2000s–2010s

I was at rear load and the first group to get in was a family who proceeded to sit in the door, blocking the rest of the boat. Since I was still holding his elbow, I asked the dad to please stand up and move to the front of the boat. He looked at me and said in a thick accent, "I'm French, I can sit wherever I like." Without thinking I said, "Win a war and then you can sit wherever you want, now move it." He immediately stood up and moved to the front of the boat.

One summer I got to be an area greeter for the westside of Disneyland. The job was a nice 8-hour shift where I was totally on my own, and I got to have a radio with an earpiece. The area greeter walked around the westside of the park and helped people. It brought me so much joy to help a guest go from sad to happy. It seemed to me like I was making magic. One day I got a call from Jungle Cruise asking me to come to the shipping office because there were two dads having an argument. I walk over there, and I'm a pretty big guy, 6'4," but I amble onto the dock with a big grin and all I see are skippers and this one shortish male guest who immediately throws his hands up in the air and starts saying, "I'm cool! I'm cool! I'm sorry!" I walk past him and talk to lead who explained that a kid on the second level dropped a drink and some of it splashed on the man with his hands up, who then began to loudly cuss and threaten the father of the kid. They wanted me there in case things got out of hand when the other dad came downstairs. So I walked over to the little dad, who put his hands up again and started saying, "Are you gonna kick my ass? I'm sorry! Please, don't take me in the back and kick my ass." It took me a moment to realize that he was being serious. I asked him, "Do you really think that's how Disneyland treats its guests?" He was totally convinced that Disneyland had a goon squad who were sent to deal with trouble makers. So I kept the smile on my face and said, "Everyone's just trying to have a fun day, and accidents happen, right?" The man, hands still in the air, nodded in agreement. "We're not going to have any trouble with you and that other dad, right?" and he just kept nodding his head up and down. So I said, "Okay, well you go have a magical day, and nobody's gonna hurt anybody. I don't want to see any fighting, okay?"

After he had gone I walked back into the shipping office and all the skippers were laughing at me. The lead said, "Ah, man, that guy was terrified of you!" All the skippers thought it was so funny, but I had no idea what made the dad act that way. I later figured that they must have told that guy some wild stories before I showed up.

Late one night I was in a boat, waiting for anyone to come to Jungle Cruise, and I was chatting with a skipper who was working rear load. At one point he asks me if I have any kids, and so, over the mic I say, "No kids that I know of." Stupid, old joke. Next thing we notice is three ladies in the queue. They heard the whole thing and were having a fit. My buddy yells, "Hit it, skip," and I take off on a deadhead. When I get back he told me that the ladies wanted my name so that they could report me to City Hall, but he didn't know my name because it was my first day. (I had been working there nearly two years at that point.)

Once I had these guests who were doing a "hidden Mickey" scavenger hunt and they got on my boat. They yelled over my loading spiel that they needed to find our hidden Mickey and that I'd better show it to them. Through the trip they kept standing up and yelling at me to tell them where it was. What got me angry is that they would loudly interrupt my jokes to ask me. I had 40 people on the boat, but these 6 or 7 people thought they were the only ones. So we'd go through a show scene and I'd ask them, "Did you see it?" They'd panic, then I'd say, "Don't worry, it wasn't there." I did this several times until they realized I was messing with them. I drove past the actual hidden Mickey spot really quickly, then asked them if they saw it, they said they hadn't, and the rest of the guests on the boat laughed.

David John Marley, 2000s

Sometimes skippers encounter guests who change their lives and their perspective of working at Disneyland and Jungle Cruise forever.

One of my first trips on my first or second week, I was driving the Uci, which is our lift boat, and and we put a child on the lift who was 8 or 9 and in a wheelchair. I noticed that the kid is laughing and so I aim some of my jokes at him so he can be a part of the experience. And we get back to the dock and his parents came up to me and said that their son is terminally ill and that was the first time in a couple of weeks that he has even smiled. The fact that that happened within my first two weeks of working at the park was my eye opener as to how awesome this job was. Seven minutes of interacting with guests, to me, is nothing, I take trips all day long. So it was great to see the impact that it can have on someone else.

Anonymous, 2000s

I think the sweetest guest experience I ever had was when an older man and his wife asked for an anniversary trip so it was just the two of them and me. Jasen the lead set it up. So it was just them and me and those trips can be kind of odd. I've done them a couple of times before that, so I asked them, "Do you just want me to talk or did you want me to do my thing and be funny? Or do you want to talk about the history of the jungle?" They told me that they wanted to do a little bit of everything. I think it was their 50th wedding anniversary, 40th or 50th, and he had an oxygen tank and wasn't doing very well. We kind of chit-chatted and they asked me about being pregnant and we did jokes and when we came back around to the dock he stood up, shook my hand, and he said, "You know I was a skipper, but that was the best cruise I've ever been on." He started to tear up and his wife started to tear up. I got really teary. That was so special. It was my favorite guest moment.

Jen Chavez, 2010s

This was the story that always reminded me of how special it was to work at Disneyland. I was working rear load one morning and I was chatting with the couple in the front of the line. The woman had on a beautiful Indian sari and I complemented her on it. She told me, "We have been here for six hours and we are so happy!" I thought that was odd because it was only 10am so the park had only been open less than two hours. I said, "We've only been open for two hours, not six." To which her husband replied, "No, no, we have been in America for six hours. We flew in from Pakistan, landed at LAX this morning, checked in our bags at the hotel, and came straight to Disneyland!" That's when it hit me. I get to spend all day in a place that people literally dream of seeing their whole lives. How can you not feel that excitement? As it turned out, I ended up being their skipper and I gave them the best trip I could. Whenever I was tired or burned out I would think of that couple and it would rev me up again.

David John Marley, 2000s

I got asked, "Do you work here?" while I was dressed exactly like the three other skippers behind me. I quickly answered, "No, but they do."

Anonymous, 2010s

The following are all actual complaints that guests have had about the Jungle Cruise over the years.

- "Everyone here was taking their job seriously, but that skipper thought everything was just a joke."
- "We got wet in the rain forest."
- "The skipper drove the boat too close to the waterfall."
- "The gun shot was too loud and it made me swear in front of my kids."

- "My son had to use the bathroom while on the ride and the skipper wouldn't let him pee into the river."
- "The skipper's jokes kept interfering with my conversation."
- An American guest complained that his skipper's English accent was "really fake." [The skipper was from England.]
- "The skipper told jokes the entire time and my child didn't learn anything."
- "The entire boat was wet." [It had been raining all day.]
- "The boat rocked too much and I almost got seasick."
- "The skipper told different jokes than the ones that I know."

[Guests who come to the Jungle Cruise sometimes ask the strangest questions.]
- "Where is Adventureland?"
- "Is that water real?"
- "Where can I buy a gun for my son like the one you shot the hippo with?"
- "Is this the Submarine Ride?"
- "Which way do these boats go?"
- "Are these the boats that go back to the parking lot?" [They must have thought they were in Florida.]
- "Where do you guys sleep at night?"
- "When does this place become Avatar?"
- "How do you play this game?"
- "Are the plants real?"
- "Is this the ride where Jaws pops out of the water?"

And then there's this exchange:
- Guest [while pointing through the queue to the boats]: How long is the train ride?
  Skipper: It is actually a boat ride through the jungles of the world and it's 10 minutes long.
  Guest: Don't lie to me, I heard a train whistle.
  Skipper: Sorry, ma'am, it is a boat ride.
  Guest: NO, IT IS NOT! IT IS A TRAIN!
  Skipper: Oh...right...yes, it is 10 minutes long...right this way.
  Lady. Do you get wet?
  Skipper: Only with tears of disappointment.

CHAPTER FIFTEEN

CELEBRITIES

It seemed to be a rule that the bigger the celebrity, the nicer they were to have as guests at the Jungle Cruise. Skippers seem to universally agree that celebrities like Michael Jackson, Johnny Depp, Robin Williams, and Tom Hanks were always a delight. It was the lower-level celebrities that could be a nightmare. They either used to be really famous and were upset that they no longer were, or they would get upset that we didn't recognize them.

Let's start with the biggest Disneyland celebrity of them all: Walt Disney. Alan Coats, son of Disney artist and Imagineer Claude Coats, became a skipper in 1962, but he remembers seeing Walt at the Jungle Cruise before opening day.

I was at Disneyland on July 4, 1955, and I rode the Jungle Cruise. It was the Penthouse Club Day. Walt invited the members of the Penthouse Club at the studio and their families to come to the park. I think he wanted to see people around the park so he could observe how it functioned before the big opening day, which was only two weeks away. I was 11 years old. That day was interesting because the Jungle Cruise had only been in operation a few days. There were no canopies on the boats yet, there was just this structure and the striped canopies were not in place. The great thing about it was that Walt got into the boat. He didn't give us the tour, but he was so nice, he stepped in the boat and said, "Thank you for coming and enjoy your day," and he was just great and then he got back out. He was too busy to take the cruise. But to have Walt with you in the boat really made the day. That was the first cruise that I ever took.

Coats also rode the Jungle Cruise on opening day, July 17, 1955.

I had my 8 mm camera with me that day and I have pictures of the Jungle Cruise on opening day and you know what? It looked pretty good. The jungle looked like a jungle. In two weeks, it wasn't just a bunch of orange trees like you hear, it was actually pretty lush. Bill Evans had worked a miracle. And the animals! At least in the pictures that I took they looked pretty good. The crocodiles in the water, they looked respectable. The giraffes, the elephants, they looked really good.

Alan Coats, 1960s

Since the Jungle Cruise was the biggest attraction at Disneyland in the early years, it makes sense that Walt would regularly visit.

I talked to Walt many times. Especially the first couple of months he was there all of the time, walking around Main Street. He would see me in my wild outfits and knew that I was from the Jungle Cruise. When he had his grandkids, he would take them in the cab of the train. You could tell when Walt was in that cab because he blew the whistle every 30 seconds. He took over the cab and had his fun. He was a nice guy. He never asked personal questions, just about how many guests we were getting. We all knew Walt.

Warren Asa, 1955

Walt would never take the wheel. He'd let us do our job. He'd usually come on a Saturday or a Sunday morning and just want to take a look. Make sure everything was being kept up and the guests were happy.

He'd sit in the back of the boat so he could see the ride and the guests' reactions to what was happening. He was friendly. He'd say hello to us. He was interested in everything.

Sometimes after we finished, he would tell us about the changes he was thinking of making to get our reaction. He'd say,"We're going to change this and we're going to add that." He was a genuinely neat guy in that way. He made us part of it all. He respected what we thought and wanted our ideas.

William Sullivan, 1950s

All the skippers were afraid that one day Walt would climb into their boat and they'd have to give a spiel to Walt Disney. Would I freeze up? Would he say anything? That never happened to anyone that I recall, but so many guys were terrified that Walt Disney would get into their boat. Most of them would have been fine.

Alan Coats, 1960s

Walt wasn't the only Disney to get a taste of a skipper's sometimes less-than-charming ways.

One day Lillian Disney [Walt's wife] was standing at the dock for some reason and one of the skippers came up to her and said, "I'm sorry, you can't stand there, this is an unload area," and she said, "I'm Mrs. Disney." She said it really nicely and the guy left her alone.

Alan Coats, 1960s

Some of the celebrities that visited the Jungle Cruise were the costumed characters that roamed the park.

One day Pinocchio, Foul Fellow, Geppetto, and Gideon came up the exit and they weren't with anybody, except for a character wrangler, and they wanted to go on the boat. So we put them on the boat at unload. We came up to front load and loaded this entire boat full of guests in with them. It was hilarious, every time I did a joke, Pinocchio would fall over laughing and Gideon would fall into Geppetto's lap. It made all of the guests laugh so hard, it was the best boat. When we got back to the dock they did the move from *Wayne's World* where they bowed to me and they were hugging me and they hugged all of the guests, and everyone got a special treat that day.

Fred Martin, 1980s

When I was there in 1996 there was a skipper who was dating a girl who often played Timon, from *The Lion King*. That summer Timon came to the dock all the time and the guests loved it. I'd be walking across Main Street on my way to the dock and if I saw Timon I'd wave. If it was her, she'd run over and mess with me, if it wasn't, they would just look at you.

David John Marley, 2000s

Real, human celebrities were almost always a thrill to have on board.

Once Pierce Brosnan was there and I had never seen so many female skippers in the shipping office waiting for him to get off the boat. One female skipper was so hell bent to talk to him, she offered to take him backstage, even though he had a plaid with him.

Amanda Case, 2000

Pierce Brosnan with his wife and kids. I felt like they had never been on the ride before because we got to the squirter and he freaked out and ducked down. You would have thought that bullets were coming down on him, so I said, "I just scared James Bond!" and his entire family laughed.

Leo Romo, 2000s

I was on the dock once when one of the famous Sherman brothers, Richard Sherman, was on a boat. As it came back to the dock, the skipper did a joke that we were not supposed to do. He said, "Please take your kids with you; if you don't, we'll take them over to It's A Small World, glue their shoes to the floor, and make them sing that horrible song over and over." The skipper had no idea that his VIP was the man who had written that song! Thankfully, Sherman laughed really hard at that joke. The plaid was not happy.

David John Marley, 2000s

I had Nic Cage and two of his friends. We took a deadhead and they didn't want me to spiel, they wanted to talk to me about a Jungle Cruise movie that he wanted to do. He was dead serious and asked me all sorts of questions. I was only 20, so I had no idea about how to make a movie about the ride. He wanted me to go as slowly as I could and he described scenes to his friends, saying things like, "My helicopters would come through here." He had this entire idea in his head. He said that it was his favorite ride at the park. He was super nice, super nice, but it was weird how obsessed he was with the ride.

Leo Romo, 2000s

I got to drive a boat for John Lasseter while he spieled for the 50th anniversary of Disneyland. He was really funny and had some good jokes.

Kaz Liput, 2000s

One evening Larry King and his family walked onto the dock. He watched as a boat left the dock, turned to me, and said, "What is this? Some sort of boat ride?"

David John Marley, 2000s

I had Hugh Jackman on the boat and I didn't recognize him, so I was chatting with his son and he was talking about having a crush on an older girl. So I told him that liking an older women was cool, and Hugh Jackman, whose wife is older than him, said, "That's how I do it!" and we high fived and I still didn't recognize him. I did notice that the plaid was giving me a death glare and I didn't know why. When they got off the boat, Hugh and his son came back and he told me how much his son enjoyed it and that I was really funny. I thanked them and as they walked away the lead came up to me and said, "You just had Wolverine on your boat," and I about died.

Kaz Liput, 2000s

I was there when Michael Jackson came to Jungle Cruise. Not only did he get a solo boat, but the boats in front and behind him were kept empty so he could enjoy the ride without getting hassled.

Anonymous, 2000s

I had Johnny Depp on my boat once and I was star struck. He was sitting a foot away from me and when we locked eyes it was magic and I realized that film does not do him justice. He was 40 and looked like he was 25.

Kaz Liput, 2000s

As a child of the 1980s, it was a thrill to have Billy Idol ride my boat in 2002. During the trip I did one of my own jokes about Orange County and how politically conservative it was. As people laughed I took a glance at Billy, who I arrogantly assumed wouldn't understand the joke. Not only did he get it, he was explaining it to his entourage of mostly English friends. I was so impressed with his explanation of the county's conservative politics that I pretty much drove the length of the Nile without saying a single joke. I just stood there, listening to Billy, smiling like an idiot.

David John Marley, 2000s

Not every celebrity trip was successful, at least not from the celebrity's point of view.

I took David Hasselhoff around the jungle and he was upset that he didn't get his own boat. But he enjoyed the trip, it was nothing spectacular, but when the ride was over he waited until everyone left the boat, reached into his back pocket, and gave me a pre-signed postcard and handed it to me. I said, "No thank you, we can't take tips."

Benny LeMaster, 1990s–2000s

I helped the basketball player Amar'e Stoudemire onto a boat. He was injured and wasn't playing. He's a bit taller than I am, and as I'm loading him, I said, "I think I could post you up right now," and he looked at me like I'd stabbed his mother. He seemed upset that I even engaged him in conversation and I was just trying to be funny.

Kipp Hart, 2000s–2010s

I had Steven Tyler of Aerosmith on my boat and another member of his band and one of his daughters was with him on a private boat. Steven Tyler looked like a Halloween skeleton that someone draped skin over. He wore a Goofy pirate bandana. We started going through the jungle and everyone was laughing except for him, and that made things extra awkward. So about a quarter of the way through the trip I was just done with him acting like a cool guy because everyone else was laughing. So I start explaining the jokes to him like he's a child and calling him by his first name, "Did you get that one, Steve? You see, it's funny because..." then I look at the Guest Relations person who looks like she is going to melt and she is begging me to stop. At the end of the trip he nods a thank you, then as he's leaving he looks at his Guest Relations lady and says something to her and the group around him. After they left the lead ran up to me and said, "Steven Tyler just said that you were the cockiest little piece of crap he has ever met in his life."

After Steven Tyler I was never allowed to have celebrities again. Literally the next week Ellen DeGeneres was getting on my boat and the plaid remembered me and had her wait for the next boat.

Trevor Kelly, 2000s

One busy summer night I was lead. A plaid comes up to me on the dock and asks for a boat for Lisa Kudrow and her guests. I tell her that I can get her in a boat fairly quickly. The plaid then says that Kudrow wants her own private boat. This is something that is usually reserved for dignitaries and major celebrities, although often super A-list celebrities, like Robin Williams and Johnny Depp, preferred to ride with regular park guests. I pointed out to the plaid that even though it was dark, we had a rare 45-minute wait, we were that busy, and we just couldn't give her a boat of her own. We had most of the upstairs of the boathouse filled.

The plaid walked back to Kudrow's party and tells her that she can't have a private boat. I clearly hear the actress raise her voice in anger, and the plaid comes back to me. "She really wants her own boat, so we're going to do that." I then mentioned all the major celebs who took boats with regular guests, hoping that could calm things down. The plaid was blunt, "I also explained that, but she wants her own boat, so it has to happen." I think I genuinely surprised her when I refused her request. The plaid, not used to hearing "no," said, "I'll call the manager if I have to." I then handed her the phone and dialed the number. The plaid talked and talked, then hung up. "The manager is on his way."

Kudrow could have already been halfway through her trip by this point.

The manager arrived, assessed the scene, and told me to give her her own boat. I told him, "If you want to do that, then you load them in, I won't do that in front of so many guests." The manager stops the next boat, loads Kudrow and her crew, and sends them off, then heads back to his office.

As the boat drives right past the loading dock and into the jungle, I heard several people complaining in the queue. So without thinking I grabbed the mic for the boathouse and said, "The lady in that boat was Lisa Kudrow and her friends and she demanded her own private boat! Remember that one time she played a dumb blonde? What an acting range! Lisa Kudrow, ladies and gentlemen!" Skippers laughed, the guests laughed, I laughed, and then the phone rang. It was the manager, now back in his office. "You do know," he said, "that you could hear your voice booming all through Adventureland, right?" I feigned ignorance. He then said, "You'd better hope she doesn't complain about that," and then hung up the phone.

David John Marley, 2000s

CHAPTER SIXTEEN

IT'S A JUNGLE OUT THERE

One of the reasons that the Jungle Cruise is so popular is that it is the most beautiful place in all of Disneyland. Ruth Shellhorn did an amazing job of turning Disneyland into a giant botanical garden, but it was Bill Evans who created what he called "the best jungle this side of Costa Rica." The jungle has grown over the decades into its own micro-climate and a garden of intense variety.

When guests would ask me how I liked working there I'd tell them that I have the most beautiful office in the world. And it was true.

Kevin Lively, 2010s

When the Jungle Cruise was new, smudge pots and giant fans were installed to keep the delicate tropical plants warm during the winter nights. By the early 1970s the jungle had grown to the point that these were rarely used, but they were still there.

When I got there in 1976 there were still smudge pots out in the jungle, though we didn't use them. Also, the tower for one of the big fans was still out there in the islands. It still had the blades on it. On the other island the tower was still there, but the motor and the blades had been taken off.

Jeff Rhoads, 1970s–1980s

Some skippers brought the jungle to work with them.

One of the skippers was Don Weir who was frail and had this big beard. He would come to work wearing chameleons. He had tied monofilament around their necks, and he'd wear three or four of them around his neck on his shirt. It really took the guests by surprise and made them feel is if they were in the wild jungle.

William Sullivan, 1950s

One skipper's favorite section of the jungle is now mostly part of the queue for the Indiana Jones Attraction.

The area from the snapping crocodile to the Indian elephant bathing pool seemed like the most isolated area in the entire park, and it's about a football field long. That section along the Cambodian shrine was the most isolated part of the entire jungle. You look ahead and never see boats ahead of you. It's a garden that we got to live in and it was the most beautiful place to be.

Fred Martin, 1980s

What is awesome to me is that when you are in Jungle Cruise, once you leave the dock and you're in it, it is so immersive and the fact that back in 1954 when they built Disneyland, the Jungle Cruise started out as the primary attraction and the one they started on first. Jungle Cruise got the most limelight off of the *Disneyland* TV show. There are still trees in there from 1955. When you are in there and if you can look through the eyes of someone who appreciates landscapes you can tell the amount of detail and precision that they used to design it.

Being at Jungle Cruise you might think that they just planted all these things and let nature take its course and it just became a jungle. But when you are there after hours you see how hard horticulture works; every tree is numbered and tagged. They turn plants around to make them look better and make the jungle look wild and overgrown. Every plant that is in there is meticulously taken care of. The next time you ride Jungle Cruise look at the plants and how they are layered. That in itself is amazing.

Another great thing about the Jungle Cruise is that each section represents a different continent, and the plants in that area pertain to that region of the world. For example, in the Indian elephant bathing pool you have a lot of broad leaf plants, plants that you would see in the tropics, but in the African veldt you see a lot more grasses and it's more sparse looking. The fact that they found these plants and got them to grow is amazing.

Anonymous, 2010s

You are immersed into this jungle environment as much as you can be immersed into anything. You are surrounded by this jungle that has been growing for 60 years. The fact is that the jungle gets better and better with age. No other attraction is like that. At other places they have to go through and spruce up things and at Jungle Cruise we just have to make sure the bamboo doesn't fall. In fact, you get disappointed when they prune back the jungle.

Kevin Lively, 2010s

I loved being in the jungle. As much as I hated having a day shift, I loved having an opening shift where you got to be one of the first three boats through the jungle. On those trips before the air got stirred up by so many boats going through, the jungle would smell so fresh. It was amazing. It was an amazing way to start your day. You would only get that one trip in the morning, then the boats would stir up the air and the place would heat up.

Mike Pucher, 2000s

My favorite time of the day is first thing in the morning, usually when you're doing the show check. Occasionally the river has a fog hanging over it. The jungle is exposed, but the river has a fog hanging over it and you're driving your boat and you're just bursting through the fog. It's surreal to be out there by yourself in a boat with no guests. It's an amazing feeling.

Kipp Hart, 2000s–2010s

The lead takes me on a skiff to clear obstacles in the river and check for animation issues. Above all else he says that we have to stay out of the view of guests and not distract from their experience. It was like a productive game of hide-from-the-guests–and-seek-for-trash while getting paid. I was 38 at the time and I felt completely like a kid, it was so much fun. Well, the boat had a tiny quarter-horsepower engine and the thing died by the elephant pool and we couldn't get it to start. Suddenly we hear a boat coming behind us, so the lead said, "Grab some leaves, we gotta get out of sight," and we pull ourselves under a banana bush. Well, we didn't quite make it all the way and what the guests saw was this little boat with our legs sticking out as we were trying to hide in the leaves. The guests were totally cracking up. The skipper was ruthless in the way he made fun of us. The lead finally separated the leaves and imitates *Star Wars* and says, "These are not the skippers you are looking for, move along!"

David Schoenwetter, 1990s–2000s

I saw a big piece of bamboo that was bending over into the river and it was going to hit that little outrigger canoe across from the load. So I asked the lead if I could go out and get it, and he said, "Yes, just be very careful." I climbed across the boats and got onto the catwalk. I climbed into one of the boats that was parked on the catwalk and from there I jumped into the jungle. I did this in the middle of the day when the queue was full. I climb all the way out there and I swing back and forth on the bamboo and I can't break it off. All the guests can see me from the boathouse and begin to laugh and cheer. I was just swinging back and forth on it.

Joey Hurley, 2000s

One morning I came onto the dock an hour before the park opened up and I'm doing all the paperwork and then I do the animation check. And by the time I come back around to the dock, I realize I see dead crawfish. So I'm back on the dock and I move the boats and you can't see water, just thousands of dead animals. Fish and crawfish everywhere. The boat engines pushed them all up. We went Code 100. [Code 100 means an attraction is unable to open at the same time as the rest of the park.] It turns out that they had applied some insecticide the night before that did all that damage. Managers approved us to open and made me open the attraction anyway. Skippers pulled out as many as we could, but the entire day was gross, you were constantly pulling dead crawfish out of the water.

Benny LeMaster, 1990s–2000s

It was a hot summer, and we had a pretty bad algae problem, and it was smelling bad, the water was pretty stagnant and it was just smelling offensive. So their solution was to dump a bunch of algae killer into the river. They dumped the stuff into the river and it killed not just the algae but every living thing in that water. So all of the fish were just floating and bobbing in the water. There are a lot more fish in that water than you think. All those bottom-feeder kind of fish. It was like an apocalypse scene. There were dead turtles, dead crawdads. No more algae, though.

Anonymous, 2010s

One morning, as the first boat of guests was still being loaded, there was a sudden roar like thunder that came booming out of the rain forest as birds flew in every direction. One of the park's original trees, now more than 50 years old, had split in half. Its massive trunk was blocking the entire river. Groundskeeping was called and arrived with small hand saws. We told them that they were going to need much bigger saws, but they didn't listen to us. Then they saw the size of the tree and immediately turned around and came back 10 minutes later with chain saws.

Since they thought it was going to take at least 5 hours to clean all the debris, the lead sent a bunch of people home. I stayed and spent the next two hours talking to guests at the entrance. The horticulture guys worked really fast and we were ready to open again in just two hours; unfortunately, we didn't have enough cast members to run the attraction.

David John Marley, 2000s

A skipper was driving in the veldt during a winter when we had a lot of rain. It might have been 2007. So he's in the veldt, on the C curve heading into the hippo pool, and he hears this big crash. A giant tree fell into the hippo pool. It engulfed the hippo pool! It was that big. It knocked out three hippos.

Kipp Hart, 2000s–2010s

I think the skipper had the best view of the entire jungle. The guests seats are down low, and they face inwards. So you're looking over your shoulder to see what's on the shore, or you're looking across the other people on the boat, but really, for what the Jungle Cruise is, that seating arrangement works. The show scenes are not that super detailed, so it's probably better for the guests that they don't have a great view; it's not like the rich detail of Pirates. The jungle is best seen by guests as a fleeting moment, and that's what makes it feel more real to them.

But as a skipper when you spend all day out in the jungle you really get a chance to appreciate the natural beauty of the place. How the plants are so richly grown in. It's such a unique location. I've never been anywhere else like it in the world. Another cool thing about being a skipper was you get to see the jungle grow. I remember seeing this one tiny plant, it was a funky little plant to the left of the lion's den. I remember watching it grow over the years and now it's all ugly and tall.

Standing in front of the boat the skipper gets this amazing panoramic view of the jungle, especially turning into Schweitzer Falls after the gorilla camp. Just seeing that unfold for you, because you're making this turn to the right, and it's almost like the plants on the right side of the boat are curtains sliding back to reveal Schweitzer Falls. There was always a nice little breeze there because of the waterfall. As you got closer, the mist from the waterfall would hit my face and that would gross me out. Otherwise, it was just the most beautiful part of the jungle.

Mike Pucher, 2000s

I had this boat and it was pretty average. It was my second shift and it was windy and everything was blowing around and suddenly you hear this snapping noise and all of this bamboo falls onto my boat. Thanks to the canopy, everyone was okay. I just looked at the guests and said, "I can't top that." When I got to the dock the guests were all cheering and a manager was on the dock and came over to congratulate me for having a good boat, and I had to tell him about the bamboo.

Ben Case, 2000s

There are lots of wild animals living in the jungle, and they can sometimes show guests Mother Nature's dark side.

During baby duck season a lead and I would go collect dead birds before the park opened. We would take a boat out with a net and collect all the dead baby ducks and then go throw them in the trashcan. It was so sad.

Joey Hurley, 2000s

One summer all the male ducks were just killing all the ducklings they could find. So there would be dozens of dead ducklings in any one show scene. You'd say, "Hey, look at that rhino," and then you'd see a bunch of dead ducklings and start yelling, "No, kids, look over here! Not at the rhino, over here!"

I remember that I was proud of this time when I said a pun so fast. It was when these two ducks swooped down super low and swerved around the boat. I yelled out, "Duck!" and nobody laughed.

Trevor Kelly, 2000s

Once a skipper and I went out to get a dead crow and we took the skiff in the back of the elephant pool. At that point it just had paddles and we were trying to get this bird and then a boat comes roaring around the corner. We didn't even hear it coming, and we just started spinning around in a circle. My buddy and I were paddling in opposing directions.

Andy McGuire, 2000s

The branches from the trees across from the loading dock had gotten really long and there was this one branch that hung high above where boats loaded. There was a crow that regularly landed on that branch, just to poop on guests sitting in the front of the boat. You'd be talking to guests as they came on board and then someone in the front would get hit with all of this white poop. We tried really hard to keep the crow from landing there. Eventually, horticulture trimmed back the plants and we made sure they cut that branch off.

Kipp Hart, 2000s–2010s

I always liked being out on a boat at sunset. It was this really magical time of day, with the ambient light from the skies dimming. It would only be there for two trips, maximum, where the brightness of the light in the sky was equal to the show lights in the jungle. So you have this really rich experience. That's when I think the jungle looked its best and it would be gone in 20 minutes. So I always tried to be in a boat when the jungle lighting was at its best. Because at night parts of the jungle would be pitch black. Those giant leaves would just soak up any available light.

Mike Pucher, 2000s

There is a beautiful spot between the gorilla camp and Schweitzer Falls. This spot is gorgeous. You have this little trickling waterfall going, you have Schweitzer Falls going, and you have a greedy gorilla, but he's quiet, and you have the gorilla camp. If you ever had a boat break down, this is the place to be. This is the most tranquil spot, plus you have the shade coming from both sides. This is the most beautiful spot in the jungle.

Kevin Lively, 2010s

The Jungle Cruise is also an attraction that runs rain or shine. It doesn't rain very often in southern California, but when it does, it's usually in torrents.

Rainy days were both fun and miserable. Few people wanted to ride, but most of those who did complained about being wet. They said this to us while we were literally soaked to our underwear. You'd be standing in the boat, soaked to the skin, while these guests would ask if you had a paper towel to dry the seat, as it was raining. The fun thing about rainy days was the canopies of the boats would sag way down and hold a ton of water. It was a good idea to regularly push up on the canopy to let the water out. Sometimes it was fun to let it stay there and if you were in a mood, you could jerk the boat at the right place and make all that water pour onto the guests sitting beneath it.

David John Marley, 2000s

My least favorite part was winter time when it was raining and it was so cold so you'd get the gloves, but they just made it worse because they acted like a sponge. You can't reload the gun with the gloves on either, so you just took them off and kept your hands in your pocket as often as you could.

Kevin Lively, 2010s

Sometimes Disneyland would put items in the Jungle Cruise if they thought a cross promotion would fit.

They had a crystal skull at Trader Sam. They had something from every movie. They had his dad's umbrella at the Trapped Safari, the headdress from the Temple of Doom was with the dancing natives, and they had a crate of stuff at the gorillas.

Kevin Lively, 2010s

One year for Jingle Cruise they put a few boxes in a scene that said, "Deliver to Arendelle" [the fictional setting of the Disney film *Frozen*], and we told them to take that out immediately. And they did.

Anonymous, 2010s

$\diamond\!\!\diamond$

ACCIDENTS WILL HAPPEN

A lead once told me that he loved working at the Jungle Cruise because when something went wrong, the cause of it was almost always a surprise.

All the attractions at Disneyland are safe, and the Jungle Cruise is safer than most. Not only is the Jungle Cruise a low-speed ride, it is also a very low-tech operation. The attraction depends on manual labor to operate and has continued running while the park experienced a power outage. However, since the ride is dependent on humans to operate it, it is the humans who end up causing the most trouble.

Some of the problems encountered at Jungle Cruise are common to any theme park, but many are unique to it. The river is the source of the ride's allure, but is also where most of the trouble happens. Mechanics issues are the other reason for trouble. Engines get worn out, boats run aground.

Many accidents at Jungle Cruise are simple and easy to fix; the more serious ones cause the attraction to go 101—code for a breakdown.

Skipper and WDI Imagineer Kevin Lively perfectly summed up the benefits of working on such a low-tech attraction as the Jungle Cruise.

I like that Jungle Cruise is a human-controlled attraction. It is as old school as you can get. If there was a problem, we were the ones who could fix it. The best tool you had at the Jungle Cruise to fix anything was a stick, which was great any time you had something like a blocked sensor. We had a row of all of these long pieces of bamboo and you'd pull one down, hop in a boat, and take a deadhead. And we brought that stick and a paddle to try to clean the sensor, because either a leaf had fallen in front of it or a duck was sitting on it. If it was a duck, you'd just splash some water to make the duck move or you'd use the bamboo. If you look at the history of the Jungle Cruise, Harper Goff designing the layout of the attraction, he used a stick, and 60 years later the best tool at that attraction is still a stick. That is the root of what the Jungle Cruise is.

Kevin Lively, 2010s

There are so many things that can happen, so many things that can go wrong that you can't possibly expect. So many! Like at most jobs the same five things go wrong a lot. At Jungle Cruise there was always something new and creative that brought the ride down. I'd think, "Huh, I'd never heard that one before. That doesn't sound possible." There was always something random.

Michael Libby, 2000s

Many of the most interesting accidents are the random and totally unexpected ones.

It's 1976 and pretty much everything in Adventureland has looked the way it looked since the park opened. The only time they ever fixed anything is when you told them that something was broken. So I'm working unload one day at the Jungle Cruise and another skipper is standing there next to me. The park wasn't very busy and we are just looking out over Adventureland and there was this balcony above the Adventureland Bazaar that was covered with a thatched roof. The support beams for the awning were made of wood. They were all rotted, and as we were watching it suddenly collapsed and landed about 8 inches away from a young couple that was walking by. If it had hit him, he would've been dead; it weighed several hundred pounds and had nails sticking out all over it. Our jaws dropped open in horror and the guy that was almost killed just kind of glances over his shoulder at it and keeps walking with his girlfriend like nothing happened. That would've been two dead bodies. So we ran over and dragged the pieces of it backstage.

Jeff Rhoads, 1970s–1980s

The clip that holds the .38 pistol to the lanyard is called the Cardenas Clip. It was put there because a guy named Dan Cardenas had his gun stolen. It happened in the middle of a trip, after he shot the hippo. The guest pulled it out of the holster, stuck it in their pocket, and took it. It was later used in a bank robbery. They took it just so they could rob the bank. So this clip was named after him. I lived with Dan my second summer and he was made a lead, even after that. He got saddled with that reputation and the story was repeated for years and years afterward.

Fred Martin, 1980s

I was at the dock and loading the gun, and if you were a sassy pants, you pre-cocked your gun and put it in the holster. I did that and it went off.

Jessica Harris–Lopez, 1990s–2000s

A heavy-set woman with diabetes got out of her ECV and into the boat. We didn't have the wheelchair boat back then. So the lady gets into the boat, and we had a great time. It was my first trip on my first shift as a Jungle Cruise skipper and it went great. We get back to the dock and she's stepping out and I hear a noise. It sounded like a zipper. And she hits the dock and just fell over. Her skin was loose and it tore from knee to ankle and everything came spilling out onto the boat and the dock. It looked like scrambled eggs and hot sauce. Her fat had spilled out everywhere. So the medical team arrives and I take a deadhead so the boats behind me can get out and I'm driving alone with all this stuff on the boat. It was really bad. They had to pull the boat off and steam clean it.

Andy McGuire, 2000s

We had this one downtime where I was at unload and I was trying to pull forward and felt this bump, so I reversed and felt it bump again. They check under the boat and they end up pulling out this piece of wood that looked like a cow heart, it was that big, it was wedged in there. That kind of thing happened anytime after horticulture did any big work because stuff would drop into the river and that would cause downtimes like a blocked sensor, or stuff falling on the track.

Kevin Lively, 2010s

Even the weather can occasionally cause the attraction to shut down.

Once the Jungle Cruise was shut down because of too much water. If you look at early pictures of Disneyland, you can see a river that flows down from the moat of Sleeping Beauty Castle, past Frontierland and into the jungle and then finally into the Rivers of America. This ribbon of water still exists, even though the section from Jungle Cruise to Rivers of America has been paved over. The water is constantly recirculated, unless one of those areas are in a dry rehab. In the early 2000s the Rivers of America was empty and it was raining very hard. Normally, the Jungle Cruise would automatically pump more water into the river where the *Mark Twain* can be found, but not on this night. The rain kept coming and the Jungle Cruise river got higher and higher. The Jungle Cruise is the only water attraction that has to be shut down if the water level is too high. If it hits a certain point, the boats won't make it under the backside of water.

Maintenance brought out two large water pumps and began dumping thousands of gallons of rain water right into the storm drains backstage. On this night, however, Mother Nature won and the Jungle Cruise had to be shut down due to too much water.

David Marley, 2000s

There are three emergency signals that skippers use their guns to warn everyone else about: 3 shot, 4 shot, and 6 shot. A 6 shot is when a boat derails. A 4 shot is for a medical emergency and is very rare, and the 3 shot is for mechanical breakdowns. When one of these emergency shots happens, the skipper puts special "break down" ammo in the gun. It's much louder than the regular ammo.

I never derailed, but my boat died once right as I was coming into the dock. I yelled, "No brakes, help!" And everyone on the dock had to run up and keep me from ramming into the boat sitting at no man's.

Trevor Kelly, 2000s

I was in the Zambezi and I 3 shot at the gorilla camp. I had talked to maintenance people about the river explosion and asked if it could go off accidentally. I was assured that there was a sensor and the jet of water wouldn't go off if a boat was over it. I believed them. It was the third day working after the rehab. The boat broke down at the squirter, and I couldn't get it to start so I had to 3 shot, then make a radio call. I tell my guests what to expect. I do the three shots and notice that I'm drifting toward the gorilla camp. I see a boat coming up behind me, they hit the sensor as I'm making my radio call, which went like this, "Jungle Central, this is the Zambezi and I'm 3 shot at the BOOOOOMMMM!" The boat lifted up, it felt like we'd been hit by a bomb. In the middle of my radio call I start screaming, "WTF was that? Oh, crap! I'm at the gorilla camp, send help." Then I looked at my boat and realized I had just swore in front of a boat load of guests. They all just looked at me and didn't react at all. In panic I hit the start button on the boat and it fired up and I went on the tour as usual. I was so filled with shame coming back to the dock. All these leads were there, and they were laughing their heads off. I was so humiliated.

Heather Wilkins, 2000s

Once my boat broke down at Schweitzer Falls at the backside of water, and I kept firing for a 3 shot but no one could hear me because the waterfall was so loud. It wasn't until boats stopped coming back to the dock that they realized something must be wrong out there and sent out a rescue boat. I had totally lost power so I couldn't use my radio or anything. The guests were really cool about the whole thing. Eventually, the boats were backed up all the way to the hippo pool. I think it was a good twenty minutes before they realized something was wrong.

Terry Eaton, 1970s–1980s

I was in a boat at the unload dock and the lead hopped up on the bow and checked the gauges on my boat's dashboard. He then tapped one dial repeatedly, then said, "Okay, move it up. Don't worry." I was by the gorilla camp when my engine died and I had to 3 shot. Soon he came roaring up in front of me to tow me back to the dock. "I'm sorry," he said, "I should have pulled your boat off." I never found out what he was looking at or why the engine died.

David John Marley, 2000s

A 6 shot is the most serious and time consuming of all the breakdowns. It can mean two different things. Either one or both of the boat's guides have come off the rail. Since the boats cannot be steered, they will randomly float or come to a grinding halt if the guide is dragging in the mud, entangled in roots, or hits fallen branches on the river bottom. A 6 shot also comes with its own worries for a skipper. If the front guide comes off, then it is usually not their fault. However, if the rear guide gets derailed, then the skipper could be in big trouble with management because that meant it was the skipper's fault.

I think the rail problem was solved during this time and the boats used to just come off the rail. The boat wasn't really attached to the rail; there was just this guide bar that kept it going along and it almost always happened at that sharp horseshoe turn going into the hippo pool, the C curve. Well, guys would take it too fast and the boat would lift up and you'd go floating into the hippo pool. It almost happened to me once. I grabbed the throttle and threw it into reverse and it sunk back onto the rail. That was an interesting part of being a skipper. You were stuck with a boat load of people. If it was a great boat you could interact with them, make a joke or something. Occasionally you'd get a boatload of deadheads that would just stare at you. They wouldn't react to anything. So I always hoped that I never got stuck with a group like that.

Alan Coats, 1960s

Before they were replaced in 1995, the old track switches could be confusing to operate, especially for rookies.

It was this big pole sticking out and it was decorated to look like a piece of bamboo. On those manual switches you always had to put the pin in to make sure the switch stayed where it was supposed to. And this happened all the time; you'd tell a rookie to pull on a boat, and they would throw the track switch but put the pin in the wrong hole, meaning the track isn't locked. So the first boat that goes over just rattles the switch and the second boat that goes over derails. Sometimes they didn't notice it right away and they would tear up the bottom of the boat. That's how a boat got sunk. I saw that happen on several different occasions. Another way it happened was when a rookie would go out through the track switch and he would get confused and wave the boat forward and the boat would immediately derail.

Jeff Rhoads, 1970s–1980s

You know how you bring boats out from the back in the morning? The lead wasn't paying attention as I brought a boat out, he didn't switch the tracks correctly. All of a sudden the boat just spins around. So the side of my boat hit the dock and both guides came out. I thought we were going to be down forever, but it was only about two hours.

Leo Romo, 2000s

I remember when the managers decided that they wanted to be skippers. There was a new manager and she derailed two boats in one week. She was so cute so we didn't say anything about it.

Andy McGuire, 2000s

I had the classic Jungle Cruise 6 shot in the hippo pool. I was also the third boat to derail in the hippo pool that day, so I think something was wrong with the track. The park was closing, it was late at night, and it was pitch black. I pulled into the hippo pool and I heard the classic "clunk." Everyone always told me when you derail you will know it because you've never heard that sound before. So I heard the clunk and I stopped the boat and then I began drifting in a way the boat has never drifted before. I fired my six shots and nobody heard them. I was so excited to load the 6 ammo into the gun. I remember looking at the gun and thinking to myself "Cool, I get to shoot all of these." So facilities came out, they got me back on the rail, and I was on my way.

Mike Pucher, 2000s

Once a boat came off the rails in front of Schweitzer Falls, the rear guide. So picture this, a boat is going behind Schweitzer at full speed loaded with guests and followed by a stern wave. Meanwhile, I'm heading to Schweitzer Falls with a light load of guests sitting mostly in the front. And the timing was just perfect. As I began my turn down the Nile, the wake from his boat hit mine, derailed the back end, and sent me right under Schweitzer Falls. The boat was just filled with water.

Jeff Rhoads, 1970s–1980s

They put the governors on the boats and it took a while to get used to them. Then they took one off of one boat to test something. They told us to be careful, and we were and had fun with it. At the end of our shift we warned the next skipper to be careful because the boat doesn't have a governor and it's got quite the kick. She said, "Fine. I'm fine." So Kaz and I were in the shipping office saying goodbye to everybody and we hear 6 shots. Then over the radio we hear her frightened little voice saying, "Hello, jungle people? I'm on land." So we go out to the hippo pool and she is nowhere near the land. She had just derailed and the back of the boat was slowly swinging around.

There was another skipper who 6 shot at the Indy queue. Her boat was vertical. She jumped the track and the wake turned her boat to block the entire river. No one had ever seen that before. I don't know how she did it. We had to calm her down, she had a panic attack. We had to do a boat-to-boat evacuation.

Benny LeMaster, 1990s–2000s

A veteran double derailed in the hippo pool. He hit the C curve and popped a guide, and he activated the animation and he couldn't stop so he hit a charging hippo which pops the other rail and now he's free floating in the hippo pool and facing backwards. They don't want to re-rail him in the hippo pool for fear he will do more damage, so we double tow him to the dock backwards. We unload the guests from the wrong side, where there are not any doors, and then we pulled it back over the track switches and three boats on each switch, and cast members on the catwalk spun the boat around 180 degrees to get it back on the rail.

Matt Nerrie, 2000s

I was bringing a boat on from boat storage and I derailed the boat, and the attraction went down. After I derailed I moved the track switch, so it looked like I was right to move my boat. They couldn't figure out how my boat derailed. I told the lead what happened years later and he said, "Ah, I knew something wasn't right with your story."

Anonymous, 2000s

I derailed one-and-a-half times. The first time I derailed was coming into the Nile and it was my front guide so it wasn't my fault. There was something on the track that caused me to hop off. The other time was when I was moving a boat back to boat storage and one of the new guys decided he was going to help me out by moving a track switch. I tried to move forward and "clunk," so neither time was it my fault.

Kevin Lively, 2010s

The most embarrassing place to derail your boat was back in boat storage, which runs along the backside of Main Street. It's embarrassing, but it happens.

I once accidentally derailed a boat in boat storage. I didn't pay attention to the lights. They open the doors to boat storage and kept calling for me to come out. I kept yelling, "One minute, one minute." I took the lanyard, the leather strap from the pistol, and worked it through the eyehole of the guide shaft and I was able to pull the shaft up and then I dropped it back down on the rail. I pulled as hard as I could and then rocked the boat back-and-forth to get it back over the rail. I was able to fix it without anyone knowing that I derailed. I knew that if they found out that I had derailed because I wasn't watching the lights that I would get written up for it. When they asked me what took so long I just told them that I was having trouble starting the boat.

Terry Eaton, 1970s–1980s

I remember one time when I was training I derailed a boat in boat storage. I had a trainee who was having a lot of trouble docking, and so we were practicing docking in boat storage. I'd push the boat around and he would have to bring it back to the starting point. So I was talking to the trainee and my hand was on the throttle and the boat slowly drifted forward onto the track switch and "clunk." I called the lead and told her what happened, and she called facilities. Not two minutes later these two facilities guys came jogging up, and I waved at them and said, "Hey, guys, I'm right here," and they just jogged right past me. Then about a minute later they came walking back. That was the first time I ever derailed a boat while I was a trainer and explaining the importance of not derailing your boat.

Anonymous, 2000s

The single most embarrassing thing that can happen to a skipper is falling into the river. It's a pretty rare event, which is amazing considering how much time skippers spend walking the dock and hopping on and off boats in all kind of weather. While Disneyland drills safety into their heads, the main motivator that keeps skippers out of the river is the constant mockery they will get from their fellow skippers.

We used to hop on boats at the exit that were heading up to the load position. So one day I'm riding on the back of this boat, and he doesn't slow down. I thought he was taking a deadhead so I hop off at load, but I missed the dock and fell into the water. The dock was too high for me to get out, so I start doing water ballet and I do a whole show for the queue and they laughed and clapped, then a skipper finally helped pull me onto the dock. People applauded.

Benny LeMaster, 1990s–2000s

One time I was at front load. There were eight boats on the river that day. I moved away from my position to check to see if the queue was sticking out into Adventureland. Back in the day there was this single rope that you put across the queue to keep guests from falling in. This time, I didn't put the rope up, which is what many skippers did. There were also these big tie-off ropes for the boats at night. I stepped on it weird and rolled my foot. I had a moment to think, "Man, I should have put the rope up." And so I fell in the water. The skipper at rear load called it "stuntman style." I fell back first into the river. I remember the water was warm and slimy. My hat was stained green forever. Ritt pulled me up. The river bed slopes up towards unload. So I was walking to the shipping office and guests were high fiving me and I see the lead and he asks if I'm okay. I said "yes" and he replied, "Good, because you look like an idiot." Then he wouldn't let me go change. He made me wait until all eight boats had passed me by so that everyone could see me, and then he let me go. I went to costuming and they asked what happened, and when I said I'd fallen in the river they asked if I had a recent tetanus shot. They gave me new clothes and a couple of towels and I took a shower and went back to work.

Chris Ramirez, 2000s

A significant part of the training process at Jungle Cruise involves making sure the guests don't fall in the river. Still, it does happen sometimes.

We used to play a game called sink or float, and one time this elderly lady hit reverse on her ECV and ran backwards into the river. As she splashed in, I swear to God that I heard the lead quietly say to himself, "Sink."

Anonymous, 2000s

One of the most famous stories about a guest falling into the river happened in 2002 when a guest fell from the second story of the boathouse into the river.

He had dropped a pair of sunglasses and they fell on a ledge above where guests load onto the dock. He climbed up the guard rail and leaned over too far and fell, first hitting the canvas awning above the loading position, then bouncing off of that and into the water where a boat had been only moments before. Several skippers remember that day well.

I remember it was dusk and a skipper was moving to load and I held him at no-man's to load a special assistance guest. Then I hear this splash and a guest had fallen from the second floor and into the water. He leaned over, broke the rail, and fell in. His family laughed and laughed and they still got onto the boat and made fun of him. Disney gave him some clothes and toys for his daughter.

Amanda Case, 2000s

I was the boat going from unload into no man's. While I was moving forward I hear a loud thump sound and see a guy cartwheel into the river. If I had been any farther up he would have crushed his skull on my boat. He quickly pulled himself out of the water and tried to casually walk away like nothing had happened. I think he was really disoriented. He was reaching over to get his sunglasses and fell from the second story into the river. It was the weirdest thing I've ever seen.

Trevor Kelly, 2000s

I was at front load and you heard the entire upstairs guests go "ooohhhh!"

Kristin McGuire, 2000s–2010s

I was the lead the day when the guest fell from the second floor. I was standing in the shipping office and I hear this bouncing sound and then a big splash. He hit the awning and the water and he was out of the river instantly! I've never seen anyone get out of the water so fast. And he tried to act like nothing had happened. He kept saying, "I'm fine, no problem" Good thing there wasn't a boat at load or he would have broken his back.

Andy McGuire, 2000s

Then there are times when random people and objects fall into the river.

A skipper was moving an ECV from the boat dock edge to where we parked it, and he backed it into the river. He didn't fall in, but the ECV went in. He hit the throttle the wrong way.

Andy McGuire, 2000s

One time Aladdin was crossing the rocks from backstage to the dock and slipped and fell into the water right in front of my boat filled with guests. He totally played it off.

Benny LeMaster, 1990s–2000s

Part of a skipper's job during a downtime was to close the queue and stand at the entrance to the attraction and talk to guests who had questions. At some of the more popular attractions, such as Indy or Splash Mountain, guests routinely get angry whenever the attraction is closed. That was rarely the case at the Jungle Cruise. This relaxed atmosphere allowed skippers to have some fun.

We used to stand outside during downtime and give complete BS excuses as to why the ride was broken down. We'd see what we could get away with. You know how you can see the rainforest from the entrance to the queue? Once I told people that a sewage line and the main water line had crossed and so the pipes were just showering feces on the guests until it could be fixed. I once told a guest, "Have you ever seen Knight Rider? Our boats are kind of like that, they are super smart and drive themselves and one of them went nuts and we're trying to catch it. We'll restart the ride after we catch it." And the guests totally bought it.

Trevor Kelly, 2000s

There were times when you would stand in front of the Jungle Cruise entrance during a downtime and talk to guests. I swear that about half the time I had to explain to guests what the attraction was. I had been at other attractions and seen guests scream at cast members because a ride was broken down as if it was their fault. That never once happened at Jungle Cruise.

David John Marley, 2000s

That was another fun position, whenever we would close. That was one of the few places where you could tell people the truth as to why it's closed and it was still a good story. "Hey, why are you guys closed?" And you'd say, "There is a bunch of bamboo blocking the river," and then they'd always say, "No, really, why are you closed?" And you'd say, "Because there is bamboo covering the river." When Indy used to break down I'd tell people, "Don't worry, we have top men working on it. Top men." The guests would usually stare at me blankly.

Kevin Lively, 2010s

For years the Jungle Cruise had one free floating boat called the skiff. It was originally kept at the end of the dock near load. The skiff was there for leads to get to an emergency quickly In the late 1990s its small outboard engine was taken out and it was moved to the Indian elephant bathing pool. It's ironic that a boat put in place to provide assistance in times of need became a source of trouble.

I remember one time a friend of mine drove the skiff right into Schweitzer Falls. It sank in two seconds. A boat comes by the backside of water and he was just standing there in the middle of the river; you couldn't see the skiff at all.

Jeff Rhoads, 1970s–1980s

When I got trained our trainer untied the skiff so the attraction would go down. It was tied off in the elephant pool. Our trainer wanted to show us what a 101 time was like.

Ben Case, 2000s

The skiff, the one behind Bertha, had come out and we had to put it back without being seen. I called a manger and said, "We have a skiff loose, can you please hold the boats." That's all I wanted. So we get the skiff back, it was a huge ordeal, but the other cast member and I are laughing about it; it took maybe 30 minutes. We walk back to the dock and security is there with the paramedics and I'm thinking, "What did I miss?" I see the manager, who looks panic stricken, and she asks me, "Did you find them?" and I said "Find who?" The manager said, "You said there was a skip loose." So I said skiff, she heard skip, and decided that it was a logical thing to act on, that she had to call all these people to come help with the escaped skipper.

Benny LeMaster, 1990s–2000s

If you were on the dock, you had a clear idea of what to do during a downtime. For the skippers out in the jungle, they were usually left to their own devices until help could arrive.

I loved the breakdowns, I lived for breakdowns. I got to be a real tour guide when that happened. I read everything I could get my hands on about Disneyland, plus my mom told me a lot of stories from her time at Disney. So when there was a breakdown I took that opportunity to just take the mic and answer any questions that people might have about the park. I would talk to them about anything they wanted to talk about. A supervisor named Joe told us we could never deviate from the script no matter what happened. Even if there was a breakdown we were supposed to maintain the show, we could only talk about stuff directly related to a jungle voyage. I thought that was pretty stupid because people knew when we are broken down. Plus he hated that when there was a breakdown we would collect our boats together and hangout. He kept telling us that we had to preserve our show spacing so that when the ride starts back up, you can continue the voyage.

I liked the breakdowns because it was something out of the ordinary to break up the monotony. The last thing you wanted to do was to be stuck on the dock during a breakdown; you want to be out in the jungle. I remember one time being at load and I heard the first two shots of what was eventually a 6 shot and I went full speed into the jungle so that I could be out there during the downtime. I remember seeing the lead trying to get me to stop my boat.

Jeff Rhoads, 1970s–1980s

When there was a 101 and you were in an empty boat we would all meet in the hippo pool, tie off, and all get into one boat and hang out. We'd smoke or whatever. I liked to have a deadhead so I could smoke a cigarette, especially at night.

Kaz Liput, 2000s

One time when all the boats were in the jungle sitting empty during a down time, we had to get the dock clear because of a 6 shot or something, and we were nose to tail from Trader Sam to the attacking natives. I was the last boat and after sitting there for 20 minutes I had to pee so badly. I moved my boat backwards to the hippo pool and was about to pee in the river when the skipper in front of me brought her boat back to see what I was doing.

David John Marley, 2000s

I remember one time I had a boat ahead of me stall and I was stuck in the jungle and it was just gorgeous. I had a boat full of people and we had fun. I had a Scottish guest and I kept asking him to say things that Scrooge McDuck would say.

Kevin Lively, 2010s

CHAPTER EIGHTEEN

HOLIDAY HIJINX

Skipper Kaz Liput said something that has been repeated by skippers for years when they are asked by guests what it is like to have to go to work on a holiday. She said, "If I couldn't be home with my family, I'd rather be at Disneyland with my second family." Here is how skippers have celebrated various holidays and history-making events at the park.

New Years Day

One year some skippers and I celebrated the New Year and drank multiple bottles of wine and I woke up at 7am for my shift. I got on the parking lot shuttle, it hit a bump, and I threw up all over myself, so I went to costuming, feeling very sick. They had a Magic Morning, all the leads of the park, and Jim Lake gathered us so that we could plan out guest control and help each other out. It was very helpful normally, but this time I sat on the castle wall and kept throwing up into the moat in front of Sleeping Beauty Castle. My friends blocked me so no one could see me. I worked at Indy that day and everyone was fine. I walked by Jungle Cruise and they were all sick. I spent the day at Indy laying down.

Benny LeMaster, 1990s–2000s

I was out on medical leave and I came into the park on New Year's Eve and I had a cast member smuggle in a bottle of rum through Harbor House [the cast member entrance to backstage Disneyland]. We met at Jungle Cruise and I get the booze and a couple of Cokes. I got the lead and a couple of skippers to take out a deadhead at 11:30 at night on New Year's Eve and we sat in the hippo pool and got drunk. Later on, managers tried to pull one of the skippers to Indy, but he was too drunk, so another skipper took his place. We then went back to one of the guy's house and drank more.

Matt Nerrie, 2000s

Valentine's Day

Valentine's Day was my favorite day to work because you've never seen so many couples fighting at the park. I think it was just too much pressure on people to be lovey.

Kaz Liput, 2000s

Fourth of July

On the Fourth of July we closed the attraction in 2003. We made the rookies stay in the boats. All of the managers left to watch the fireworks on the River Belle Terrace and left us to our own devices. So we shut down the attraction and went up to the second level and watched the fireworks and the second they were over we raced back to our positions and the managers never knew anything.

Chris Ramirez, 2000s

Halloween

I had a creepy solo cruise on Halloween. I pulled up to the dock and there was nobody waiting; it was dead because people were all going to see the fireworks. The lead asked me if I would take this woman around the jungle alone. I was like, "Sure, that's cool." She gets in the boat and I ask her what would she like me to do, and she said, "Just pretend there are people on the boat and do your thing." I took her out and she had a notepad and a pen and she was writing the whole time and I was so uncomfortable. I'm doing my thing and she was quiet and just wrote notes.

We came around to the dock and it was dead so we stopped at unload and I talked to her for a little bit. I said, "Can you tell me what's going on with the note pad?" She said, "Oh, I'm trying to get in contact with my boyfriend who passed away last year and his favorite ride was Jungle Cruise. I thought if I went on this boat I could do what is that called automatic writing. I started doing automatic writing to see if he would come through to me on Halloween." I didn't pry too much because I had to move up the boat, but I said, " I hope you got in contact with him," and she said that she had. So I just said, "Okay, have a great night. I'm sorry to hear about your boyfriend." And she went on merry way.

The skipper that was in front of me said, "I knew what she was doing and I didn't want it on my boat. It scared me." That was interesting and was kind of the creepiest thing that ever happened.

Jen Chavez, 2010s

Last year we had a group of guests who came to Jungle Cruise dressed like the attacking natives. It was the coolest thing I'd ever seen.

Anonymous, 2010s

Christmas

Being there on Christmas was so much fun and it was great to make other people's holidays brighter. For a long time I was the only one authorized to decorate my boat for Christmas. I asked the managers and they said okay, and I bought decorations that fit the theme, battery-operated lights that looked like berries. The next year a skipper named Sherri made all of those Jungle Cruise Santa hats and it was great. This was years before Jingle Cruise.

Kaz Liput, 2000s

Christmas is my favorite day to work because everyone is in a good mood. The atmosphere is just different, it's my favorite day to work Jungle Cruise.

Kipp Hart, 2000s–2010s

I agreed to extend on Christmas Eve and they kept me in a mid-shift. So I had to get there really early to get a new costume and get to the dock by 10am. I get there on Christmas Day and the lead sends me out to be greeter since Jungle Cruise was 101. It was super windy that day. What the lead didn't tell me was that most of the westside was also closed. So I had people coming to me who had been turned away from Splash and Indy. Everyone was so angry.

Amanda Case, 2000s

One time we were filling a stocking for a charity around Christmas time. Management gave us a list of supplies and each attraction had a stocking to fill that would be donated. Well, somebody put one of the guns in the stocking, and it was so funny seeing it hanging there, that a family would be given a gun from Disneyland.

Benny LeMaster, 1990s–2000s

It was Christmas of 2002 or 2003 and it was raining sideways and they still wanted us to run the Jungle Cruise because the park was busy. And this big piece of bamboo came crashing down so six of us took a boat out and cut it down and brought it back like we were jousting. We were all soaking wet and laughing so hard.

Joshua Sudock, 2000s

One year for the two weeks before Christmas it seemed like every boat was dead. It might be an exaggeration, but that's how it seemed. I was trying my best and no one was having it. I'd do this joke to test the boats at the dock. At the rain forest I'd say, "Welcome to the Jungle Cruise, this is where reality and disappointment come together." It's not the best joke ever, but it always got a chuckle and it would give me a good idea about the boat. One night I tell that joke and it was dead silent, and I lost it. So I turned and said, "That's right, kids, there's no Santa Claus." And as soon as I said it I thought, "Yep, I've just lost my job." I was sure at that moment that I was going to get fired. You should have heard the reaction; the boat was filled with kids and parents. One parent yelled, "Watch it," and you could just feel the anger. I get to the Cambodian shrine and I've been telling jokes but getting no response. You could feel the heavy cloud. So I started to sing "Santa Claus is Coming to Town." That didn't help, they want nothing to do with me. By the time we got back to the dock they'd either forgotten or weren't motivated enough to complain. I honestly thought I'd lost my job.

Kipp Hart, 2000s–2010s

Jingle Cruise

The Jingle Cruise is a Christmas-themed overlay that was started in 2013. The Jingle Cruise was the brainchild of a skipper who left the park to work for Walt Disney Imagineering, also just called WDI, Kevin Lively.

The Jingle Cruise branched out from my emails with Kevin Rafferty when I was working at the park. We originally had someone else doing the scripts but she retired, and I reached out to Kevin because I knew him from my interviews at WDI. I asked him who was the Jungle Cruise's new point of contact, and he said, "I guess it's me." Whenever we would submit jokes I would email him and I had these long chains of emails. During Christmas we had a string of emails that were a series of puns about the Jungle Cruise and Christmas. He said, "No more! Save them until I can pay you for them."

So fast forward to when I'm working here at WDI and I had some open time in my schedule so I went to the head of Blue Sky at the time and said, "Rafferty and I used to do these Christmas jokes and I have an idea for an overlay, can I get some funding for this?" He said, "Sure, take eight hours." So I took those hours and I created a presentation and then I championed the idea for the next year. Our entire budget to create a pitch was only eight hours and we were able to sell it to both parks. I told them that this is a rare opportunity were we can do a very simple thing that will empower the cast and crew to carry a show for you. I wanted to make sure that the original set of jokes was in the family so they were written by me, Casey Collins, Kyle Reed, and a bunch of other skippers who work here at WDI. We were able to get the initial wave of jokes up. From there we reached out to the skippers and they are able to submit things every year.

Kevin Lively, 2010s

I love the Jingle Cruise. I liked it best the first year when it was more subdued as far as the decoration, because it fits the story better. The gorilla camp was just a little bit decorated. They had pumped it up in marketing to make it seem like it was going to be Christmas everywhere and the guests were disappointed. People would say stuff like, "I thought there were going to be more decorations." That was how it evolved into what it is right now. They listened to the guests. The decorations went from one extreme to the other. It is over the top. As soon as you hit the rain forest there is stuff everywhere. The guests loved it much better. I thought that was weird.

Kipp Hart, 2000s–2010s

I was there for the first year when it was just an idea they were playing with and it wasn't enough. The decorations weren't enough, they'd played it up really big when they marketed it, and it wasn't what people were expecting. The queue was awesome, but I don't think they knew what to do with the jungle yet. The first year of Jingle Cruise was 2013 and they had a give-away where guests could get a poster on the first day and it was really busy and I just remember guests saying,"Oh, that's not what we thought we were getting" when they went through the jungle. They required us to learn an entire spiel of Christmas or holiday jokes, but we only had to use 20 or 30% of the spiel. So a lot people just didn't embrace it. I totally embraced it and they had a contest for the best Jingle Cruise spiel nightly. The leads put that together to kinda push us to do it more. And I won three nights in a row. I won best jingle spiel because I just embraced it and had fun with it.

The only part of Jingle Cruise that skippers didn't seem to care for was when the Christmas holiday celebration was extended into January.

I remember being excited to do Jingle Cruise and then I couldn't wait till we went back to normal. They extended it for two weeks after the holidays and it was really odd because we're still making these Christmas, holiday jokes and it had passed. I started to make jokes about how this is kind of weird and no longer relevant. We just kind of played along with it and we would say things like, "Okay, this would've been cool two weeks ago."

Jen Chavez, 2010s

Gay Day

Gay Day began in 1991 at Walt Disney World. Disneyland had a special party night for gays, which was cancelled in 1998. This brought about the start of Gay Days at Disneyland. The event is now a weekend long event, but Gay Day is the first Saturday in October. Usually about 30,000 gays come to the park, wearing red shirts to identify themselves. While this is an unofficial day, Disneyland offers discounted tickets and hotel rates for the event. There are always lots of complaints on Gay Day from people who didn't know what was going on. For many skippers, it was one of their favorite days to work at Disneyland. Decades before Gay Day became an officially unofficial event, there were surreptitious private evening parties, where the park was closed to all but a select group of ticket holders.

Companies would reserve a night and buy a bunch of tickets, but it turned out sometimes these are fake companies that were getting lots of tickets to sell. One of these companies bought tickets for one night and turned it into a gay night. It didn't bother me. The guys at the Jungle Cruise were a little concerned because back then there was lots of homophobia going on. They were not happy about it. The company was called, "Greater American Yankee," or GAY. That was funny.

Terry Eaton, 1970s–1980s

I loved working Gay Day or Red Shirt Day, mostly because of the straight men who showed up wearing red and were not happy about it. One day this really big guy in a red Marines shirt got on the boat with his wife and family. I said, "You picked the wrong day to wear that shirt," and everyone laughed and he just glared at me. I then looked at him and said, "Don't ask, don't tell." Again the guests laughed, his wife laughed, and he did not.

David John Marley, 2000s

The best was Gay Day, which is also called Red Shirt Day. I had an entire boat of guests in red shirts and they were really fun. As I stood on the captain's crate one of them grabbed my butt as I was doing the Crocodile Hunter impersonation.

Joey Hurley, 2000s

Once on a Red Shirt weekend I got my butt pinched by a very large lesbian. She did it several times. When I did the backside of water, she yelled, "The backside of Karen!"

Karen McGuire-Vogelvang, 2000s

The first Pirates of the Caribbean movie premiered at Disneyland with a day-long event. A red carpet ran the length of Main Street and thousands of people came just to catch a glimpse of the many celebrities who had been invited to watch the movie, which was shown on a giant screen on the end of Tom Sawyer Island. For most cast members the day just meant more crowds and people unhappy that most of the westside of the park was closed off. For most of it, but not all, the Jungle Cruise stayed open.

During the summer of 2003 the first Pirates of the Caribbean movie premiered at Disneyland. Since the screening was to be shown on the Rivers of America, and there was a red carpet that literally ran the length of Main Street, most guests assumed that the entire westside of the park was closed. However, the Jungle Cruise was perhaps the only attraction still open. Maybe Indy was open, too; I forget. What I do remember is that no one came to Jungle Cruise. It was so great. We got paid to just hang out all day and occasionally take out a boat. When the movie started a couple of us skippers went upstairs to the Adventureland offices and watched the beginning of the movie from the balcony.

David John Marley, 2000s

Not only do holidays leave an impact on skippers, but just being at the park during times of national emergencies or world-shaking events can have a life-changing impact.

I was at Jungle Cruise the night that John Lennon was killed. The Disneyland Christmas party was that night and they had sent us guys who had been working the day shift to help out these guys from the Disney studio. We gave them a crash course in how to be Jungle Cruise skippers. It was some animators and other people from up there. It was December 8, 1980. So it was a very easy night, the park wasn't crowded, I was working unload, and my parents were in the park. It was a special event where if you brought in a toy, you got in free. It was a very fun night at the park.

I was standing at unload and this other skipper comes back from the break area. They were showing a Monday Night Football game, and he comes over and tells me that there was a breaking news story that John Lennon had just been killed. This was a time before cellphones and stuff like that, but the news spread around the park really quickly. My parents were across the park and came over to the Jungle Cruise when they heard. They where worried about how I'd take the news. My biggest memory of that night was about the music. I remember seeing this sea of people walking down Main Street toward the exit and the music was so loud because the crowd was so quiet. Then you get in your car and every station was playing Beatles music.

It was that night when I realized that I needed to get serious about music. Before that it had been a goof, something to get girls or just have fun. But that night I decided to get serious about music. That was the night that I became a professional entertainer. I left about six months later. Every year on Facebook I post a picture of me at the unload dock at Jungle Cruise, in memory of the day I made that decision.

George Trullinger, 1970s–1980s

September 11, 2001, was one of the worst days in American history, and it had a strong impact on the cast members of Disneyland.

On 9/11 I got a call telling me not to come in because the park was closed. The entire Jungle Cruise community was in contact with each other. We all ended up hanging out at a skipper's house eating pizza. It was frightening because we closed due to terrorist attack and we realized it could have been us. The first couple of days back were rough. Everyone was quiet, even the guests. Everyone was solemn; foreign guests offered condolences constantly. Maybe a week later Disneyland had a moment of silence. Every attraction closed at noon and everyone stood outside and there was a moment of silence. It was an intense emotional moment.

Benny LeMaster, 1990s–2000s

I got a call from the lead early in the morning who told me that Disneyland was closed. That is when I turned on the news and learned about the attacks. Gerry had skippers do a phone tree to inform all the other skippers. I was stunned that Disneyland was closed. That's how I knew that something terrible had happened.

After 9/11 it was so tough, and many people, many skippers, deal with grief by making jokes. So we made jokes, but kept it backstage as a way to deal with our grief. You stopped asking people where you are from because if they said New York, then it was nothing. It brought everybody down. It was great having other skippers there to talk about our fears and help work through our fears.

Kaz Liput, 2000s

After 9/11 there were so many guests who wanted us to be robots. We were open on 9/12 and guests wanted us to be happy. I ran into guests who were really angry that we shut all the rides down for a moment of silence.

Amanda Case, 2000s

Management came down on us after 9/11. We were not allowed to ask people where they were from, because they might say New York. You couldn't do the "fully loaded" joke, you couldn't do "Did you take an airplane here? Did you give it back?" All of those were banned. I was supposed to fly to Walt Disney World on 9/11 and got kicked out of the Long Beach airport. So we went to Disneyland. We used our passes to get into the back and went to the Indy break room and hung out and watched the events on TV. I remember how weird it was to see the park empty during the day. For the next four months it was so dead at the park. We would just cycle boats through and it felt weird being funny. After New Years things got better. There were days where they would scramble fighter jets over the park and you'd be in your boat and look up and see an F-16 roar past. It was a weird time. I think that is why we all got to know each other so well because there were no guests.

Chris Ramirez, 2000s

Right around then I was in the boat and there was a Ziploc bag of white stuff and I couldn't tell what it was and it scared the crap out of me. This was during the anthrax scare. So they sent me on a bunch of deadheads until security showed up. It was baby powder and a towel.

Ben Case, 2000s

It was a week after 9/11 and everyone was on edge and all the cast members were worried because we thought Disneyland was a target. So I was out in the jungle and I heard a loud boom and everyone just stopped. I honestly thought, "Well, here it is, the terror attack." What had happened was one of the boilers on a steam train blew out and made this huge boom through our side of the park. People thought a plane had just crashed into Sleeping Beauty Castle. It was loud. So I was thinking, "Do I bring the boat back to the dock or stay here or what?"

Trevor Kelly, 2000s

After 9/11 they were looking for attractions cast members to do back checks. It was a 4-hour training with a KA [knowledge assessment] and PA [performance assessment] and I told them I would fail the 5-question test because I didn't want to look through people's bags. This was right after 9/11 when anthrax was around and people were worried about everything. I was just a mall rat, not a security guard.

Andy McGuire, 2000s

CHAPTER NINETEEN

GRAD NITES

Grad Nites are a rite of passage for southern California high-schoolers and a special level of hell for the cast members who work at the park. It all began in 1961, and by 2009 Disneyland welcomed it's five-millionth Grad Nite guest. Grad Nites were not Disneyland's idea. In 1961 the park was approached by the PTAs of three high schools from the San Fernando Valley. They were looking for something fun and safe for their graduating seniors to do since the year before a few kids had been killed in a drunk driving accident. In 1961 the park invited 8,000 students from 28 Los Angeles high schools to a special after-hours party at the park. It was popular and became an instant hit. Usually, the park would close at 8pm and then be transformed into Grad Nite. Disneyland would then reopen at 10pm and run until 6am.

Grad Nite was especially tough for skippers because they had to be alone with crazy and sometimes half-drunk high school kids all night long. It was also the time when they were the most at risk of being assaulted or harassed, especially the female skippers.

During a Grad Nite not all of the attractions were open, and those that were allowed cast members to loosen the rules just a bit. Normally, Disneyland is concerned with guest counts, in the hopes of allowing as many people as possible to ride as many attractions as they can during their visit. For years this same standard wasn't kept for Grad Nites which at Jungle Cruise yielded predictable results.

One of the most famous secrets about the Jungle Cruise and Grad Nite is the existence of an adult version of the spiel, the infamous Grad Nite Spiel. What I've come to find is that while most every skipper knew about these dirty jokes, very few ever did any of them.

Grad Nites were an ordeal. I think they went until 6 in the morning.

Alan Coats, 1960s

I worked a Grad Nite when I was a senior in high school. I missed my own Grad Nite and worked at Jungle Cruise instead. Everyone hated working Grad Nites. I was at the veldt and I was being hassled the entire time through the jungle. So when I get to the Veldt I turn on the outside lights and a skipper walks out from behind the lion's den, one appears by the baboons, and a third from behind a hill, so three skippers come out and each of them are wielding two guns each that were fully loaded. They shot all 36 rounds at my boat and it scared the hell out of me. I jumped to the bottom of the boat, the kids were all laughing and screaming. I get back to the dock and standing there is a manager with security and the Anaheim police. The manager walked up to me and said, "We heard explosions or gunshots. We think it was probably firecrackers." Then he just stared at me and so I said, "Oh, yes, I saw firecrackers, somebody threw them into the jungle." So the police left as the three skippers walked back on the dock and put the guns back without being noticed. They never even bothered to check the gun cabinet to see if any of the guns were missing.

Benny LeMaster, 1990s–2000s

There was this one time that there was a special event for a Grad Nite where they put all these plush toys of Simba from *The Lion King* all around the jungle. They want to make it a game where you could look for Simba. But the Simbas kept falling into the water and getting messed up by the boats and they were just floating down the river.

Joey Hurley, 2000s

I worked a lot of Grad Nites. I loved them. They were the easiest shift to work. Most of the time people didn't want to hear a spiel so I would get into the jungle, then say, "I'm going to turn the outside lights on and just drive, you people do what you're going to do, and I'll flash the lights twice and that will give you time to finish. I would also do the dirty spiel, everybody loved that. I worked a bunch of Grad Nites with a lead who was our age so there was basically no supervision.

Leo Romo, 2000s

Skipper Heather Wilkins' father had been a skipper back in the 1970s and the lessons that he taught her about working Jungle during a Grad Nite came in handy.

One Grad Nite I did something that my dad told me they did back in the 1970s. I used to smoke and as we left the dock I told the boat that I was going to smoke and drive, and they can have the next seven minutes to themselves as long as they promised to clap and scream and laugh once we got back to the dock. It worked every time. I never did the dirty jokes, and they didn't respond to the regular spiel, so I took my dad's idea.

Heather Wilkins, 2000s

Late one Grad Nite the entire crew of the Jungle Cruise got bored and the lead had the idea of putting a boat through the jungle, but without a skipper. So we turned on the outside lights, so we could track it, and set it off on a slow, but steady pace. Off into the rainforest it went as we laughed hysterically. We saw it pass the gorilla camp and waited. We saw the lights of the boat again as it came through the rapids, and toward the dock. As the boat approached Trader Sam, a manager walked on the dock. The lead, thinking amazingly fast, put his arm around the manager and said, "I'm glad you're here, there is a guest concern over at Tiki." And with that he spun the manager around and walked away. He looked over his shoulder and smiled. We caught the boat as it came back to the dock. Thankfully for us, the manager didn't remember that the Tiki Room wasn't open during Grad Nite.

David John Marley, 2000s

A skipper friend of mine was working that night and he brought a boom box and we put the mic up to it and we played this one Janet Jackson song on an endless loop. We'd yell, "It's the party boat!" and flash the light as we left the dock and then play that song on repeat. We'd all be dancing and anytime there was a lull we'd yell at them and make them dance. After seven minutes they were ready to get off the boat.

Trevor Kelly, 2000s

We used to do lots of dock jokes, stuff you could do at night but during a Grad Nite we just went nuts. There was no supervision, which is really weird because they had a lot of employees who were all in their late teens and early twenties and they scheduled them to work these late-night shifts with all of these high school girls. It's just going to end poorly.

Leo Romo, 2000s

One year the skippers were given boxes of flashlights and stuffed animals were hidden in the jungle so that the teenage guests could play flashlight tag. Most of the flashlights ended up in the river. Some skippers even took bets on how long a flashlight would stay on while underwater.

Anonymous, 2000s

I remember that it was fun because if there was a sassy teenager, you could destroy them in front of the boat with no fear of retribution whatsoever.

Trevor Kelly, 2000s

I don't have any crazy Grad Nite stories. I think because I was always so crazy on the boat, I didn't see this as a reason to get crazier. I would just do more pop culture references. Sometimes later at night I would shut off all the lights and drive through the jungle quietly. It was very relaxing on a Grad Nite since they were all so tired. By 3am, they were all so tired.

Joey Hurley, 2000s

My first Grad Nite was one to remember because I had one of my worst boats and best boats literally one after the other. My first boat featured these kids from two rival schools. These two girls got into a screaming and cussing fight with each other as the kids in the middle of the boat tried to keep them apart. I was unsure of what to do, so I just threw the throttle forward and got back to the dock as quickly as I could. We got back to the dock and one of the girls said, "You didn't even say any jokes!" and I just said, "Get out." I thought that if this is how Grad Nites are going to be, I won't make it through the night. I pulled up to load to get my next guests and they started laughing at my jokes as they got on board. The boat was laughing and paying attention and I hadn't even left the dock yet. I did my tour, which they loved, and when we got back to the dock I got a standing ovation and a couple of kids came up to take photos with me. At that point I got bumped out of the boat and while in the shipping office the lead asked me how my first Grad Nite was going. I told him I honestly had no idea what had just happened to me.

David John Marley, 2000s

I worked one Grad Nite ever. I picked up a shift from someone because I thought I should do it once. They had turned Aladdin's Oasis into a house dance club with deep bass and it gave me a killer migraine. You could go off script like crazy on Grad Nites; you just had to be smart and most skippers were not smart about it. You had to ask if there were any chaperones on the boat. If you asked if there were any chaperones they wouldn't say, so I said, "Who's graduating this year! Who graduated years ago!" And then any chaperones that were there would laugh. And then I asked them if they wanted a spiel, or I could shut off the lights and drive. Driving with the lights off was fun because eventually there would be a few couples just going at it, full make out, and I would point the spotlight on them and say "This is a park for families, not a park where you make a family."

Kaz Liput, 2000s

I remember it was the day of a Grad Nite and a kid came up in a big jacket and he was all sweaty and it looked like he was trying to hide something in the bushes by the exit. He thought no one saw him. He left and we had security dig it up and take the booze away.

Kaz Liput, 2000s

I didn't like working Grad Nite because I got pinched a lot.

Karen McGuire-Vogelvang, 2000s

My first three years being a lead during Grad Nights were a blast. We'd run three boats, maybe five, then we'd send people to go on other rides. I'd bring donuts and we got loaded up on sugar and got our job done.

On one Grad Nite the lead dropped to one boat and our wait was over an hour and a half. The entire boathouse queue was full as well as the Indy loop. This manager comes by and says, "You've got a long line there." The lead just said, "Yep." Then the manager asked, "How many boats are you running?" and the lead said, "One." The manager cracked up and walked away.

My other favorite Grad Nite story is once we found weed on this kid and we're hassling him about it. "You brought weed into my jungle?" and the kid started to cry, he thought he was going to jail. So we take his weed and threw it into the water and told him to leave. We found a lot of weed. We also caught kids that had snuck into the jungle to have sex.

We mostly tried to get the female skippers off of the boats on Grad Nite. We didn't like letting them go alone. Kids are dumb.

Andy McGuire, 2000s

During one Grad Nite we were on the Nile and this boy started grabbing me. I spun around and stopped him and told him that I was going to call his chaperone. He said, "You're not much older than I am." Like that made it okay. He kept verbally harassing me, then a rival from another school started a fight with the first kid. He was my white knight, but I got back to the dock, got out of the boat, and never took another Grad Nite trip.

Kristin McGuire, 2000s–2010s

I didn't like Grad Nites. Staying up all night and working nights is not fun. I worked back-to-back Grad Nites one time with my day job. So I worked 8 to 6, drove to work, worked all day, then straight to Disneyland for another Grad Nite, then back to work. I made it half-way through that second work day and I told my boss that I had to go home. I was exhausted.

Kipp Hart, 2000s–2010s

I was working Grad Nite and there were kids who were trying to tell all my jokes for me, like they do. So I switched them up and started telling the joke about how the snakes always travel in fours. "Look, there's one, two, three, oh, no, where's the fourth one!" The kid shouts, "It's in my pants!" To which I reply into the mic, "Nah, kid, we're looking for big ones." I was instantly mortified and swore that was what would get me fired, but all his friends started punching him and he became the one that got heckled the rest of the cruise and not me, which was a relief.

Anonymous, 2010s

CHAPTER TWENTY

◇◇◇

SAFARI SO GOODIE

The Jungle Cruise is a beautiful garden, a real jungle. So in addition to the animatronic animals, some wild ones have taken up residence there as well. The plant life grows and changes with the seasons, and it is actually its own mini ecosystem. Because it is so beautiful and because skippers spend so much time out there, it is only natural for them to want to explore the jungle on foot.

For years going on safari, as it is called, was encouraged. The theory was that skippers had to be familiar with their attraction. Everyone else gets to walk around their attraction, why not skippers? As time passed, going on safari was increasingly frowned upon, and now is essentially forbidden. This hasn't stopped skippers from venturing out into the jungle; it just makes them more sneaky.

Despite Disneyland management's claims that banning safaris is a safety issue, having skippers who don't know anything about the land they are driving around is not any safer. There were leads who allowed a skipper to go on safari as long as they asked permission first. This kept the chaos to a minimum. As you shall see, going on safari, exploring this natural wonder, is a rite of passage for skippers.

I didn't go out there much, I didn't even get to either of the islands, as I recall. I never did any safaris. I did get out on the skiff once, which was always parked by the loading area. The manager told me to go out and fix something.

Alan Coats, 1960s

I used to go on safari all of the time. I'm one of those people that like to know how things work. There're a couple of times when I would climb up on the rocks at the baboons and imitate them to see if anybody would notice. Sometimes instead on the veldt, or by the pole with the rhino, just to see if anybody would notice. Most of the time the guests never even see me and I was just standing there. Sometimes the skippers would see me, sometimes they wouldn't. Sometimes if a skipper saw me they would yell out, "Look, a gorilla!"

Terry Eaton, 1970s–1980s

A couple of skippers wore swimsuits under their costumes and during their lunch break they went up to the top of Schweitzer Falls and sat in the water with drinks in their hands and made it seem like they were having a Jacuzzi party up there. They'd wave to the boats and walk around to make sure that they were seen by all the boats.

Jeff Rhoads, 1970s–1980s

We used to go out to the jungle in the morning and take funny pictures. A skipper named Ed went to Notre Dame and was going to be a doctor. My favorite photo, it sums up the Jungle Cruise in one photo, is Ed dressed as a doctor, giving an exam to the dead zebra.

Sue Barnaby - 1980s–1990s

It was not uncommon for skippers on break to go out and dance with the dancing natives. Once a skipper beheaded one of the dancing natives. He tried to take the hat off one of them and the entire head came off. That was never reported as skipper error, it was just reported that the head fell off. The skipper felt so guilty for a long time after that.

Benny LeMaster, 1990s–2000s

Some leads were more lenient than others when it came to letting skippers go on safari.

My rule was, "Don't break the jungle," but I bet you felt a closer connection to the attraction because you knew it so well.

Andy McGuire, 2000s

Sometimes if I was on a break or didn't have anything to do, I would go over to the Indy queue and hop over the little fence and then jump on to the crocodile that was right behind the first archway in the Cambodian shrine. I would straddle that crocodile and as boats went by I would imitate the Crocodile Hunter. "Crikey! Look at the size of this beauty!"

Joey Hurley, 2000s

One night Ritt dropped me off on Catalina Island and I made my way over to the attacking natives and I found a big stick and I would attack with the rest of the natives. When they would attack I would rise up with them and I would keep going as they went down to cycle back and I'd start yelling at them, "C'mon, guys. Guys! C'mon, attack them!" and then I would act all sad and just half-heartedly throw my stick at the boat and then I ducked back down. That was fun until the boat had passed and you're stuck on Catalina in the pitch black of night and you have to wait five more minutes for the deadhead to come back around. It was terrifying. That jungle is terrifying.

Trevor Kelly, 2000s

One time I laid down next to the zebra in the lion's cave and pretended to be dead. We used to do stuff like that all the time until management caught on and threatened us that they were going to hide out there and catch us.

Leo Romo, 2000s

I loved being in the jungle, it's a really cool place. It's unfortunate that managers were so dead set against having skippers in the jungle. I think that only made it more special to me. It was so cool to go sit out there in the jungle and it would be so quiet out there in between the boats. You could hear the sound of the leaves in the wind and the jungle noises that had been piped in.

Mike Pucher, 2000s

I loved to do the "Mom joke" at the hippo pool. You'd tell a skipper that you'd be out there at night so they knew to do it. That was always fun. I danced with the natives once. It was crazy because it was the first time I had been back there on my own. It was so fun.

Leo Romo, 2000s

There was a skipper who ratted out a couple of skippers she saw go on safari while she was working another attraction. She went and called Adventureland managers and got these guys busted. A month later she was made a lead at Jungle Cruise and took some friends out on a safari to the same spot, after telling everyone that safaris were banned. Word of that got around.

Anonymous, 2000s

We crawled under the jeep at the gorilla camp and cried for help when boats came by. We mostly did stuff like that to the rookies to see how they'd react. Seeing how fast you could run from scene to scene without getting dirty or caught was also really fun.

Kaz Liput, 2000s

The first time I went on safari it just blew my mind. When I was lead, I used to go on safaris more. I would take my breaks out there. One time I stood on top of Schweitzer Falls and there is one angle where you kind of really can see everything. The jungle is sort of a figure eight bent at 90 degrees, and you can see the entire thing from the top of the waterfall. I took a moment to take it all in and it was a great feeling.

Michael Libby, 2000s

Once a trainer had some trainees and he was running in the jungle from Bertha to the gorilla camp at night and they came out and were covered in spiders! It was like that famous scene in *Indiana Jones and the Temple of Doom*.

Kaz Liput, 2000s

Late one night a skipper and I decide to get into the skull canoe, by the dancing natives. That was easier said than done, but we got in and brought a big tow rope with us. We then wrapped it around our hands to look like captives. As a boat pulls around we begin yelling for help. That first boat was piloted by a skipper who may have had some social skills disorder, and it was on full display that night. As we yelled for help, he brought the boat to a dead stop and said, "Hey, guys, what's going on?" We yelled stuff like, "The cannibals captured us and are going to eat us! Help." And he just stood there and stared at us until even his guests began to look at him strangely. I gave up and just yelled, "Move it up, skip." And off he went.

The next boat was great, the female skipper totally went along with the joke and promised to bring back help. It was then that I foolishly decided to wait for one more boat, since the first one was so bad. It was the first skipper again, and he did exactly the same thing as he did the first time.

David John Marley, 2000s

Once Ritt and I went on a deadhead sitting on the bow of the boat telling stories. As we passed the attacking natives we hear a rustle in the bushes and this skipper slides down to the edge of the water and says "Hey, guys," so Ritt fired the gun at him and the gun shot made him slip into the water.

Kriztina Varga, 2000s

I made it a regular habit to go on safari at least once during each shift. Sometimes I would eat my lunch out there, sometimes while sitting above Schweitzer Falls, and watch the boats go by. I loved being out in nature. Usually I would bring my camera and take photos. There are lots of places where you can see boats go by and the guests never know. The skippers sometimes saw me, but no one else did. I found it to be a great way to relax, especially when the park was really busy. It was so quiet, peaceful, and beautiful out there.

David John Marley, 2000s

I went out there because I wanted to get pictures of me on the rhino. I was wearing my costume, the khaki slacks and shirt. So I'm up there and I'm getting my picture taken, and as I hop off the rhino I see that my pants are now completely black. And it was sticky, it wasn't dirt that you can dust off. I had to go back to the dock like that. I had to work the rest of my shift wearing those pants and nobody said anything.

Kipp Hart, 2000s–2010s

I asked one current (2016) skipper how management keeps skippers from going on safari.

Fear. And the people that worked there now just don't have that drive to be adventurous because they're afraid of getting in trouble. I'm pretty sure that they'd fire you on the spot right now. This safety initiative that they have now is all inclusive even on things that are safe. Things like safaris are under the safety umbrella that gives them the authority to do things like fire people.

Anonymous, 2010s

CHAPTER TWENTY-ONE

<><><><><><><><><><><><><><><><><><><><><><><><><><><><><><><><><><><><><><><><><><>

THE LOVE BOAT...OR CRUISE

The Jungle Cruise had many different names as the park was being developed and even after Disneyland opened. One of its early names was the Rivers of Romance and it's easy to see why, especially at night on a warm southern California evening the jungle is one of the most tranquil and romantic places at Disneyland. This romantic feeling applies to both guests and skippers.

Disneyland was great because there were so many girls who worked there, mainly in the ticket booths. It was easy to ask them out to spend time at the park after our shifts were over. You could get free food and treats with your Disneyland ID. We went on all the rides.

Warren Asa, 1955

You'd say to your buddy, "Did you see my Uncle Herman?" and the other guy would ask, "Where is he?" and you'd say, "He's driving a red Porsche." That meant you were looking for a girl in a red shirt. And if you said he was driving a Porsche 914 it meant she didn't have a bra on. Totally harmless if a guest heard it.

George Trullinger, 1970s–1980s

I liked working at the Tiki Room because there were girls who worked at the Dole Whip stand and it was the only time you would see girls while you were at work. There was one girl who worked there and I had eyes for her; I think she had eyes for me, too. We used to joke back and forth. They worked in foods and their office was some place different from where the attractions office was, so I never saw her other than at the Dole Whip stand. It was like this non-romance.

Fred Martin, 1980s

I was working load one night and this entire cheerleader squad came up and I could have fit them into the boat, but I just sent it. The skipper was a girl and said there was room, but I made her go, so I could spend 10 minutes talking with the cute cheerleaders.

Trevor Kelly, 2000s

There were some brave girls who dared to socialize with us and they would get all of the attention. I do not mean to imply that they had loose morals in anyway, they just enjoyed the company of the skippers. There was one girl who worked as a sweeper and she would come by and hang out with us and we thought she was very cool. This other girl worked at Pirates and she would come over and hang out with us in our break area.

Fred Martin, 1980s

Some Skippers, like Ben and Amanda Case met and fell in love at the Jungle Cruise.

I got cross-trained at Jungle Cruise because Pirates was down. I met Amanda after a shift or two and then I wasn't at Jungle Cruise much. Then one day I was wondering about Amanda and I go into work and we end up working together for a few hours. We both walked at the same time and we spent 40 minutes in K-Lot talking. I was late to a meeting with some friends at a coffee house. One of the guys ended up officiating at our wedding.

Ben Case, 2000s

We exchanged numbers and I invited him to hang out with the skippers because we always hang out. So I call him to see if he wants to go to TGI Fridays with a group and he says, "I'm sorry, but I have to do homework." So I thought he was blowing me off; turns out he is just an honest guy.

Amanda Case, 2000s

Eventually they began to date, and then got married.

There was a random book in the tower of the boat house and Amanda and I found a blank page and signed it together. I hope it's still there.

Our house is decorated all Jungle Cruise. In our wedding ceremony we wrote our own vows, and used Jungle Cruise puns in them. Things like, "I promise not to take you for granite." We called it the World Famous Case Wedding. Our love for the Jungle Cruise will always be there.

Ben Case, 2000s

Some skippers were second or third generation cast members. Not only does Jessica Harris-Lopez's great grandfather, George Mills, Sr., have a window on Main Street, her parents met while they worked at the park.

I dated one boy all through high school so Jungle Cruise was like a smorgasbord. You do date Disney. I'm surprised that I didn't meet my husband at Disneyland. It was neat to see those relationships grow. Eventually I came to the philosophy that "you don't date the dock."

Jessica Harris-Lopez, 1990s–2000s

The guy I trained with was a Mormon who looked like Drew Carey and he told us he wanted to work at Disneyland because he had turned 18 and it was time to start dating. He asked every girl out over and over.

Amanda Case, 2000s

There was one skipper who was always hitting on the girls. He creeped most of us girls out. Then one day his wife and child come up to the dock. No one knew he was married, he'd never mentioned it. He quickly got them on his boat.

Anonymous, 2010s

One time I had a breakup on my boat. I had a couple full on fighting before they got on my boat and they sat right next to me. She was telling him, "I didn't know you felt that way." And he said, "Ah, come on, babe." Then she said, "Well, you can get your stuff when you get home and you can go." Meanwhile, I was thinking, "Oh my God, you're doing this right now on my boat." It was so uncomfortable. They stopped talking and I just kind of ignored them and I didn't know what to do. I knew that something serious was happening, though. They were quiet the whole time and it was miserable.

Jen Chavez, 2010s

One day at Disneyland my lead at Jungle Cruise introduced me to a guest who told me that he wanted to propose to his girlfriend at the backside of water. We talked about how we would do it, and he said he would return with her in an hour. I asked my lead why he had me do it, and he said it was because I was the only skipper who was married. I told my lead that if his girlfriend said "yes" that I would flash my lights as I approached the dock. No lights meant she said "no."

So an hour comes and I see them on the dock. They got on my boat at the exit and scooted up to sit at the front next to me. I pretty much ignored them. I filled the boat with people at the load area, and I put on the best show that I could. The lead had told the other boats that I was going to need space, so they held the other boats at the dock while I headed toward the backside of water.

As I gave my tour, I was nuts. I did my best jokes, did crazy voices, made fun of the people in line at Indy. I gave my best performance. It was all part of my plan. When the boat got to the hippo pool I did a couple of dumb jokes, and fewer people laughed. We passed the dancing natives and I did worse jokes, nobody laughed. Then at the attacking natives I was as unfunny as I could be, and people just stared at me.

"So," I said, "you guys don't think I'm funny anymore? You think you could do this better than me? Well, why don't you try it!" With that I handed the microphone to the man who was going to propose. The boat laughed when he took it. I then sat down and said, "Go ahead." And more people laughed when he stood up. As I had planned it, the boat had now coasted to the backside of water and stopped there.

When the man started to talk, people laughed, and then people began to realize what was going on. His girlfriend began to cry, a group of junior high girls who were sitting in the back really began to cry. The man pulled out the ring, she jumped up and said yes, and everyone, including me, had tears in their eyes. It was awesome and everything worked out just as we had planned. I forgot one thing: what am I going to do for the rest of the trip? The dock was two minutes away and I couldn't go back to doing jokes about the jungle, it wouldn't work. So I did what I do all the time. I spent the two minutes making fun of the couple. They were from Las Vegas, so that gave me lots of material.

As the boat approached Trader Sam I flashed the lights on the boat and as we came around the corner, all of the skippers were on the dock clapping. They then handed the couple Mickey Mouse ears on bride-and-groom hats, and their names were already on them. We took lots of pictures, they gave me big hugs, even the manager came and hugged me, then after they exited I moved the boat to the loading area and took 45 more people out to the jungle.

For reasons that I still don't understand, if you saw a cute girl you would raise your hand, make it into a C shape, and say "courtesy," and then the other skippers would look around for her. One evening I was standing in the shipping office with a lead when he looked over my shoulder, nudged me, and flashed the courtesy sign. I turned and saw that it was my wife. The lead was mortified.

David John Marley, 2000s

For many skippers, the Jungle Cruise was the best place to pick up girls in the park.

I met a girl once who hooked up with me solely because I was a Jungle Cruise skipper. There was this group of girls that I had met and I got off work right before Fantasmic and we ended up making out in the Haunted Mansion and I ended up losing my phone and she apparently had it. She showed up at the dock the next day and in the light she was not as attractive as I had previously thought. So I saw her in line and she said, "I have your phone," and I was horrified and I just left the park and never got my phone back. The Jungle Cruise is a very attractively lit place at night.

Trevor Kelly, 2000s

One of the leads that I worked with would find a young lady to help him "close the treehouse" with him. He'd tell them that Fantasmic was about to start and we'd be on the dock and wonder who he was going to pick tonight.

Michael Libby, 2000s

But there was always a dark side to young love.

This family came to the dock and declared that the next skipper that pulled up was the one God wanted to marry their daughter. And this poor skipper named Chad pulled up and in this girl's mind he was betrothed to her. She was crazy. The whole family was crazy. They used to come to Big Thunder and stalk him. I was the devil to them, because I was often the lead and I shooed them away. I told them, "I can't have you standing there staring at my cast member, you're making him nervous." At first we thought that they were harmless and cute and then it got to be like crazy psychotic stalking. They gave everybody a nickname. I was the devil. They used to write these long letters to a manager named Garth who tried to be nice to them. But then they wrote him a letter saying that he had changed and turned into the devil and this and that. They were nuts and we kept asking management to ban them. Eventually, one of them slapped a security guard. We were wondering what it would take for Disneyland to ban them. I think Chad had to do a formal complaint with the police because they had found out where he lived. They were crazy. We used to have to hide Chad when they showed up. We had to hide him in the office until they left.

The daughter once told me, "God told me that the next skipper is going to be my husband," and poor Chad. I think she was in love with another skipper before that. It was during the summer of 1992, I think, maybe 1993.

Sue Barnaby, 1980s–1990s

CHAPTER TWENTY-TWO

<<<<<<<<<<<<<<<<<<<<<<<<<<<<<<<<<<<<<<<<<<<<<<<<<<<<<<<<<<<<<<<<<<<<<<<<<<<<<<<<<<<<<<<<<

SKIPPERS OFF THE CLOCK

Part of the fun of working at Disneyland, and especially at the Jungle Cruise, is the wild times that happen once the work day is over. From stand-up comedy shows to wild drunken parties with more than a thousand people, skippers have done it all.

There were these two skippers who would go on safari after the park closed and skippers would pile into a boat and these two guys would act out every scene. When they got to the dancing natives one of them was dancing naked. He had this stuffed monkey that he kept with him and he used that as a loin cloth.

Amanda Case, 2000s

Skippers were famous for wild times off property as well as the pranks they pulled while at work.

We lived in the apartment complex on Walnut, right across from Disneyland. You could hear the *Mark Twain* toot in the morning, so you knew when you were late. Times were crazy, we were dirt poor, we were sleeping on the floor, and we spent all of our money on fun early in the week and then we'd be scooping the bottom of It's A Small World for change in order to buy tortillas and refried beans.

Fred Martin, 1980s

A bunch of skippers lived in an apartment down on Orangewood and I swear every Friday and Saturday night there'd be a huge party at their place. And it was cool because they were Jungle Cruise skippers and they invited us to their party. That was like the good ol' boys club type thing

Sue Barnaby, 1980s–1990s

During one of our many Jungle Cruise Halloween parties the Anaheim cops showed up to bust the party. They found out that we worked at Disneyland and asked for free park tickets, so we rounded up 3 comp tickets. Then they told us to keep it down and to have a good night.

Chris Ramirez, 2000s

One of my favorite things about my wedding was all the skippers had their own table and they were so much fun.

Karen Vogelvang, 2000s

Once I was selected for jury duty and I got picked to be a juror. So I'm in the box and they ask what I did for a living and I said I was a Jungle Cruise skipper and the judge says, "No way, so was I!" He was a skipper in the late 60s. In Orange County, you never know who was a skipper.

Andy McGuire, 2000s

I was teaching a Friday night-Saturday morning US History class that met over four weekends at Cerritos College. On the Friday morning of the second weekend, I was in the middle of a trip through the jungle when I realized that I hadn't brought a change of clothes to work with me. I was wearing khaki shorts and a khaki shirt with khaki socks and black shoes. How was I going to teach for 4 hours that night dressed like that?

After my shift was over I went to Disneyland costuming and checked out the costume worn by a parade lead. This outfit consisted of black slacks, white shirt, and a blue-and-red stripped tie. Normally they would scan your ID when you checked out clothes to make sure that you were allowed to have that particular set of clothes. I guess people were taking costume pieces from attractions that they didn't know. So in a panic I developed a story about how I was an emergency lead and I was getting trained, which is why it didn't show up on my records. Thankfully the lady didn't bat an eye, just checked me out. I got changed and taught my class. I was terrified that a student would recognize the costume, but no one did.

David John Marley, 2000s

Without a doubt the most epic parties that skippers ever held were the infamous Banana Ball parties that were the rage for a decade starting in the mid 1970s.

I had friends named John and Jim and there was this party called the Banana Ball and originally it was only Jungle Cruise skippers who could go. That was part of the cachet back then. You had to wear your Jungle Cruise costume if you wanted to go to the Banana Ball. The last one of those was back in 1969 or 1970. So the girl that you brought, and you had to bring a girl, had to wear a formal gown. You had these Jungle Cruise skippers and these well-dressed ladies in kind of like a banquet.

When I got there in 1976, someone wanted to bring back the Banana Ball and make it like Custer's Last Stand which was a party put on by the Canoe guys and some of the Indians. It was a fun beer drinking party. So they made the Banana Ball of 1976 as a park-wide party where anybody could go. It was held at the Orange County Fairgrounds in Costa Mesa. I went that first year in 1976 thinking, "What a bunch of drunken idiots." It was such a mess.

In 1977 somebody else took it over and made it a disco bash with fog machines and disco music and my friend Mark asked me to help him. I ended up serving booze. Then in 1978 my friend Jim told me that no one was planning on doing the Banana Ball this year and so he and I should do it.

Jeff Rhoads, 1970s–1980s

It was just a lot of people getting drunk out of their minds. I think a lot of children were conceived at the Banana Ball, or just outside in the parking lot. We rented a big building from the OC Fairgrounds. We paid the rent and told them that we would have security and all these safety measures in place. We did in a way; it was just a very loose way. There were a bunch of us that put it together. Sometimes we had a band, but we usually just had a DJ. It was at the Banana Ball that they premiered the Mr. Bill film.

Terry Eaton, 1970s–1980s

Let me tell you something about the Banana Ball. You were going to throw a party for a thousand of your best friends, and most of them are not 21 and there is going to be beer and wine served. So you know what is going to happen. I did it in 1978, 79, 80. We would have to put up all of the money for the thing, rent the hall, buy the booze, print the tickets, and advertise before any money started rolling in. That made us nervous.

People start showing up and drinking beer. Our biggest one had 1,500 people with 40 kegs of beer, half of which was spilled on the floor. As the producer of the show you don't get to go to the party; you manage it. I remember walking up to the beer truck with these taps on the side. There were guys who would volunteer to serve beer and there was a metal table along the side of the truck. The truck was refrigerated and was having electrical problems. People would walk up to the table, with an inch of beer on the ground, and they'd touch the table and get electrocuted. The servers thought it was funny, but I said, "You can't let this happen!" So I had to deal with that.

One year after the party was over, we turned on the lights and there was a sea of plastic cups and trash all over the floor. As we cleaned up, we found a guy laying face down in the beer, totally passed out. He was covered in crap from head to toe. W had to drag him out. Every year there was damage done to the place. One year there was $3,000 worth of damage done to the fairgrounds building. There was a ticket booth they used for the OC Fair, which was a fiberglass orange, and somebody drove their car into it and destroyed it. We had to pay for that. Then one year a maintenance truck disappeared. I got a call from the OC Fair people and they said one of their maintenance trucks had been stolen, and I told them that I didn't know where it was or what happened. Then I drive to Disneyland and there was the OC Fair Maintenance truck parked at the Disneyland employee section. So I called them and told them where their truck was.

One time there was this girl that came walking up to another guy who produced the show with me, and she's got a bone sticking out of her arm. She was so drunk and she said, "I fell down and I think I hurt my arm." It was fractured pretty bad. One guy wants to call an ambulance and we ask how old she is and she said, "Sixteen," and I thought, "We are so screwed." He puts her in his car, drives her down to Hoag Hospital to the emergency room, and they're checking her in and getting her information and when they ask about insurance, she says that her mom has insurance, and at this point my friend John interrupts and says, "We'd like to handle this without insurance if that is possible." And he pulls out a huge wad of money and they said okay. So he peels off $600 in cash and she comes out in a cast and she keeps apologizing and John is just happy that she didn't die. That was the worst thing that ever happened. Each year, after the dust settled, we made money. A couple of thousand bucks total to split between four guys.

The other thing about the Banana Ball was that you wanted people to show up, but you wanted them to have fun, and you wanted them to come dressed Hawaiian style. We always said that there would be a best costume contest, but we never had the contest because everyone would get so drunk. One year we decide that we are actually going to do the contest, but we needed prizes to hand out. So Jim noticed that the submarine ride was down for rehab and they were painting all of the fish in the paint shop. He was back there and said, "Man, all that stuff is just sitting there and it would be a perfect gift if we could just get one of those sharks." In boat storage they had extra rudders for the Jungle Cruise boats. He said, "Could you just imagine giving a Jungle Cruise boat rudder away as a prize? That would be awesome."

At that time Sunkist was still in the park and Jim was friends with one of guys who worked there. He said, "Could you drive us in the Sunkist van to make a couple of stops and then drive us out of the park?" And he said okay. So we get the van before the park opens and we take a rudder from boat storage and we run it over to Sunkist, and then we drove over to the staff shop and Jimmy runs out and grabs a shark which was about 6 feet long and he throws it into the van. The driver isn't leaving until later that day, so we go back to work. I was in my *Columbia* costume and Jim was in his *Mark Twain* costume. We got the van and he drove us across the street to Howard Johnson's where we had our cars parked and load everything into a friend's truck. The Sunkist guy said he couldn't drive us back into the park, so we had to get over there ourselves.

Now we were both in costume and back in those days you did not leave the park in costume. We walk across Harbor Blvd and into the Harbor gate, say hello to the security guards, and go back to work. A little bit later we got a call from our supervisor, telling us to come up to the office. He says to us, "I just got a call from security saying you were outside the park in your costumes. He said you said you were over at Howard Johnson's. Were you guys over there drinking? So we told him that the guy from Sunkist donated a bunch of cups for the Banana Ball and we were putting them into our truck. We both got suspended for being out of the park in our costumes. The very next day the foreman got sick and I was made foreman on the *Mark Twain*. The very next day. That was my big suspension, one whole day. I get called in from suspension to get my promotion, and one of the managers is there and he says, "Look, I know what's going on around here and if there was anyway we could prove it, you guys would all be fired," then he made me supervisor of the *Mark Twain*.

Jeff Rhoads, 1970s–1980s

The deal was that if you bought your tickets in advance they were $7 and then $10 at the door. And they would get the most beautiful girls and give them a stack of ten or twenty tickets and get all that money for the Banana Ball to rent the hall and the beer trucks to back in there. They were paying for all of it, but it was a big operation. So there was like 2 inches of beer on the floor with 1,500 people there.

I went to my first Banana Ball in 1979 and told the guys running it, "I'm in a band, we can play here next year." We played there in 1980 and 1981, then took a couple years off. I was doing a Hollywood legend show at the Hollywood Palladium in 1984 for the Olympics. One of the nights we were performing was the same night as the Banana Ball. I got permission to get out early because my old band is playing at the Banana Ball. I didn't have to do the final encore. I did my Buddy Holly act, got in my car, and jammed down to Orange County. That was the last one we played.

George Trullinger, 1970s–1980s

There was this thing we called Jungle Juice. It was a giant punch bowl and we stirred it with paddles that we took from the river. The Jungle Juice was a combination of cheap champagne and fruit juice. Then as people came in they would just pour some of whatever they brought with them into the bowl. The first sip may have not been great but after four or five you didn't care. We also had lots of kegs of beer. People would go to this event either barefoot or in flip-flops and there was so much spilled beer and dirt on the floor and your feet were dirty for at least 24 hours afterwards.

Terry Eaton, 1970s–1980s

It was seen as dishonorable to call in sick just because you've been drinking. If you called in sick because you were extremely hung over, you would never hear the end of it. That was the attitude of pretty much everybody on the westside of the park. I remember once being at Davy Crockett Explorer Canoes and I was in the back and I slowly bent over the back of the boat and threw up into the river but I kept paddling. Yeah, it was disgrace to call in sick after the Banana Ball because everybody knew where you were and what you had been doing.

Terry Eaton, 1970s–1980s

Another popular series of parties were the annual Weekend at Benny's parties that were held in the early 2000s. These parties would literally last an entire weekend.

Weekend at Benny's was an annual party that would start on a Thursday and end on Sunday morning. My family would leave the house in Buena Park. The parties were stocked with booze. I'd buy about $2,000 worth of alcohol and bowls of condoms. It was a weekend where skippers could show up and party and then sleep it off and go back to work. I know of a number of people who hooked up at the party and are still together.

One time I'm sitting in the backyard and there were these two guys in their early 20s and nobody knew who they were. I talked to them. They were Disneyland guests from Canada who found a flyer on the ground on Main Street and decided to show up to the party. The cops never showed up; it was lovely.

Benny LeMaster, 1990s–2000s

The first Skipper Show (originally called Skipper Stand-Up) was born in June 2006 and has been a regular show appearing around Orange County ever since.

I left the Jungle Cruise in late 2004 when my first daughter was born, and I quickly realized that I needed an outlet for my comedy. I love teaching history in college, but at some point you have to stop telling jokes and get to the history, so I thought I'd try stand up. I did my first stand-up gig about two months after leaving the park. Eventually, I was running a show in Fullerton with a couple of really funny guys, and our show was great, but getting people to show up was a grind. I pitched the idea for a show where all the performers were current or former skippers, and the Skipper Show was born. We sold out our first show, so for our next one I doubled the ticket price, all the way up to $10! I thought it was a one-time deal, but we ended up doing five Skipper Shows a year for years. We took it on the road around Orange County and even the Bay Area.

The show is fun because every skipper has already taken a master class in being funny. Some of them do jokes about Disneyland while some never mention it, but the results are always hysterical. I give pretty much any skipper one chance to try it out. Sometimes they get bitten by the stand-up bug and try to make a real career out of it. We call it the "comedy womb" because the audiences are always so supportive.

I've written books, articles, all kinds of academic stuff and nothing has brought me more press than the Skipper Show.

David John Marley, 2000s

Kipp Hart performed at the first Skipper Show when it started in 2006. Since then he has gone on to perform stand up across California.

I always loved comedians, but it never dawned on me that that was something I could do until I was asked to do the Skipper Show. I did the very first show. It never even dawned on me that was a possibility. I knew I had something because of Jungle Cruise. I only had six weeks to write eight minutes, and the response was great. And for the next couple of years, all I did was skipper shows. It's such a nice, safe audience. But eventually I wanted to see if I can do stand-up in front of a different audience, not a crowd that knew who I was and would be more forgiving. So I went up to Pasadena to the Ice House and I auditioned for a show there and got it and it was fun. And then I got bitten by the bug. That is how my comedy career started and it has been phenomenal.

Jungle Cruise is such a leg up when it comes to starting comedy. I never would have been able to develop the timing and understanding of a crowd. It's essentially the shortcut. You are forced to have a new crowd every eight minutes, and if you want to have fun you have to be engaged the entire time. I was fortunate to learn that I can learn from my guests. I don't get mad at them; if they didn't get a joke, it was my fault, not theirs. I didn't communicate it clearly enough.

Kipp Hart, 2000s–2010s

In the years after I left Disneyland I had an annual pass and frequently took my young daughters to the park. One time I was there with my wife, who was tired of me constantly hanging out at the Jungle Cruise. She said, "One day you're going to come to Jungle Cruise and not recognize anyone, and I'll be so happy." One day we came to the dock with my family, looked around, and I knew no one. I told my wife, so she could enjoy the moment, but her joy was short-lived. A boat pulled up to unload and the skipper, who I did not recognize, looked at me and exclaimed, "Hey, you're the guy who runs the Skipper Show!"

My wife, who has sworn three times in her entire life, quietly muttered, "Dammit."

David John Marley, 2000s

CHAPTER TWENTY-THREE

◇◇

LIFE AFTER JUNGLE CRUISE

I've never met a cast member who didn't have at least one good story to tell about their time working at Disneyland. It seems like skippers have more stories than most. Working at Disneyland and at Jungle Cruise specifically can be a life-changing experience and they take the lessons that they learned out in the jungle into the world.

After my Disneyland time I was back living in Portland and I got a job helped opening the first Disney Store there. It was a slow day in the store and these two Japanese tourists came in. They were two girls and they were looking at me and giggling and laughing and then they finally got the courage to come up and talk to me. They didn't speak English, but one of the girls said "Disneyland" and pulled a book out of her bag. She flipped through pictures and there is a picture of me with these two girls on a boat in the Jungle Cruise taken about eight months earlier.

Fred Martin, 1980s

I've done all kinds of things in my career, but no matter what I've done, people will always say, "You used to work at Disneyland?" That's the big one.

Ron Robledo, 1980s

I have a great job now, but when I used to have this really stressful job and I couldn't sleep, I wouldn't count sheep, I would do the Jungle Cruise spiel in my head. I would close my eyes and picture the jungle and I'd usually be asleep by the time I got to the elephant pool.

Fred Martin, 1980s

Jungle Cruise ruined me at every other job I've ever had since. It's like going to a VFW meeting where only other vets knew your experiences.

I didn't want to make friends at other jobs because there was never that same feeling of togetherness there.

Chris Ramirez, 2000s

I was so introverted and shy. My boyfriend in high school and I were so withdrawn and shy and I got this job at the Jungle Cruise which opened up this whole new avenue to me and my boyfriend couldn't keep up with me. I started coming out of my shell, going to concerts, and going to skipper parties. Then I moved in with two other skippers.

Jessica Harris-Lopez, 1990s–2000s

A couple of years after I left Disneyland I stopped by the Jungle Cruise dock to visit with my friends. I had my daughter Olivia with me, who was maybe 2 years old at the time. As I was chatting with the skippers my daughter took off running toward Adventureland. I yelled to her, "Hold it up, Skip!" and she came to a complete halt and put her fist in the air like skippers are supposed to when stopping their boat. I was so proud of her and my friends laughed so hard.

David John Marley, 2000s

The friends that I made at Jungle Cruise still amaze me. It's been 15 years and I still see them about every other day. I was told that the people you meet in your college years will be your friends forever, and that was true for me. It wasn't my college, but my work. I never thought I'd find people with my sense of humor. The kind of stuff my brother and I would laugh at when we were kids and now I have 15 friends who are just like that. We eat together, we party together, we go to Vegas together. It is something very special.

Joey Hurley, 2000s

I went to Florida years ago and I did four Disney parks in one day. The last thing I did was I went to Jungle Cruise and told them that I was a former skipper from back in the 1980s. And for some reason being from the 1980s really impressed them. We all went out on a boat and they even let me spiel. It was a totally female crew that night and a bunch of them got on my boat. The river is really different and I would ask them, "What do you say here?" and they would yell out various jokes. It was a such a great memory. Even the lead came on the boat with me.

Fred Martin, 1980s

I was at a history convention in Kentucky when the following conversation happened:

Lady: You worked at Disneyland?

Me: Yes, I used to.

Lady: You were a Jungle Cruise skipper, weren't you?

Me: How could you tell?

Lady: You can spot those guys a mile away.

David John Marley, 2000s

I can say that my experience in the park in general has been really helpful. There is such an interesting mix of people at WDI. You have people with engineering degrees from really prestigious schools, or they worked in film, and I went to Cal State Fullerton and worked at Disneyland for five years. I bring in that dynamic that when they make plans, I can tell them how it worked in the real world. Working at the park has helped. I know how spiels work, I'm a huge advocate of getting into the parks and trying to team up with the crews as much as possible. That's why we got the spiel teams in place. I got the spiel box moved over to Florida. I know how important communication is between WDI and the cast if you wanna have a successful product. The director has to talk to the crew in a play. There cannot be a disconnect.

Kevin Lively, 2010s

Working at the Jungle Cruise has led to skippers getting a chance to make the break to television and internet podcasting.

We pitched a TV show idea to a production company owned by Jason Alexander. It was called *Welcome to the Jungle*. It's about a group of people that work on a ride in a theme park. It was basically things that really happened to us in the jungle; going to parties, hanging out with the people, and all the different personalities that worked there. We wrote all of our friends as characters. I still have a few scripts that we actually finished. It was going to be a 22-minute sit-com. We actually filmed the pilot episode for it. We went to Louisiana to film it on a swamp tour so we could have access to water and a boat. I'm not very proud of the pilot; I don't think we did a good job. We were trying to make it funny for people who have worked at Jungle Cruise. We should have tried to make it funny for the United States. It didn't work because so many of the jokes were inside jokes.

Joey Hurley, 2000s

In 2011 I got an email asking me if I'd be interested in appearing in a TV show. They had me sign all kinds of non-disclosure agreements and forms before they'd tell me anything about the show. It was a show about famous people in history and what they ate. The show was called *History, It's Food!* The idea was brilliant and I'm still amazed that no one picked it up.

The producer said they wanted a Ph.D. in history to host the show, which was why they were talking to me. I assumed that they'd seen me on the History Channel show, *The Nostradamus Effect*; they hadn't. I then fig-ured that they heard of my 2007 book about Pat Robertson; they hadn't. I couldn't figure out how they found me. It turned out that they found me because the show's creator, in an effort to find a funny host who was also a historian, typed some combination of the words "history, comedy, Ph.D" (and a few others) into Google and the first thing that popped up was the Skipper Show. So once again, the years I spent in grad school have shown themselves to be a waste of time. Or at least mainly a waste of time.

They flew me to Florida to shoot the pilot, and I had the time of my life. I had no idea what I was doing, but they hired a director with a solid background in theatre so she could explain TV production to me in terms that I understood.

David John Marley, 2000s

During my time at Disney, I got to know a great number of other cast members, and made a lot of friends and connections. After I left the resort, I kept in touch with as many skippers as possible, and Facebook made that easier. In 2009–2010, the podcast explosion was just barely starting. I had met one of the hosts of The Nerdist podcast, and it really got me into the concept of podcasts. I saw that the project could serve as the first real oral history of the Jungle Cruise, and over the next six years the show expanded greatly. I have since recorded 143 episodes of the podcast, including interviews with over 100 skippers from eras spanning the entire history of Disneyland. We have had two Skippers who worked on Day 1 of the park's opening, and a handful that worked at Disneyland while Walt was at the park. We have had skippers from three different Disney parks. There are currently nearly 130 hours of content on the website, and we feel that we have created something that has become the definitive way to understand the experience of not only working at Jungle Cruise, but working at Disney attractions. As of now, we have had 1.75 million down-loads by nearly 40,000 unique listeners.

Kyle Crocker, 2000s

Skippers have also found ways to create art, merchandise, and even games based on their love of the Jungle Cruise.

Working at the Jungle Cruise led me to starting my own small business. My daughters wanted a fort in our small backyard. Since I was already making it look like a jungle out there, I made them a playhouse that looked like the boathouse at Jungle Cruise. I then decorated it with signs and small tikis that I tried to carve. My wife kept telling me that I should sell them online, but I thought that she was just being nice. Then one day my friend and former skipper Joshua Sudock came over, saw my work, and told me that I should sell my stuff online. I thought, "He must be telling the truth, he has no reason to be nice to me." So I opened stores on ETSY and Amazon Handmade, and I sell all kinds of stuff inspired by my love of Disneyland and the Jungle Cruise. (etsy.com/shop/DrSkippersJungleHut)

David John Marley, 2000s

In 2015, we started to branch out with merchandising. Our first idea was to take t-shirt designs from skippers and create a "for Skipper, by Skipper" t-shirt shop, where any skipper can contribute designs and sell their shirts. We have eight designers who have given us designs, and we have nearly 50 different designs on the site. Some directly pay homage to the Jungle Cruise, and others are fun, adventure-themed shirts. We have sold hundreds of shirts to date, and we continue to put up new ones, particularly mash-up designs with Jungle Cruise and other pop culture properties.

Kyle Crocker, 2000s

Sometimes, very rarely, a skipper who no longer works at the park will get the chance to spiel again. What is it like going back home again?

A while ago I was hanging out at the exit talking with a skipper and he told me that he was about to bump back in and I could take a boat. So I stood there and my wife watched me be silent for 15 minutes while I thought of what I would say. I went over every joke that I had wanted to do for the last ten years. So we get in the boat and as we turn the corner away from the dock he says, "We have a very special guest today," and hands me the mic. He worked the throttle while I did the tour. He said he knew that he had made a mistake when I did the drunk cobra joke. When I did that joke he took off his name tag and I preceded to do the tour I had wanted to do for 10 years.

Trevor Kelly, 2000s

I used to take my History of Disneyland class to the park and the leads were always kind enough to let us take a couple of trips on the Jungle Cruise. I'd have my class take a boat with guests first, so they could experience it fresh, then the lead would let me take a boat with just my class and a skipper. I could spiel, but I couldn't control the throttle. Not being able to control the throttle really threw off my timing, since I used it as a sort of rim-shot to my jokes.

David John Marley, 2000s

The jokes that skippers do for trip after trip get stuck in their brains and they end up doing them in some random places.

I've take the Jungle Cruise spiel on the road. I did it on a bus in Belarus for a bunch of older American women on a trip. I got to spiel on a river in Uganda. We were on a big boat sailing to see the big animals in Queen Elizabeth Park. I have a picture of me at the wheel. I did it twice, in 2007 and 2013. The second time we went a hippo popped up right by the boat, he was like Jungle Cruise distance away from us. He wasn't attacking us, he was just making himself known. We got a picture of that. People on the boat asked me, "Did he wiggle his ears?"

Fred Martin, 1980s

ACKNOWLEDGMENTS

There are a number of people I'd like to thank for their help during the course of this project. First of all, I'd like to thank Didier Ghez, Todd James Pierce, and all my friends at the Hyperion Historical Alliance. I appreciate the support from my fellow faculty at California State University Fullerton's History Department, especially, Nancy Fitch, and Ronald Rietveld.

A skipper told me that working at Jungle Cruise is like joining the Illuminati. That must be true because I was helped by a network of skippers that only seemed to grow while working on this book. Thanks to Alan Coats for talking with me about the park while Walt Disney was alive. Thanks also go to Kyle Crocker for his *Tales From The Jungle Crews* podcast. All the quotes from opening day skipper Warren Asa were taken from Kyle's podcast. I appreciate all skippers past and present, especially those named and anonymous ones who helped make this book possible. Thanks to Jasen Lewis for letting me into the tower of the boathouse for my author's photo.

Thanks to Trevor Kelly for his great artwork on the cover. All the quotes from William "Sully" Sullivan were taken from his book *From Jungle Cruise Skipper to Disney Legend: 40 Years of Magical Memories at Disney*, available from Theme Park Press. Former skipper and current *OC Register* reporter and photographer Joshua Sudock helped me track down some famous skippers, while Jason Schultz from the Richard Nixon Presidential Library dug out information about skipper turned Nixon press secretary Ron Ziegler. My dear friend Alexandra Kindell mostly dodged the editorial bullet this time; I hope you enjoyed the break. A special thanks to Karen Nishie, who was a dear friend to me on a campus filled with bullies and cowards.

My wonderful family was supportive during this project, especially Erla Curtin, Jeri South, Lin and Tony Fern, Terry Wolfsen, and my beautiful, talented, and overly patient wife, Deb Marley. My sister-in-law Sara Thede provided me with much needed editorial help.

A number of students and former students assisted me in this project as well. Thanks to Natasha Sheriff who served as "non-skipper" reader to make sure this book made sense to people who never worked at Disneyland.

I'd also like to thank all my students in my Fall 2016 classes at Cal State Fullerton who got to class early to read chapters from the book and hear me tell some of the stories. I am especially thankful to all the students in my Fall 2016 Historical Thinking class who helped me organize one huge chapter into two smaller and better-focused ones.

I'd also like to thank a number of people who helped me in many ways during this project: Sandra Jacobs, Kelly Wells, Mike Pucher, Kipp Hart, Tony Clifton, Jessica Kelly, Daisy Rain Martin, Jason Lamoreaux, John and Alaina Eames, Chip MacGregor, Paul McGraw, David Koenig, David Schoenwetter, and of course, Trader Sam.

About the Author

David John Marley, a former Disneyland Jungle Cruise skipper has a Ph.D. in modern American History from George Washington University. He taught for several years at California State University, Fullerton. Marley is the creator of the first-ever class specifically on the history of Disneyland. Marley has appeared on the History Channel, published articles in scholarly journals, a chapter for an anthology on the civil rights movement, over a dozen book reviews, and editorials for the History News Network. He has worked as a performer and comedy writer for Disneyland and is the producer of the popular Jungle Cruise based comedy show The Skipper Show (facebook.com/skippershow).

Made in the USA
Monee, IL
15 February 2023

27842631R00138